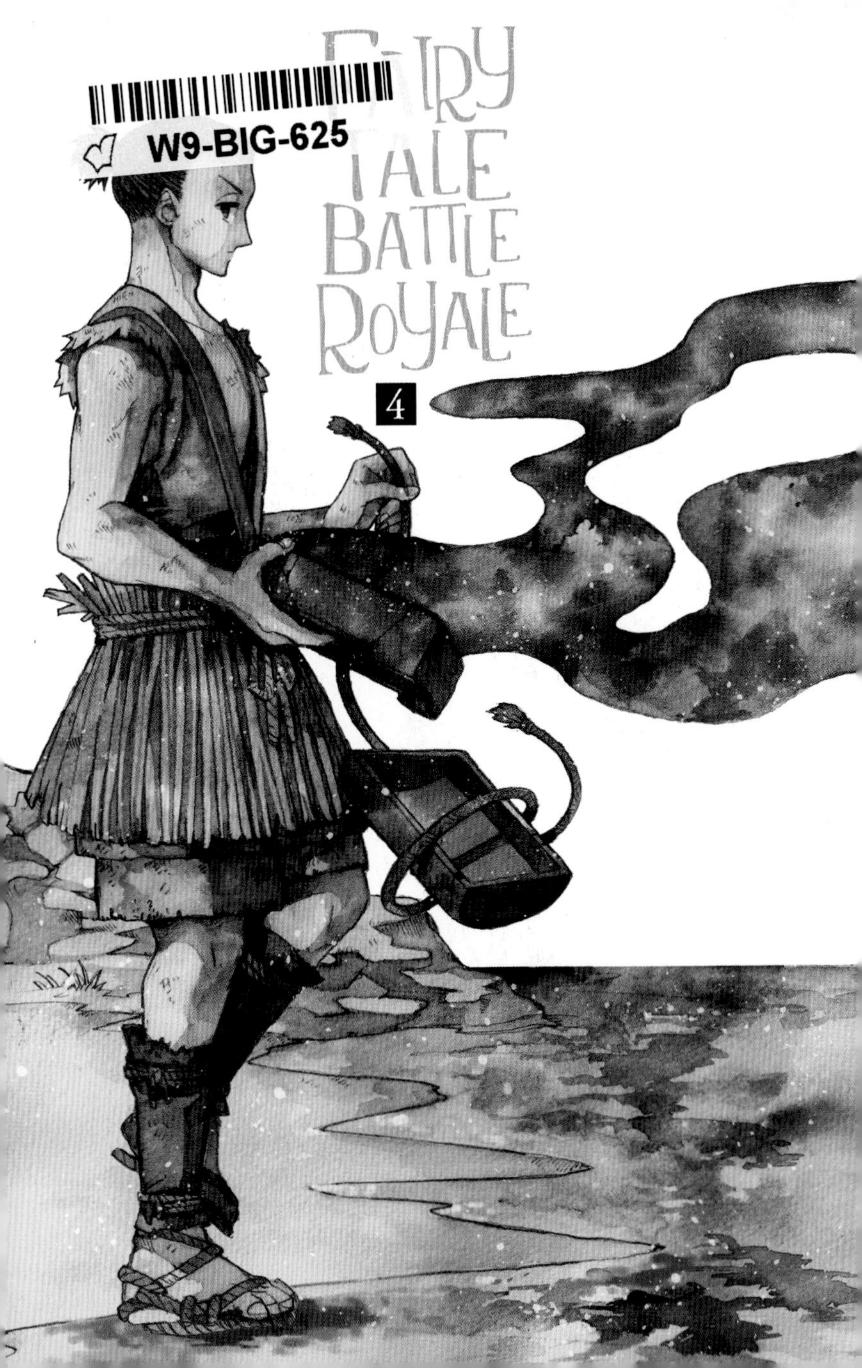
FAIRY
TALE
BATTLE
ROYALE
4

Contents

Chapter 13: Emblem

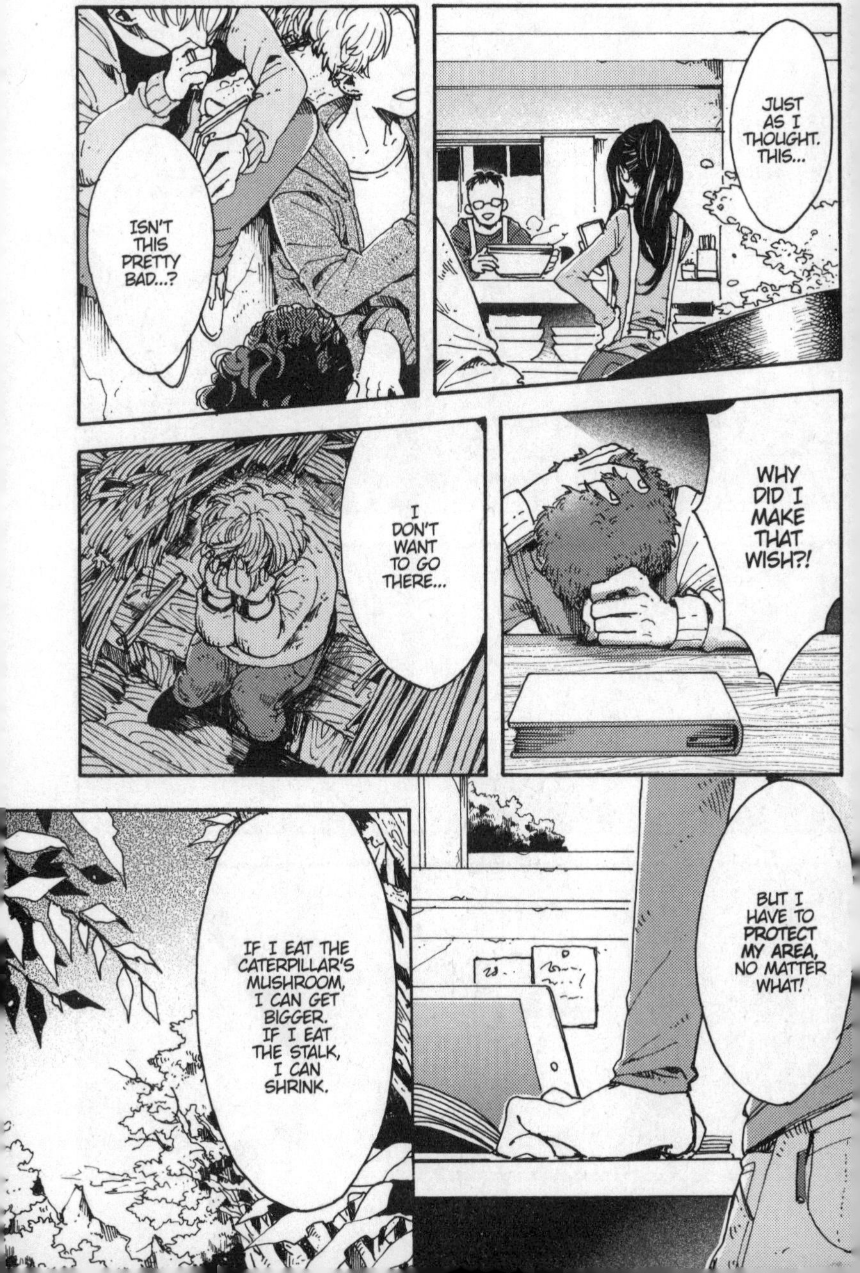
JUST AS I THOUGHT. THIS...
ISN'T THIS PRETTY BAD...?
WHY DID I MAKE THAT WISH?!
I DON'T WANT TO GO THERE...
BUT I HAVE TO PROTECT MY AREA, NO MATTER WHAT!
IF I EAT THE CATERPILLAR'S MUSHROOM, I CAN GET BIGGER. IF I EAT THE STALK, I CAN SHRINK.

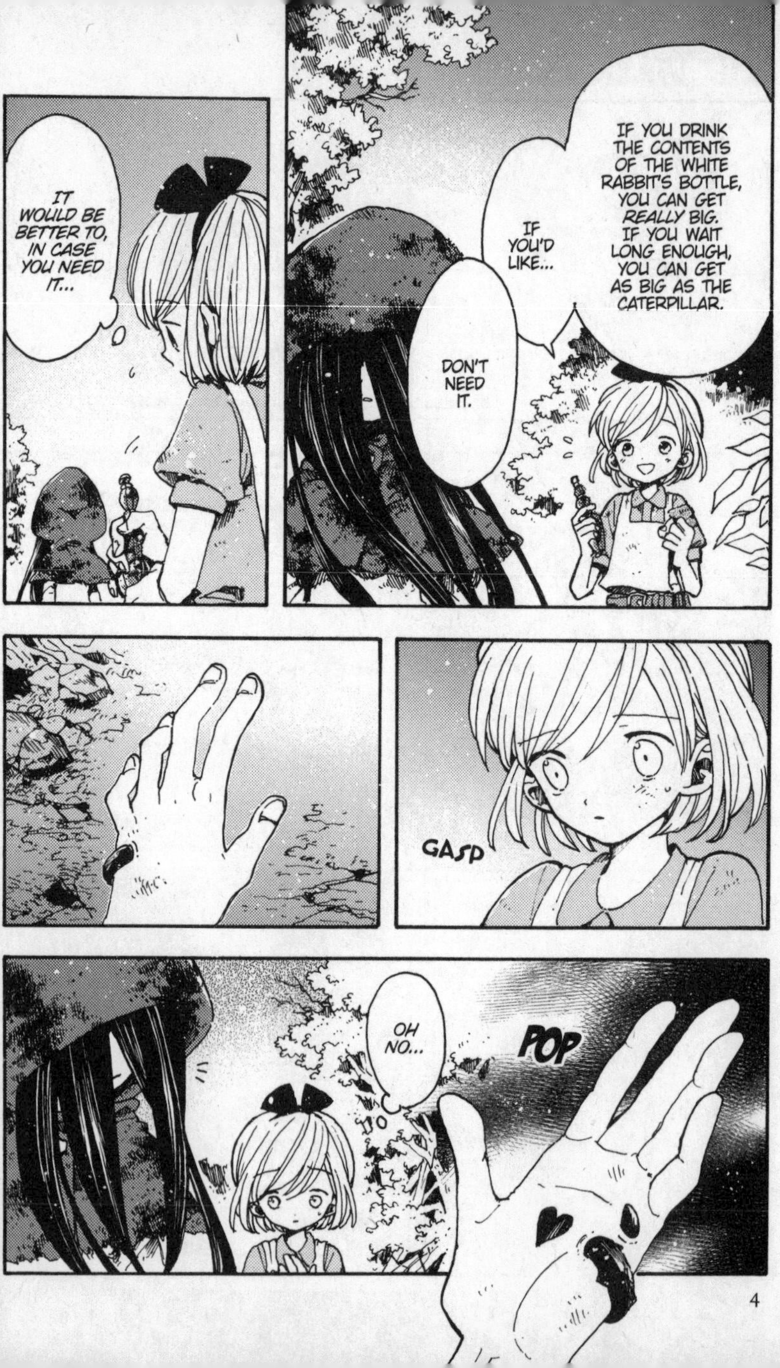
IF YOU DRINK THE CONTENTS OF THE WHITE RABBIT'S BOTTLE, YOU CAN GET *REALLY* BIG. IF YOU WAIT LONG ENOUGH, YOU CAN GET AS BIG AS THE CATERPILLAR.
IF YOU'D LIKE...
DON'T NEED IT.
IT WOULD BE BETTER TO, IN CASE YOU NEED IT...
GASP
POP
OH NO...

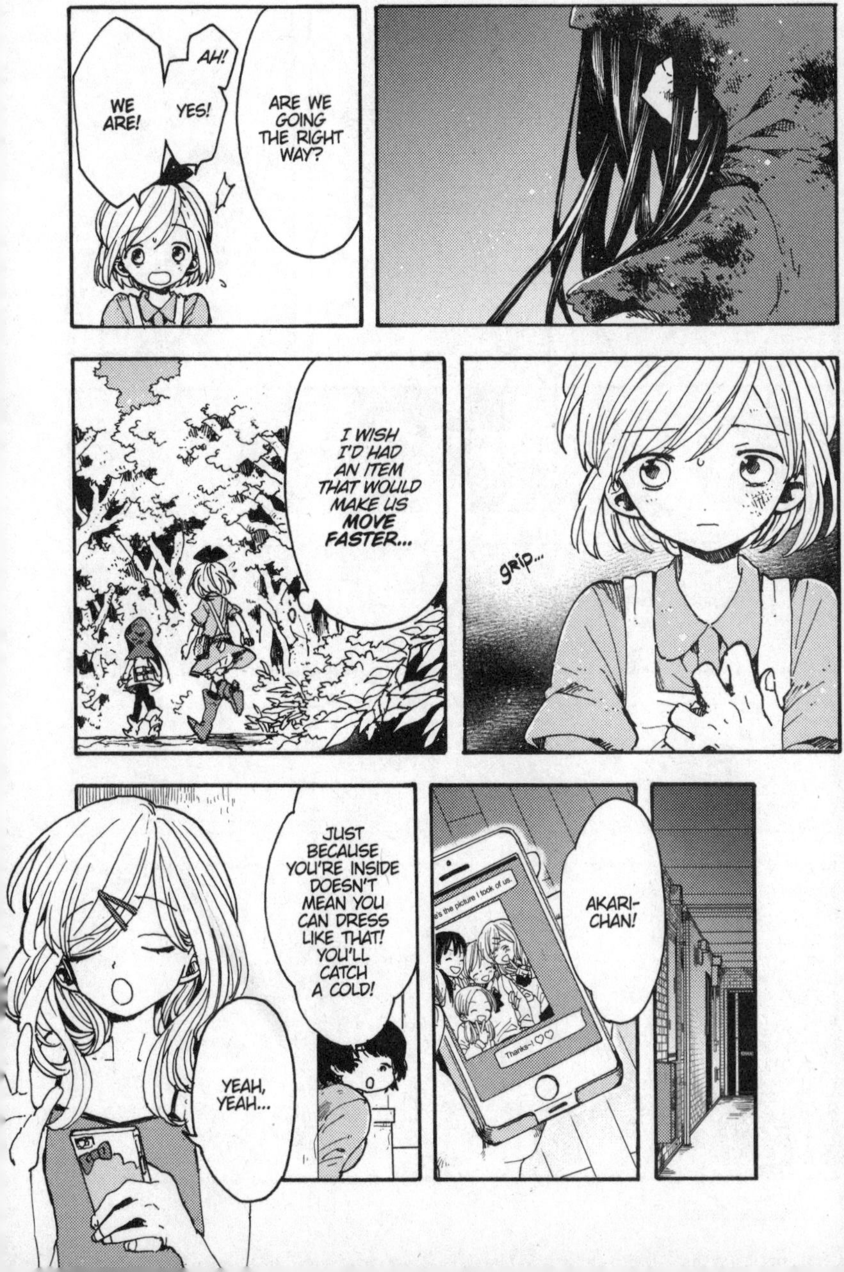
ARE WE GOING THE RIGHT WAY?
AH!
YES!
WE ARE!
grip...
I WISH I'D HAD AN ITEM THAT WOULD MAKE US MOVE FASTER...
AKARI-CHAN!
Thanks~! ♡♡
JUST BECAUSE YOU'RE INSIDE DOESN'T MEAN YOU CAN DRESS LIKE THAT! YOU'LL CATCH A COLD!
YEAH, YEAH...

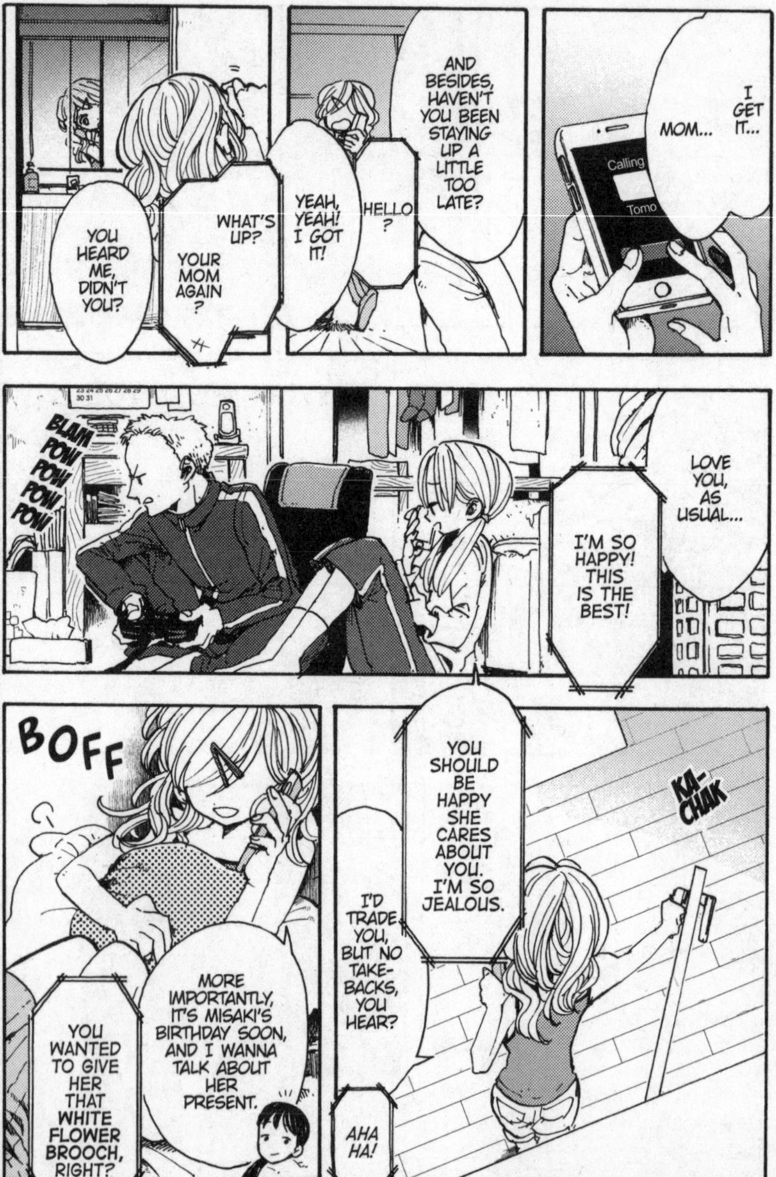
I GET IT...
MOM...
Calling
Tomo
AND BESIDES, HAVEN'T YOU BEEN STAYING UP A LITTLE TOO LATE?
HELLO?
YEAH, YEAH! I GOT IT!
WHAT'S UP?
YOUR MOM AGAIN?
YOU HEARD ME, DIDN'T YOU?
LOVE YOU, AS USUAL...
I'M SO HAPPY! THIS IS THE BEST!
BLAM POW POW POW POW
YOU SHOULD BE HAPPY SHE CARES ABOUT YOU. I'M SO JEALOUS.
KA-CHAK
I'D TRADE YOU, BUT NO TAKE-BACKS, YOU HEAR?
AHA HA!
BOFF
MORE IMPORTANTLY, IT'S MISAKI'S BIRTHDAY SOON, AND I WANNA TALK ABOUT HER PRESENT.
YOU WANTED TO GIVE HER THAT WHITE FLOWER BROOCH, RIGHT?

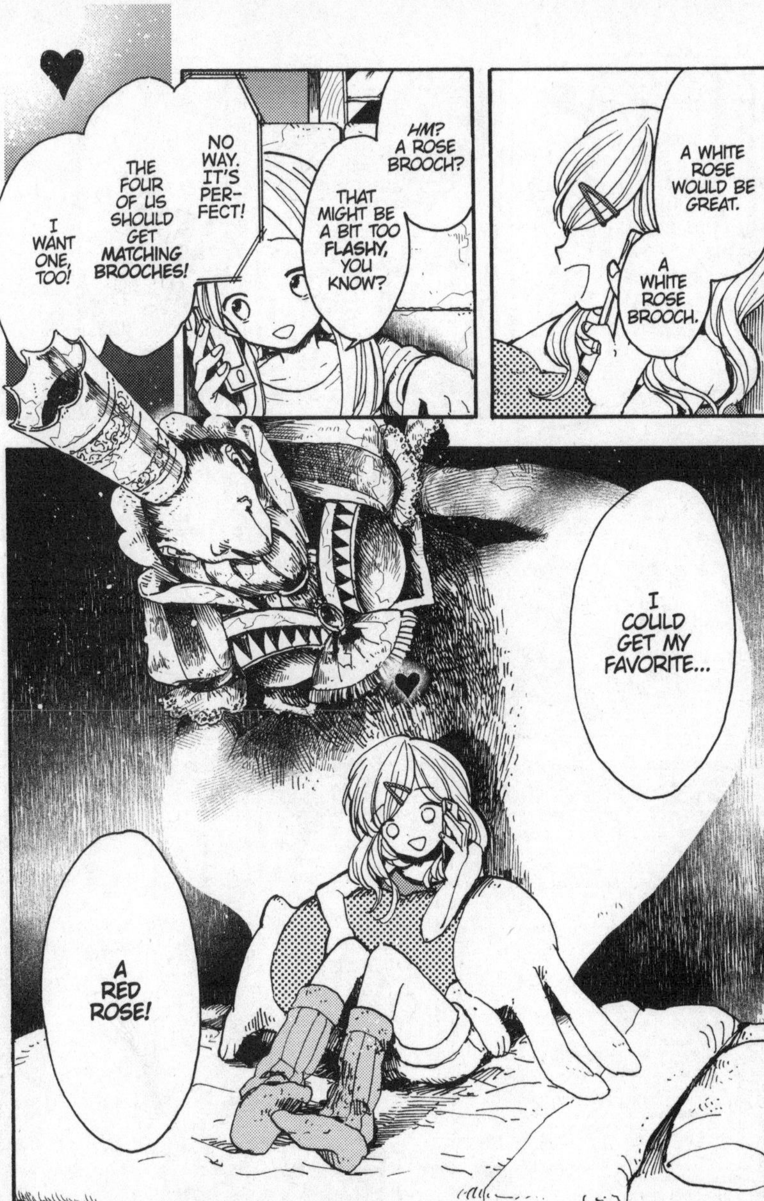
A WHITE ROSE WOULD BE GREAT.
A WHITE ROSE BROOCH.
HM? A ROSE BROOCH?
THAT MIGHT BE A BIT TOO FLASHY, YOU KNOW?
NO WAY. IT'S PER-FECT!
THE FOUR OF US SHOULD GET MATCHING BROOCHES!
I WANT ONE, TOO!
I COULD GET MY FAVORITE...
A RED ROSE!

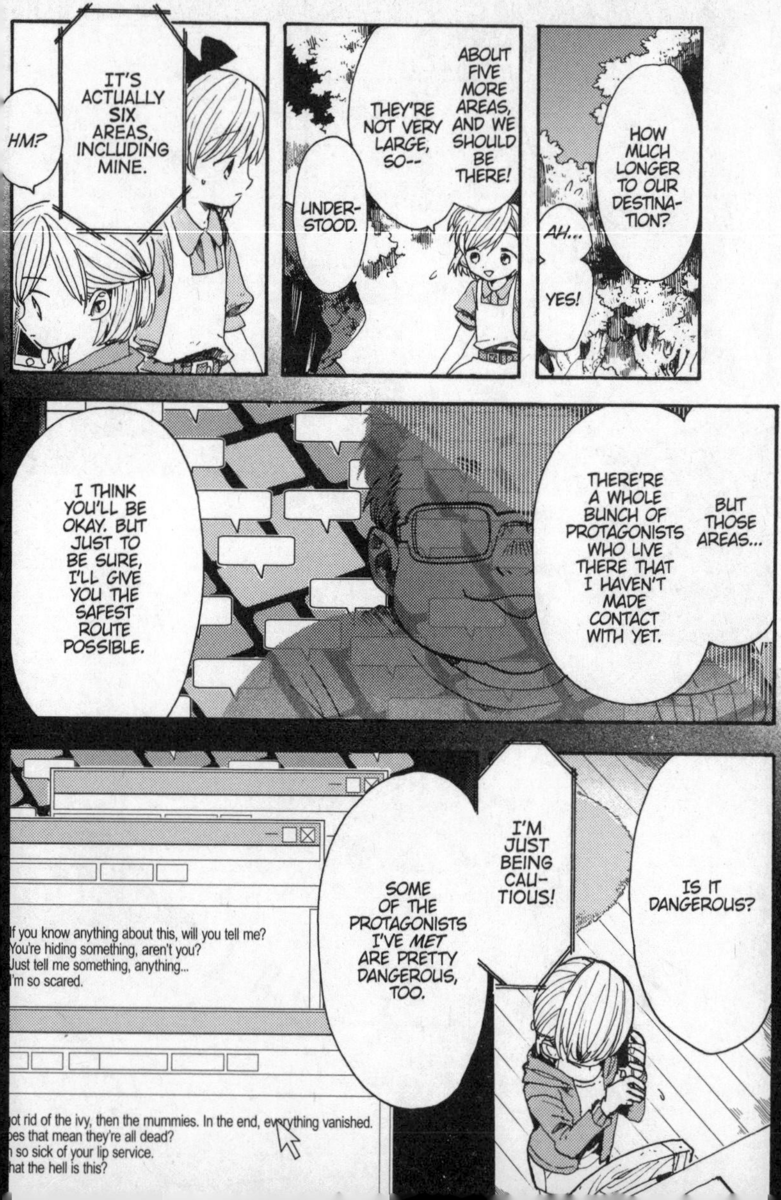
HOW MUCH LONGER TO OUR DESTINA-TION?
AH... YES!
ABOUT FIVE MORE AREAS, AND WE SHOULD BE THERE!
THEY'RE NOT VERY LARGE, SO--
UNDER-STOOD.
IT'S ACTUALLY SIX AREAS, INCLUDING MINE.
HM?
BUT THOSE AREAS...
THERE'RE A WHOLE BUNCH OF PROTAGONISTS WHO LIVE THERE THAT I HAVEN'T MADE CONTACT WITH YET.
I THINK YOU'LL BE OKAY. BUT JUST TO BE SURE, I'LL GIVE YOU THE SAFEST ROUTE POSSIBLE.
IS IT DANGEROUS?
I'M JUST BEING CAU-TIOUS!
SOME OF THE PROTAGONISTS I'VE *MET* ARE PRETTY DANGEROUS, TOO.
If you know anything about this, will you tell me?
You're hiding something, aren't you?
Just tell me something, anything...
I'm so scared.
ot rid of the ivy, then the mummies. In the end, everything vanished.
oes that mean they're all dead?
n so sick of your lip service.
hat the hell is this?

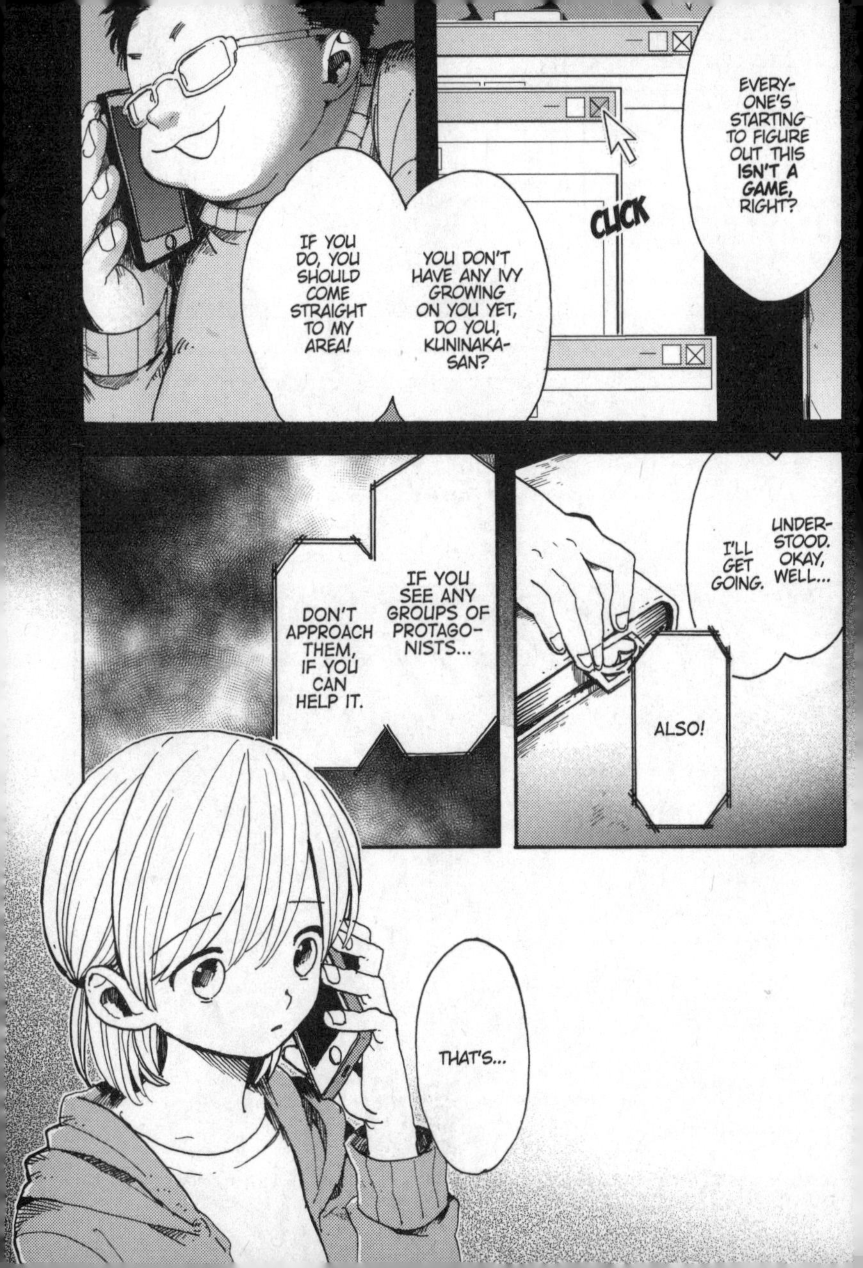
EVERYONE'S STARTING TO FIGURE OUT THIS ISN'T A GAME, RIGHT?
CLICK
YOU DON'T HAVE ANY IVY GROWING ON YOU YET, DO YOU, KUNINAKA-SAN?
IF YOU DO, YOU SHOULD COME STRAIGHT TO MY AREA!
UNDERSTOOD. OKAY, WELL...
I'LL GET GOING.
ALSO!
IF YOU SEE ANY GROUPS OF PROTAGONISTS...
DON'T APPROACH THEM, IF YOU CAN HELP IT.
THAT'S...

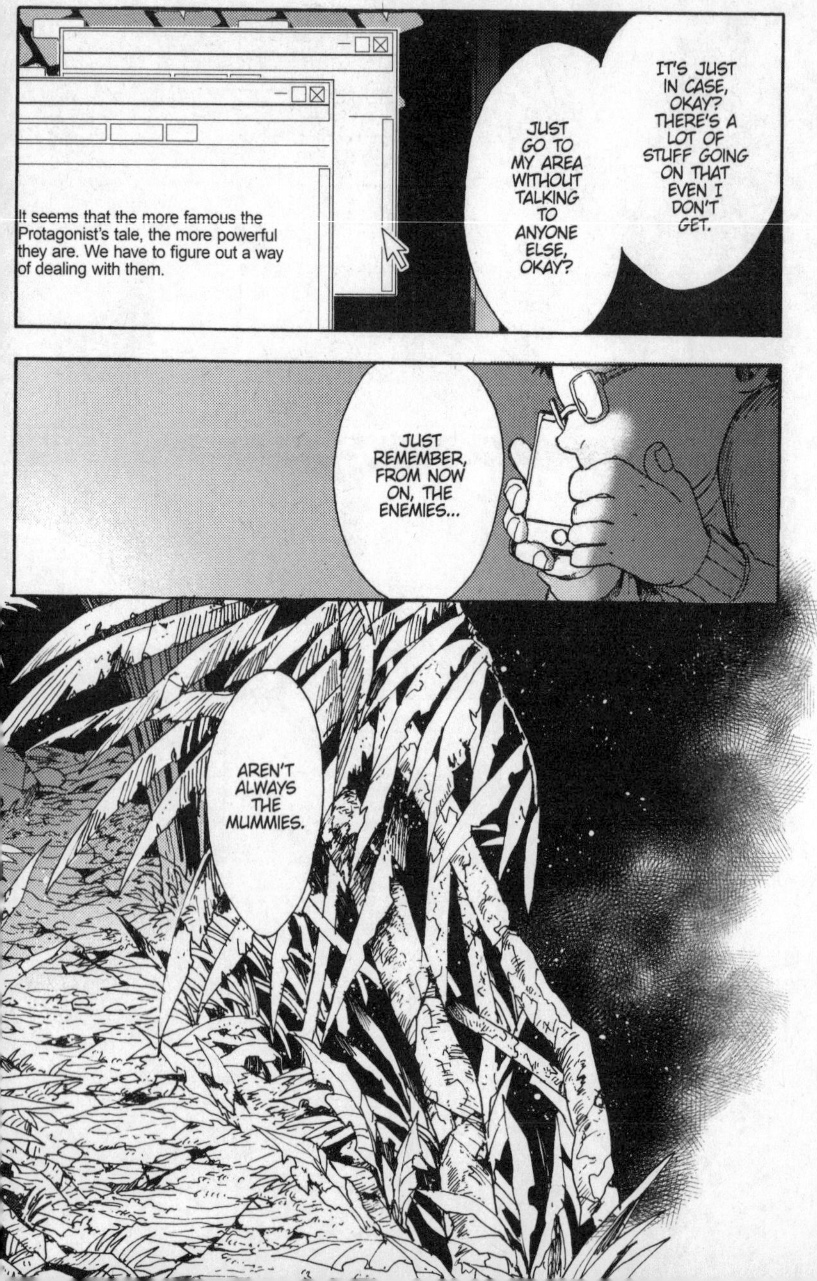
IT'S JUST IN CASE, OKAY? THERE'S A LOT OF STUFF GOING ON THAT EVEN I DON'T GET.
JUST GO TO MY AREA WITHOUT TALKING TO ANYONE ELSE, OKAY?
It seems that the more famous the Protagonist's tale, the more powerful they are. We have to figure out a way of dealing with them.
JUST REMEMBER, FROM NOW ON, THE ENEMIES...
AREN'T ALWAYS THE MUMMIES.

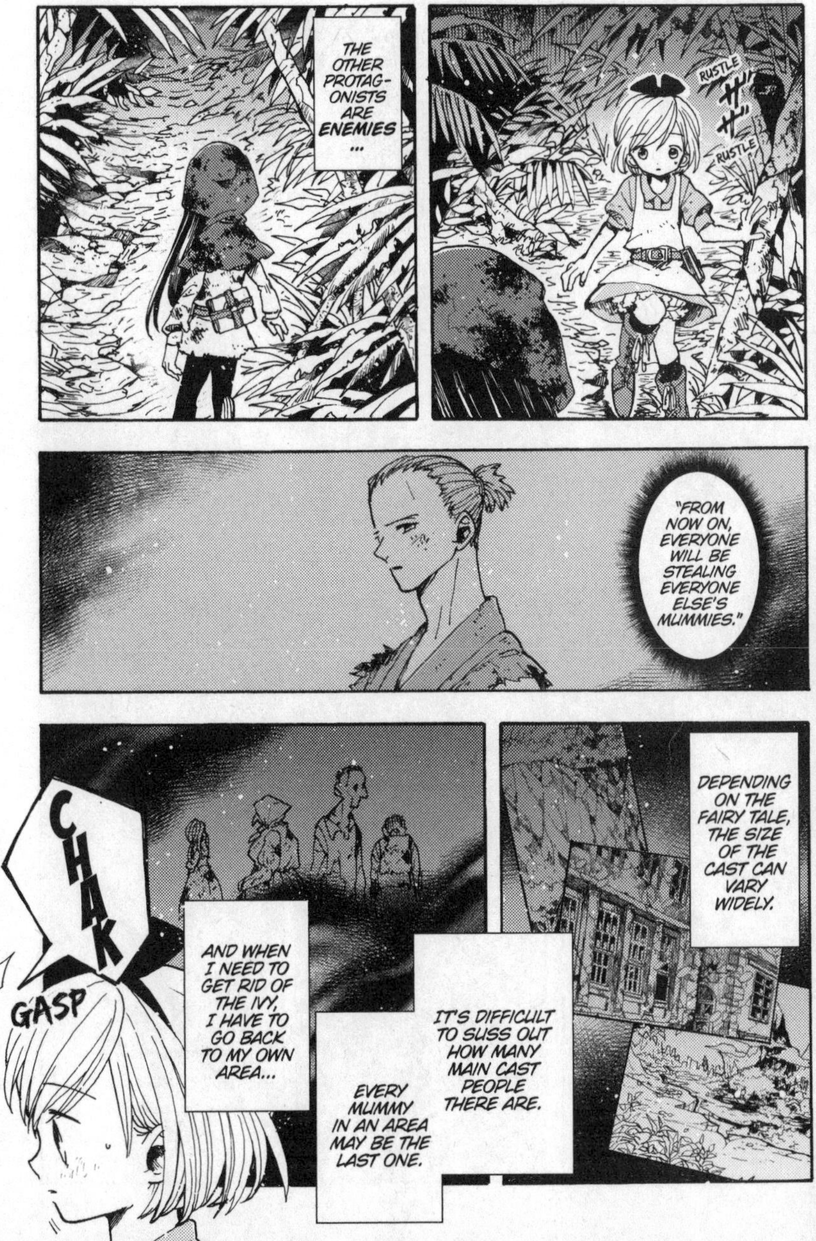
RUSTLE
RUSTLE
THE OTHER PROTAG-ONISTS ARE ENEMIES ...
"FROM NOW ON, EVERYONE WILL BE STEALING EVERYONE ELSE'S MUMMIES."
DEPENDING ON THE FAIRY TALE, THE SIZE OF THE CAST CAN VARY WIDELY.
IT'S DIFFICULT TO SUSS OUT HOW MANY MAIN CAST PEOPLE THERE ARE.
EVERY MUMMY IN AN AREA MAY BE THE LAST ONE.
AND WHEN I NEED TO GET RID OF THE IVY, I HAVE TO GO BACK TO MY OWN AREA...
CHAK
GASP

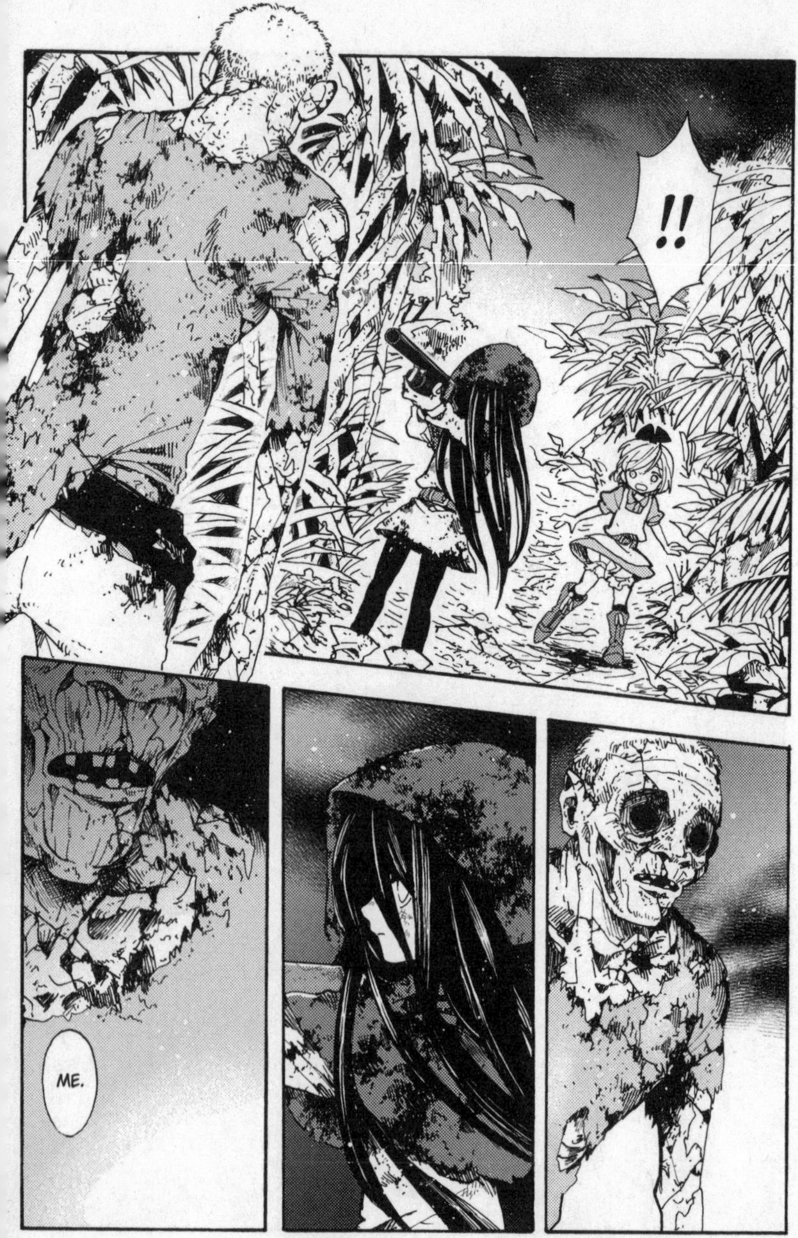
!!
ME.

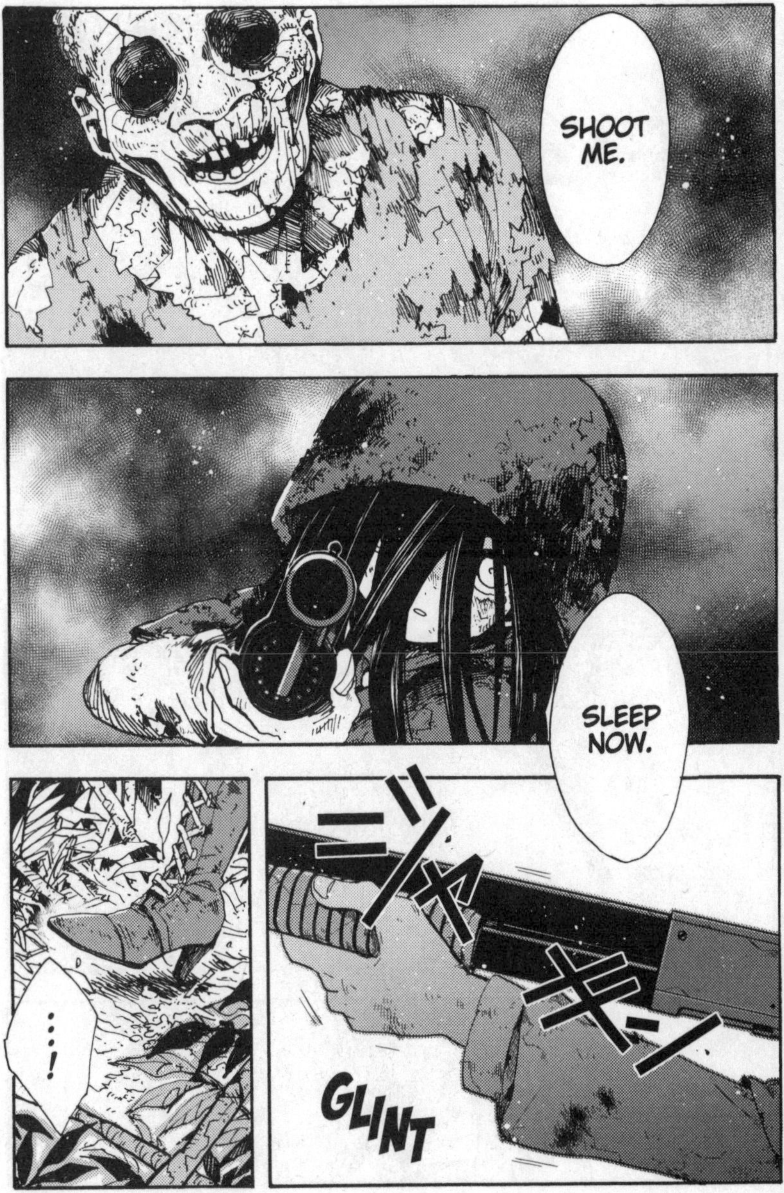
SHOOT ME.
SLEEP NOW.
GLINT
...!

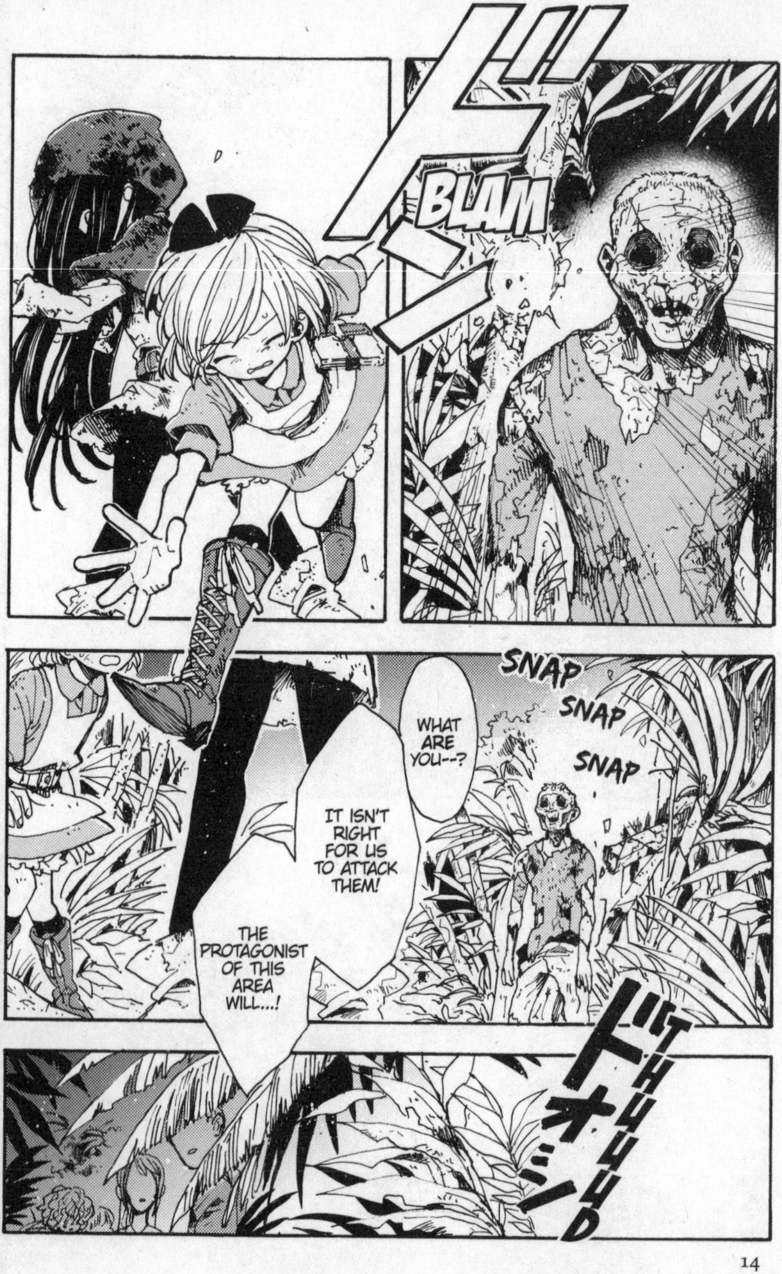
BLAM
SNAP
SNAP
SNAP
WHAT ARE YOU--?
IT ISN'T RIGHT FOR US TO ATTACK THEM!
THE PROTAGONIST OF THIS AREA WILL...!
THUUUUUD

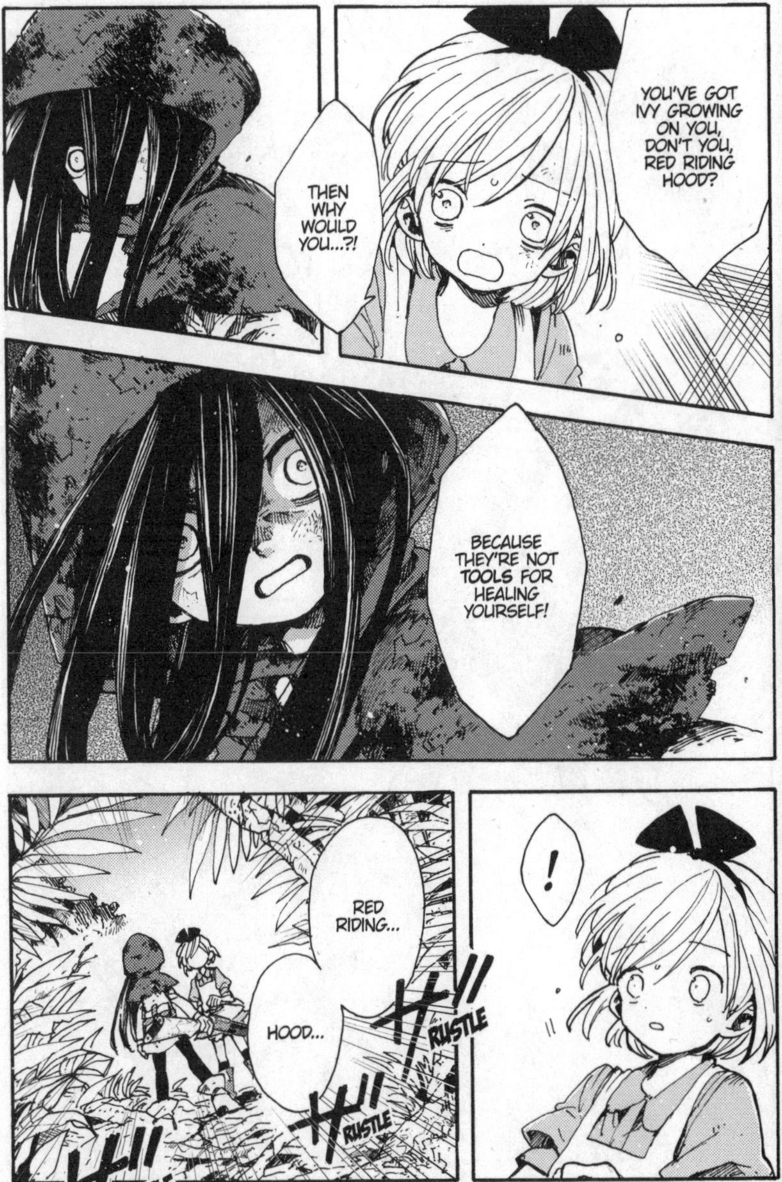
YOU'VE GOT IVY GROWING ON YOU, DON'T YOU, RED RIDING HOOD?
THEN WHY WOULD YOU...?!
BECAUSE THEY'RE NOT TOOLS FOR HEALING YOURSELF!
!
RED RIDING...
HOOD...
RUSTLE
RUSTLE
RUSTLE

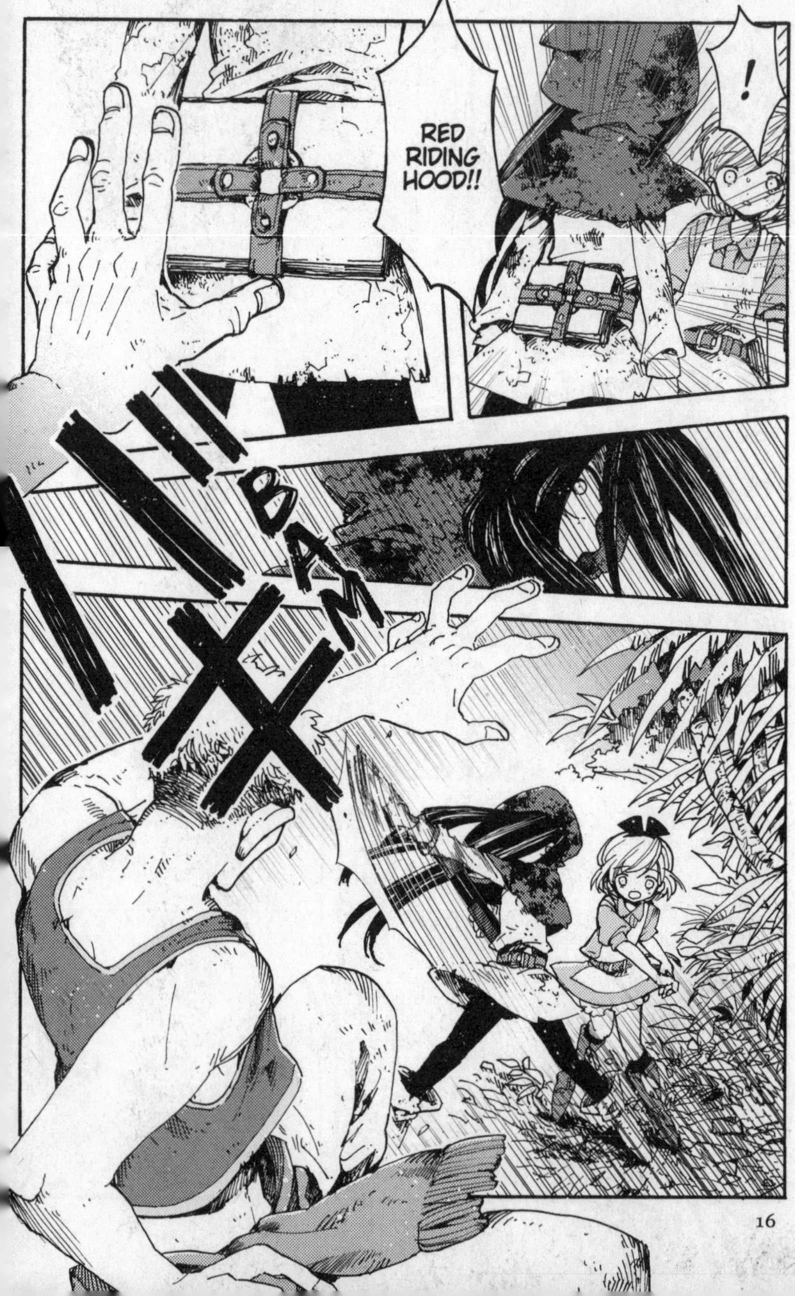
!
RED RIDING HOOD!!
BAM

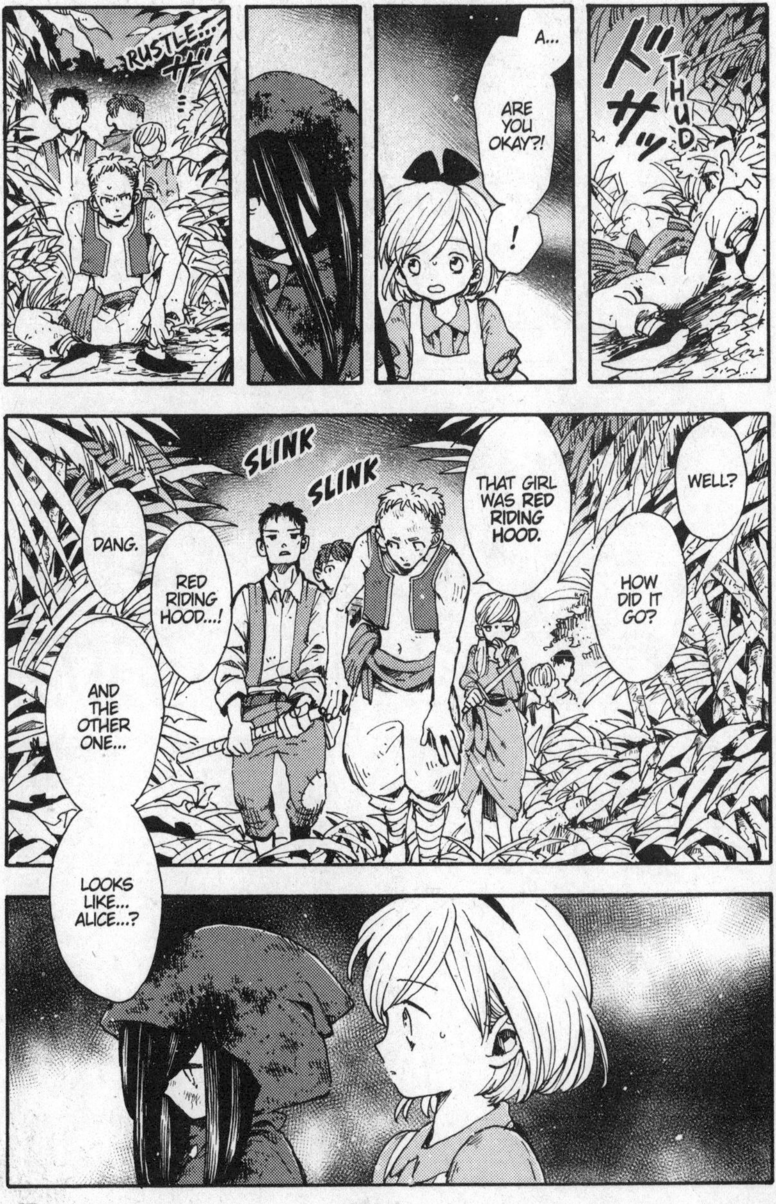
THUD
A...
ARE YOU OKAY?!
!
RUSTLE...
WELL?
HOW DID IT GO?
THAT GIRL WAS RED RIDING HOOD.
SLINK
SLINK
DANG.
RED RIDING HOOD...!
...
AND THE OTHER ONE...
LOOKS LIKE... ALICE...?

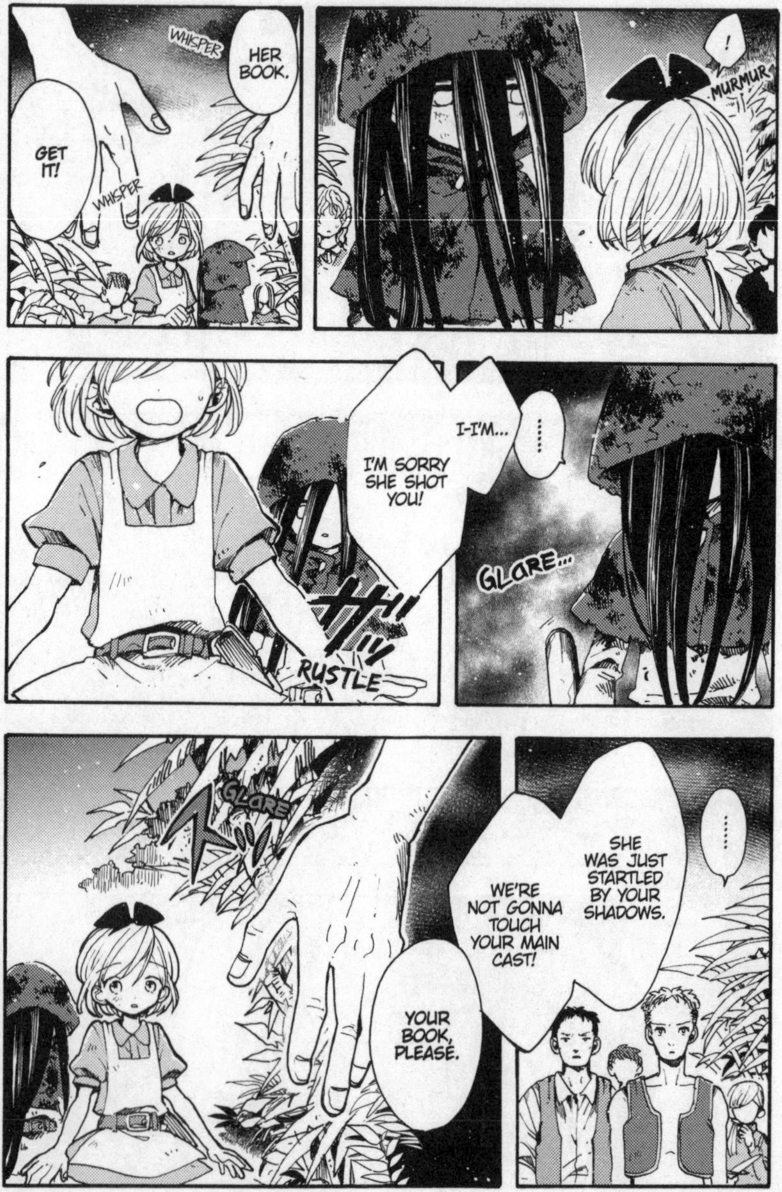
!
MURMUR
HER BOOK.
WHISPER
GET IT!
WHISPER
......
GLARE...
I-I'M... I'M SORRY SHE SHOT YOU!
RUSTLE
......
SHE WAS JUST STARTLED BY YOUR SHADOWS.
WE'RE NOT GONNA TOUCH YOUR MAIN CAST!
GLARE
YOUR BOOK, PLEASE.

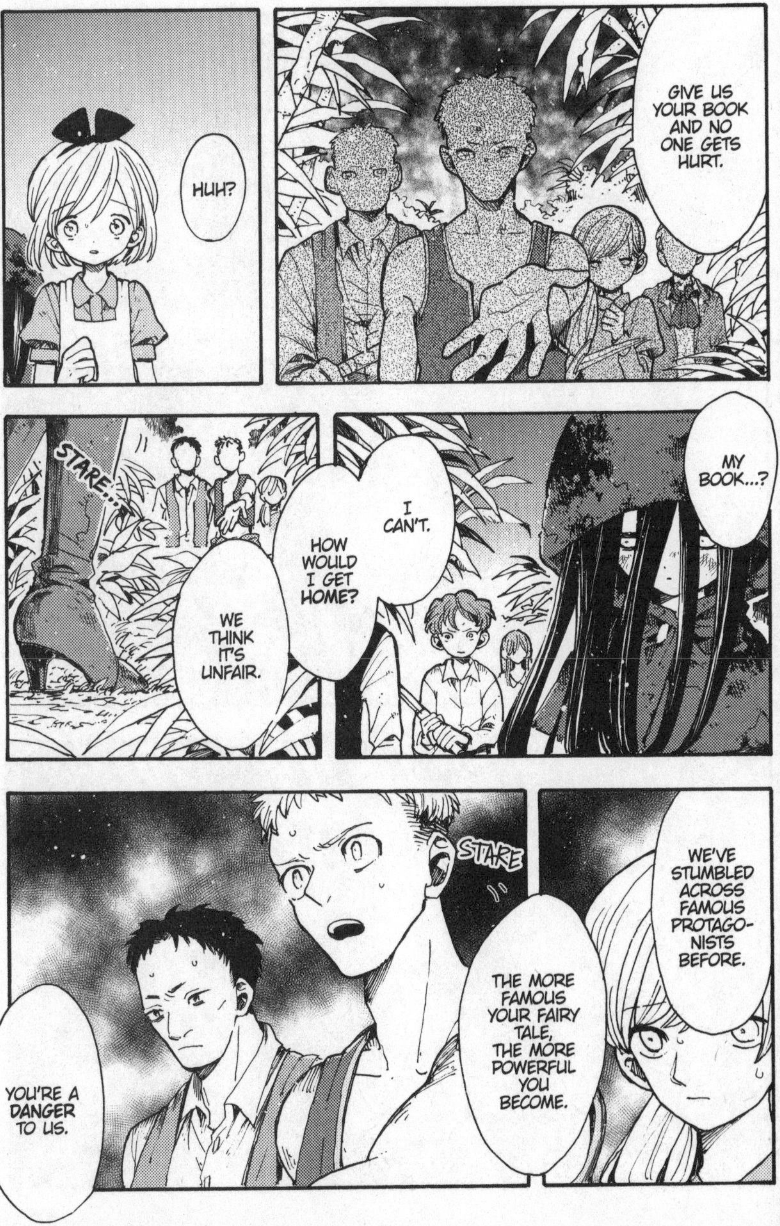
GIVE US YOUR BOOK AND NO ONE GETS HURT.
HUH?
MY BOOK...?
I CAN'T.
HOW WOULD I GET HOME?
WE THINK IT'S UNFAIR.
STARE...
WE'VE STUMBLED ACROSS FAMOUS PROTAGO-NISTS BEFORE.
THE MORE FAMOUS YOUR FAIRY TALE, THE MORE POWERFUL YOU BECOME.
STARE
YOU'RE A DANGER TO US.

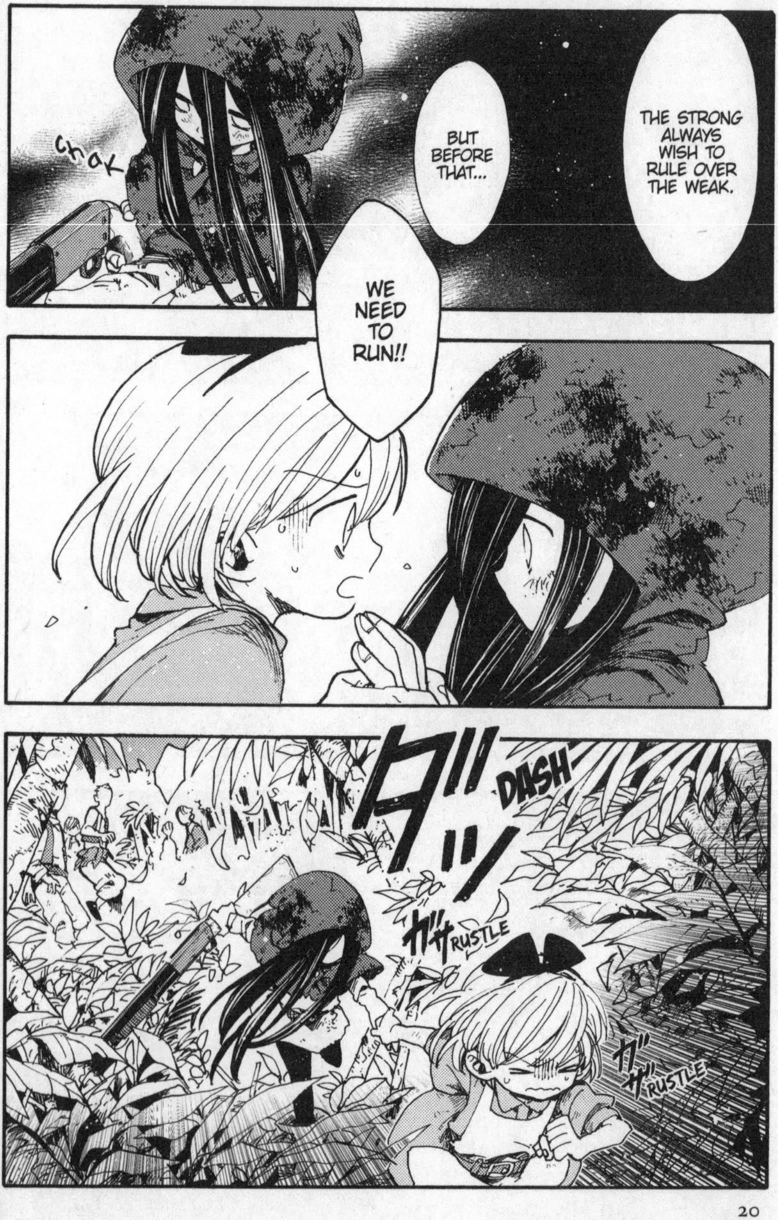
THE STRONG ALWAYS WISH TO RULE OVER THE WEAK.
BUT BEFORE THAT...
chak
WE NEED TO RUN!!
ダッ
DASH
ガサ
RUSTLE
ガザ
RUSTLE

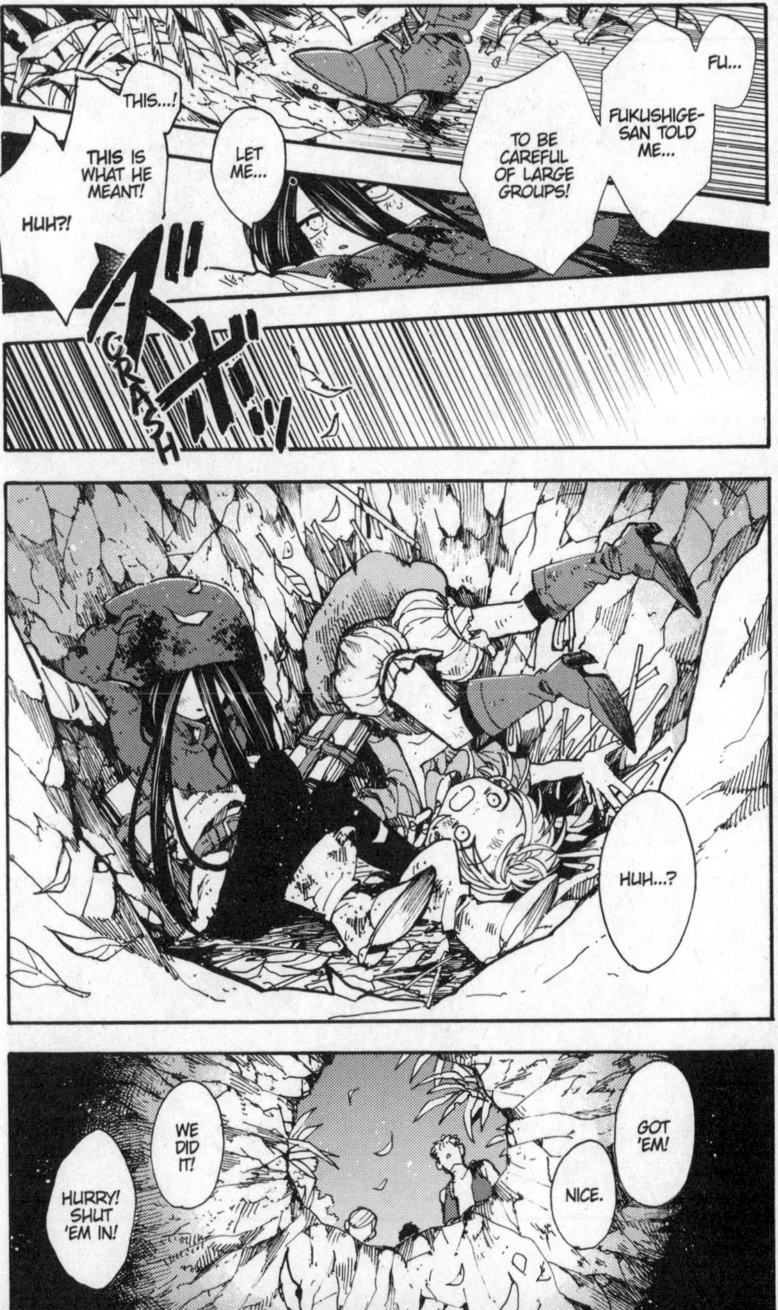
FU...
FUKUSHIGE-SAN TOLD ME...
TO BE CAREFUL OF LARGE GROUPS!
LET ME...
THIS...!
THIS IS WHAT HE MEANT!
HUH?!
CRASH
HUH...?
GOT 'EM!
NICE.
WE DID IT!
HURRY! SHUT 'EM IN!

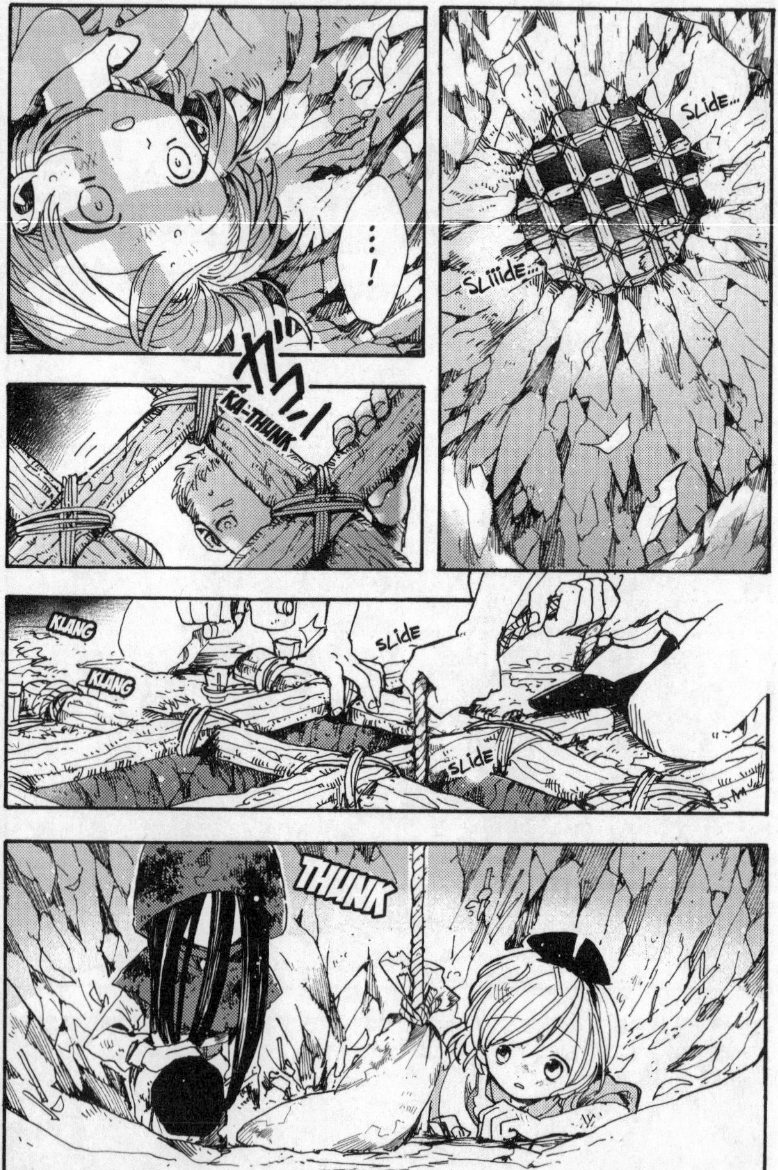
Slide...
Sliiide...
...!
ガコッ
KA-THUNK
slide
slide
KLANG
KLANG
THUNK

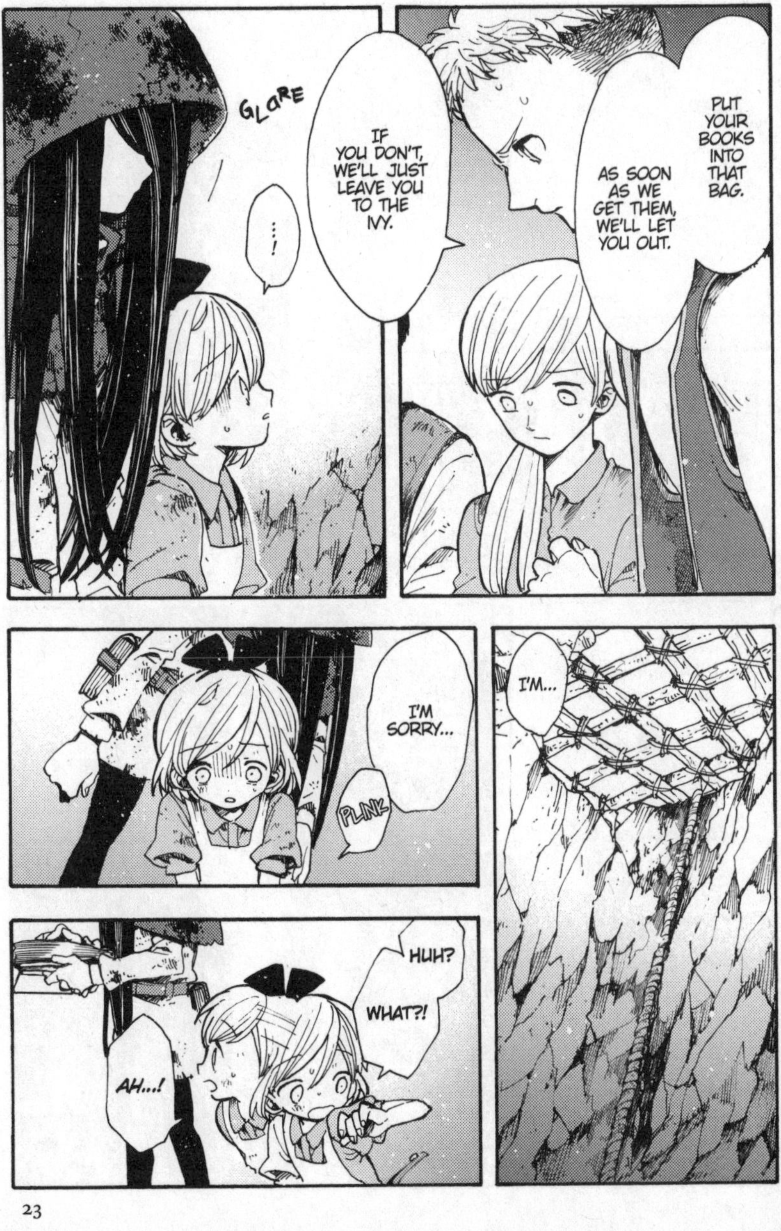
PUT YOUR BOOKS INTO THAT BAG.
AS SOON AS WE GET THEM, WE'LL LET YOU OUT.
IF YOU DON'T, WE'LL JUST LEAVE YOU TO THE IVY.
GLARE
...!
I'M...
I'M SORRY...
PLINK
HUH?
WHAT?!
AH...!

THAT'S MY...!
YOU SHOULD GO HOME.
Fwip
p://toitter.com/Noah!..
Noah!!
GO HOME?!
WHAT ABOUT YOU, RED...?
COME BACK IN A LITTLE WHILE.
BUT THIS... IT'S MY...!
YOU'RE IN MY WAY.
WAIT...!

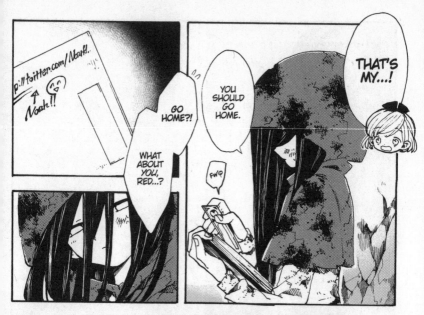

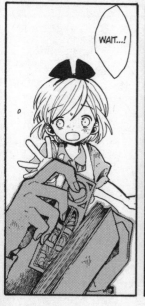

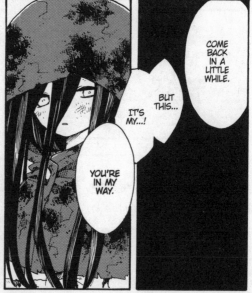

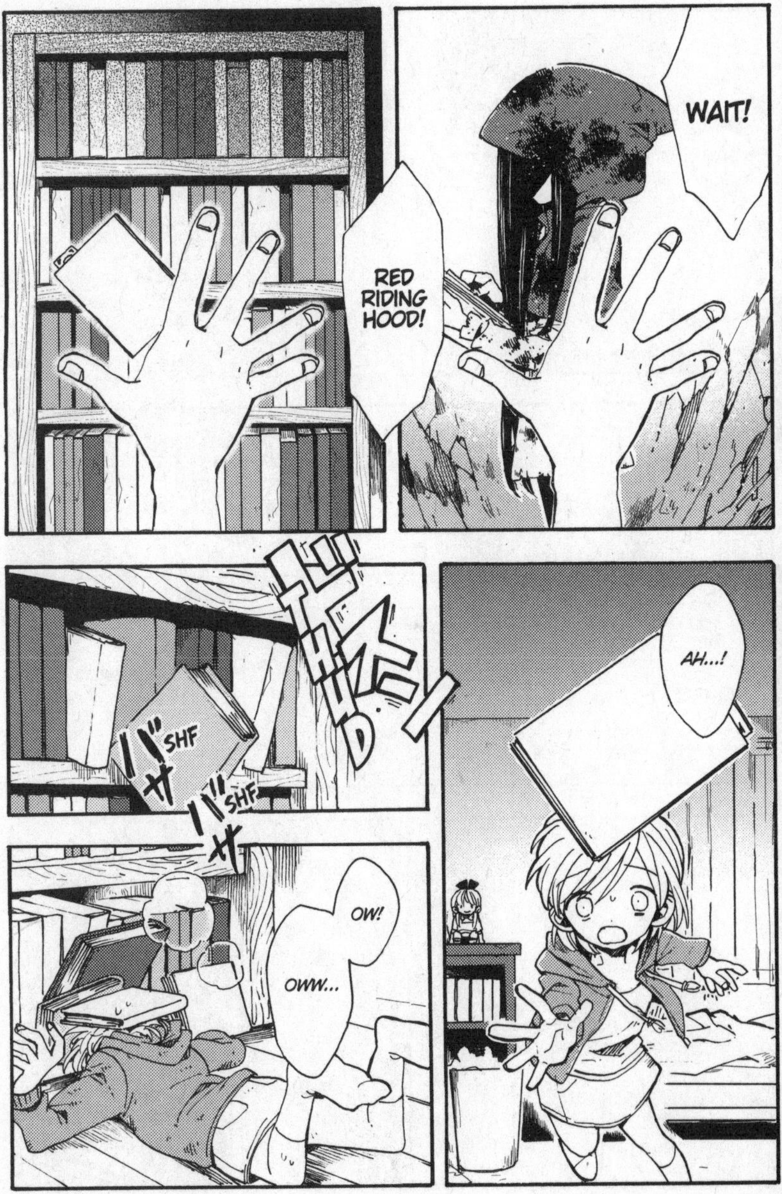
WAIT!
RED RIDING HOOD!
AH...!
THUD
SHF
SHF
OW!
OWW...

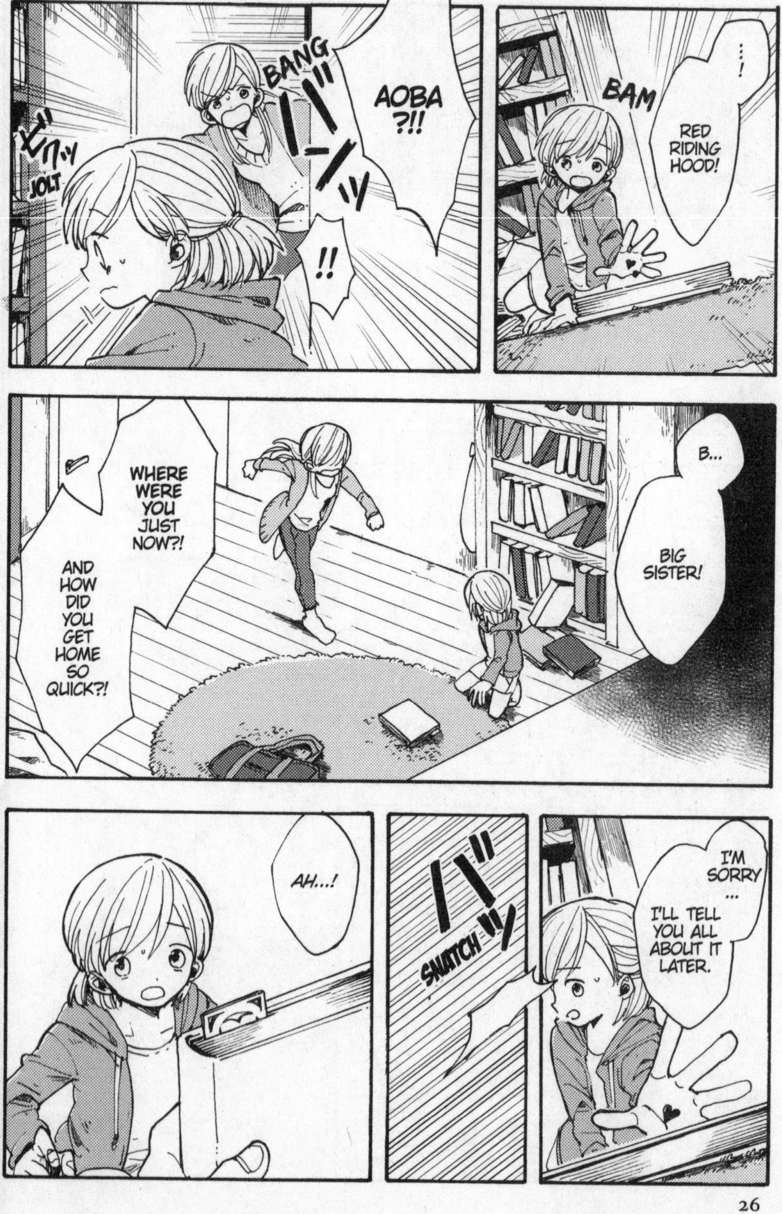
BAM
...!
RED RIDING HOOD!
BANG
AOBA ?!!
!!
ビクッ
JOLT
B...
BIG SISTER!
WHERE WERE YOU JUST NOW?!
AND HOW DID YOU GET HOME SO QUICK?!
I'M SORRY ...
I'LL TELL YOU ALL ABOUT IT LATER.
SNATCH
AH...!

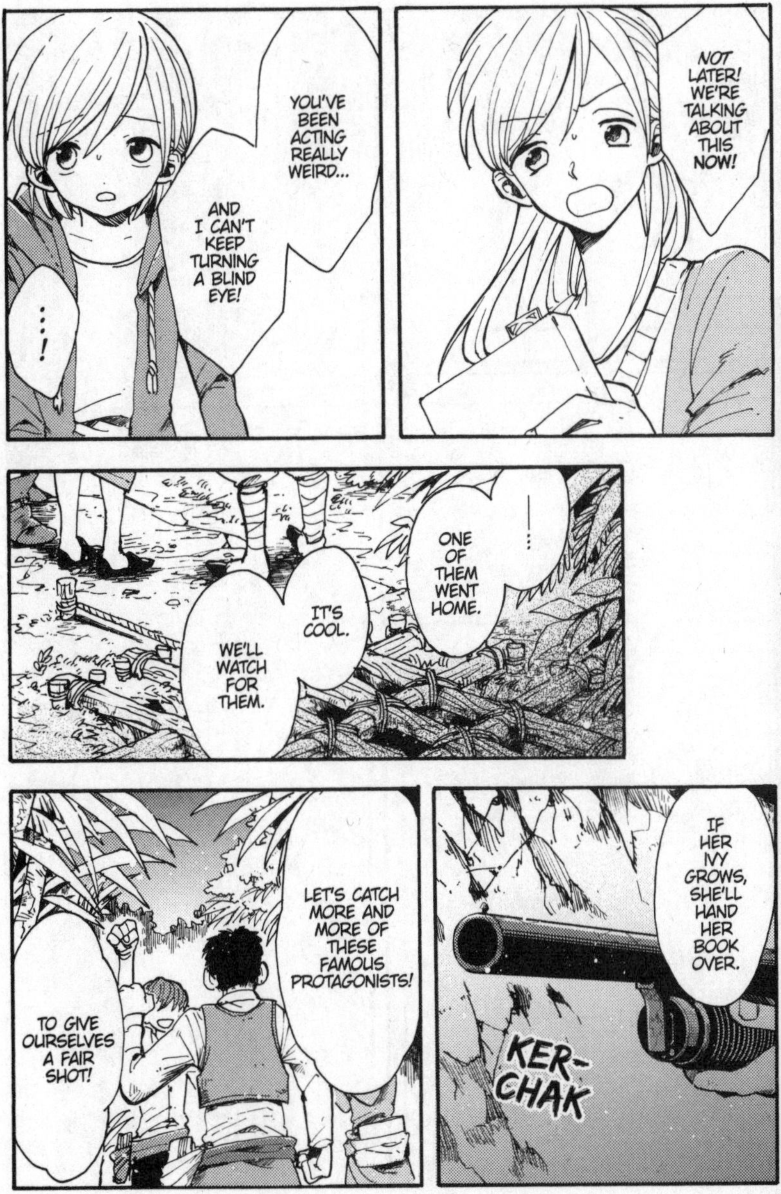

NOT LATER! WE'RE TALKING ABOUT THIS NOW!
YOU'VE BEEN ACTING REALLY WEIRD...
AND I CAN'T KEEP TURNING A BLIND EYE!
...!
...!
ONE OF THEM WENT HOME.
IT'S COOL.
WE'LL WATCH FOR THEM.
IF HER IVY GROWS, SHE'LL HAND HER BOOK OVER.
KER-CHAK
LET'S CATCH MORE AND MORE OF THESE FAMOUS PROTAGONISTS!
TO GIVE OURSELVES A FAIR SHOT!

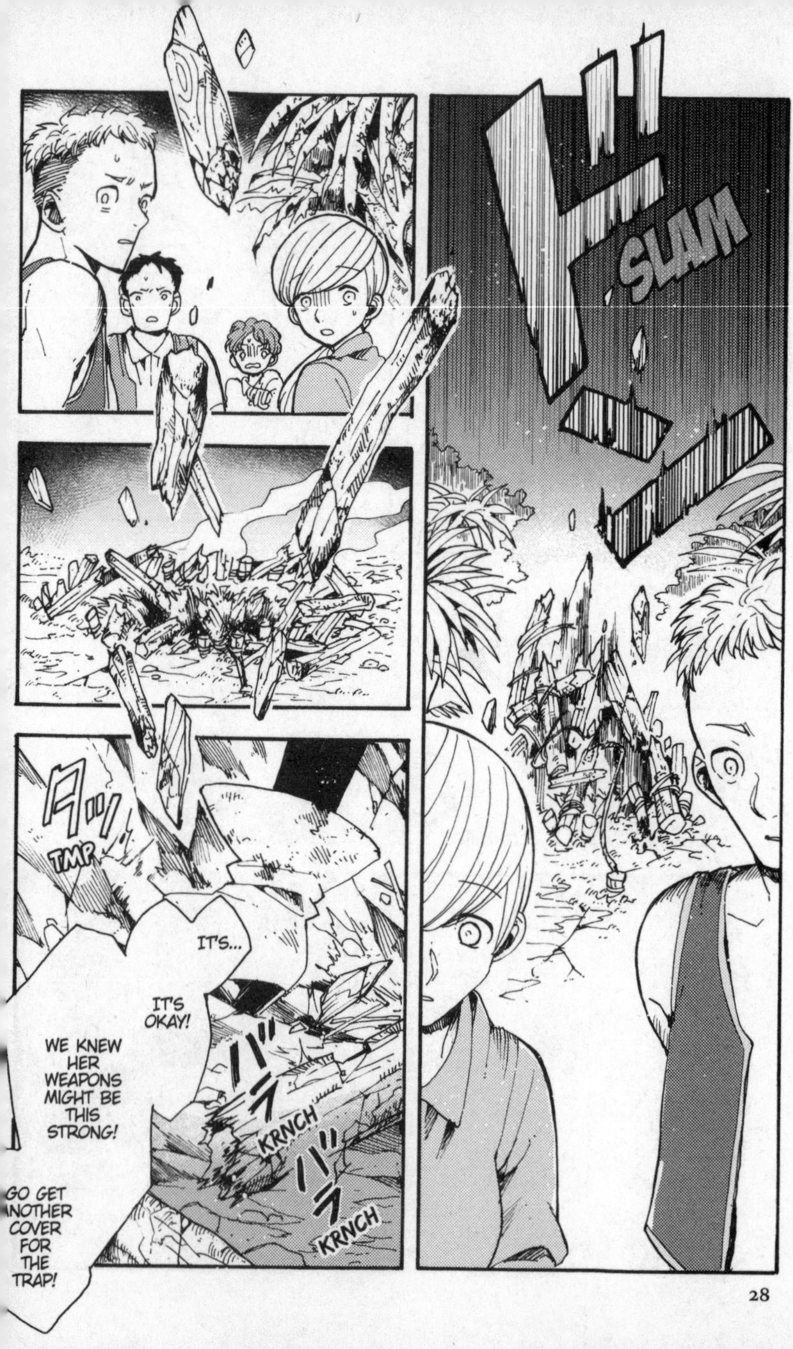
SLAM
TMP
IT'S...
IT'S OKAY!
WE KNEW HER WEAPONS MIGHT BE THIS STRONG!
GO GET ANOTHER COVER FOR THE TRAP!
KRNCH
KRNCH

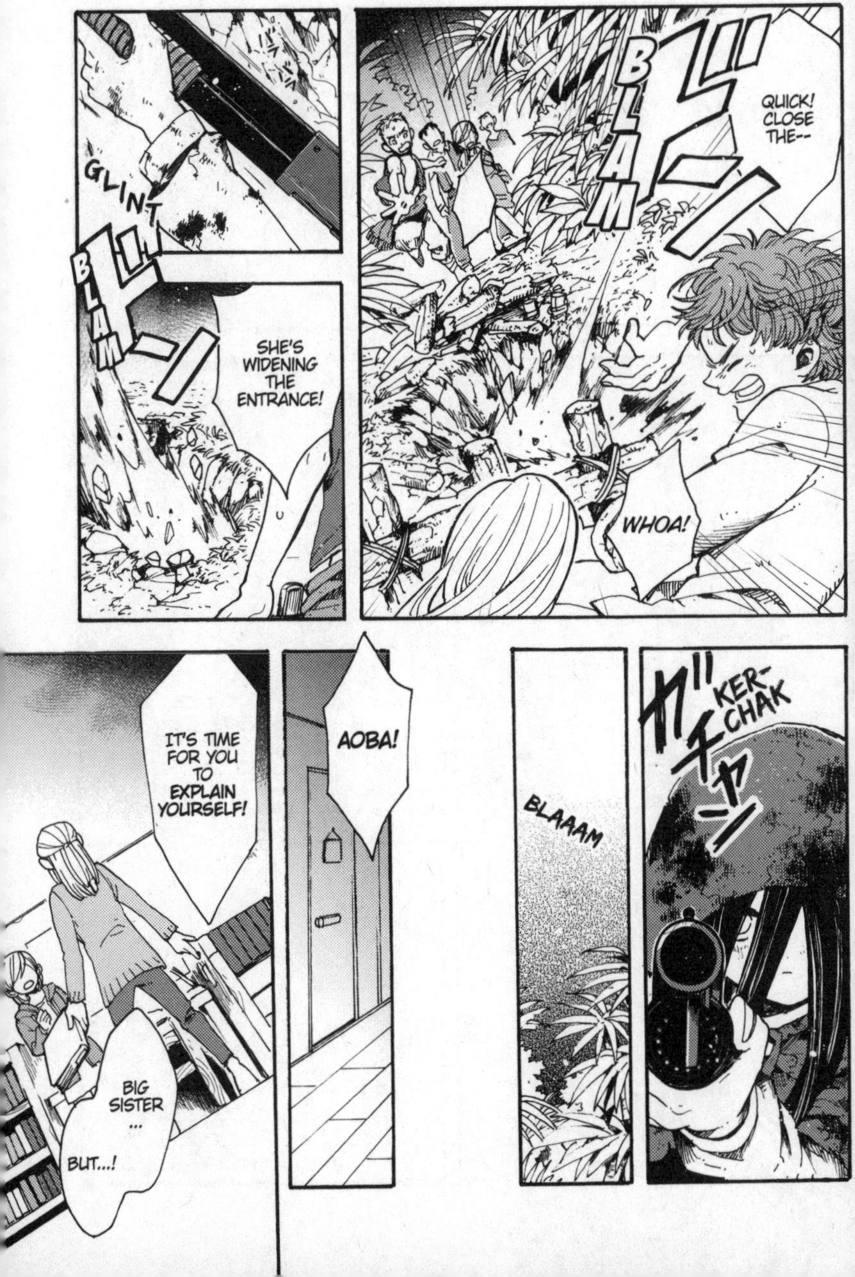
BLAM
QUICK! CLOSE THE--
WHOA!
GLINT
BLAM
SHE'S WIDENING THE ENTRANCE!
KER-CHAK
BLAAAM
AOBA!
IT'S TIME FOR YOU TO EXPLAIN YOURSELF!
BIG SISTER ...
BUT...!

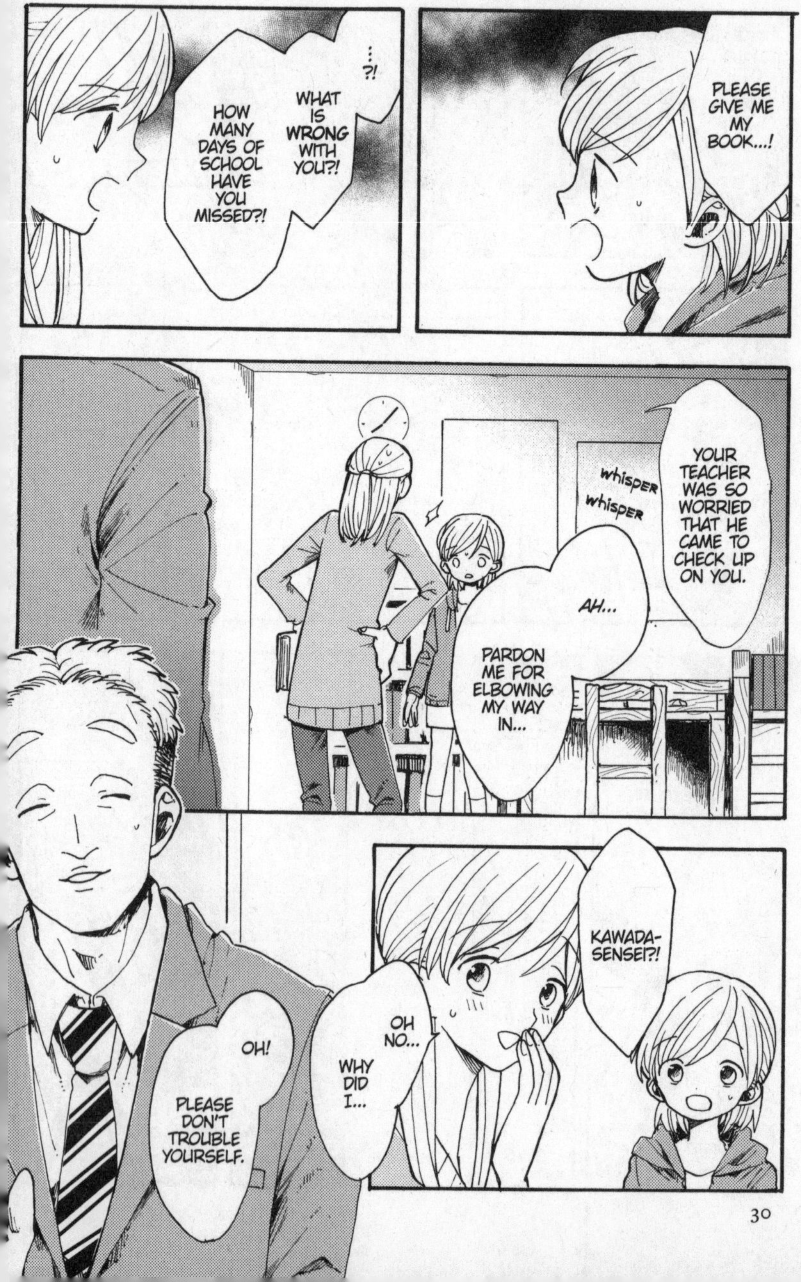
PLEASE GIVE ME MY BOOK...!
...?!
WHAT IS WRONG WITH YOU?!
HOW MANY DAYS OF SCHOOL HAVE YOU MISSED?!
YOUR TEACHER WAS SO WORRIED THAT HE CAME TO CHECK UP ON YOU.
whisper
whisper
AH...
PARDON ME FOR ELBOWING MY WAY IN...
KAWADA-SENSEI!?!
OH NO...
WHY DID I...
OH!
PLEASE DON'T TROUBLE YOURSELF.

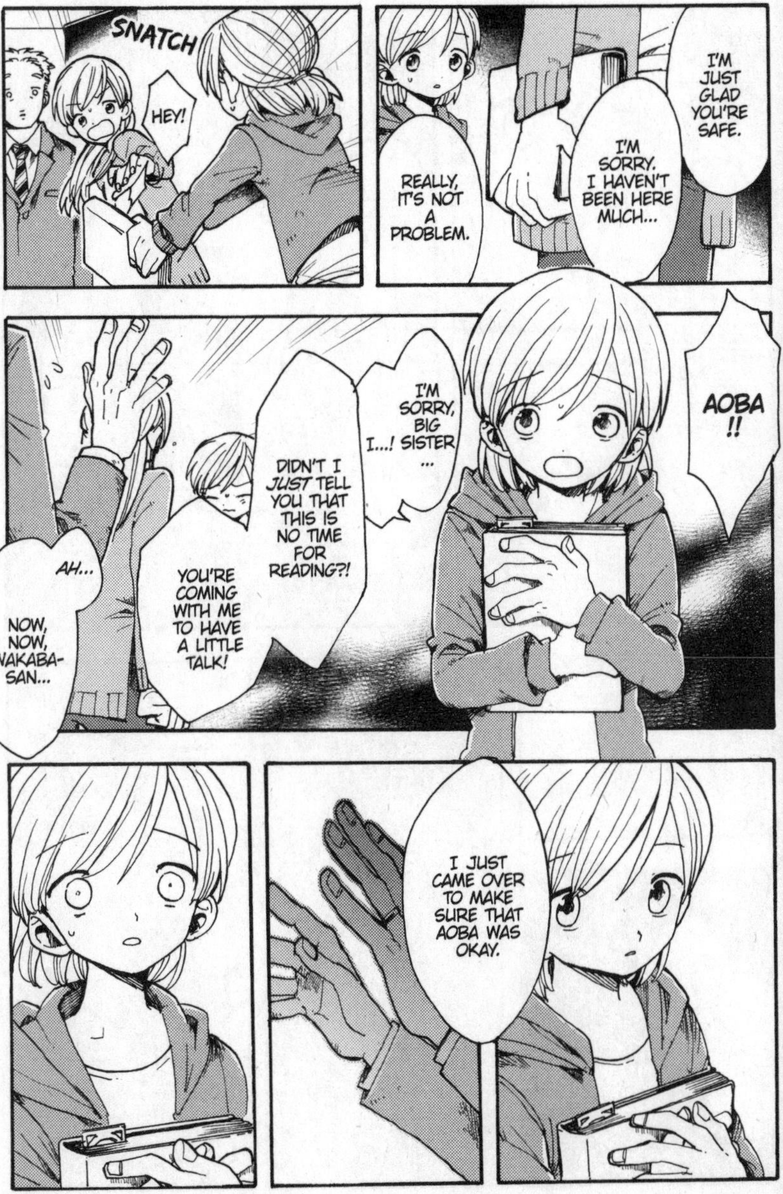
I'M JUST GLAD YOU'RE SAFE.
I'M SORRY. I HAVEN'T BEEN HERE MUCH...
REALLY, IT'S NOT A PROBLEM.
SNATCH
HEY!
AOBA!!
I'M SORRY, BIG SISTER...
I...!
DIDN'T I *JUST* TELL YOU THAT THIS IS NO TIME FOR READING?!
YOU'RE COMING WITH ME TO HAVE A LITTLE TALK!
AH...
NOW, NOW, WAKABA-SAN...
I JUST CAME OVER TO MAKE SURE THAT AOBA WAS OKAY.

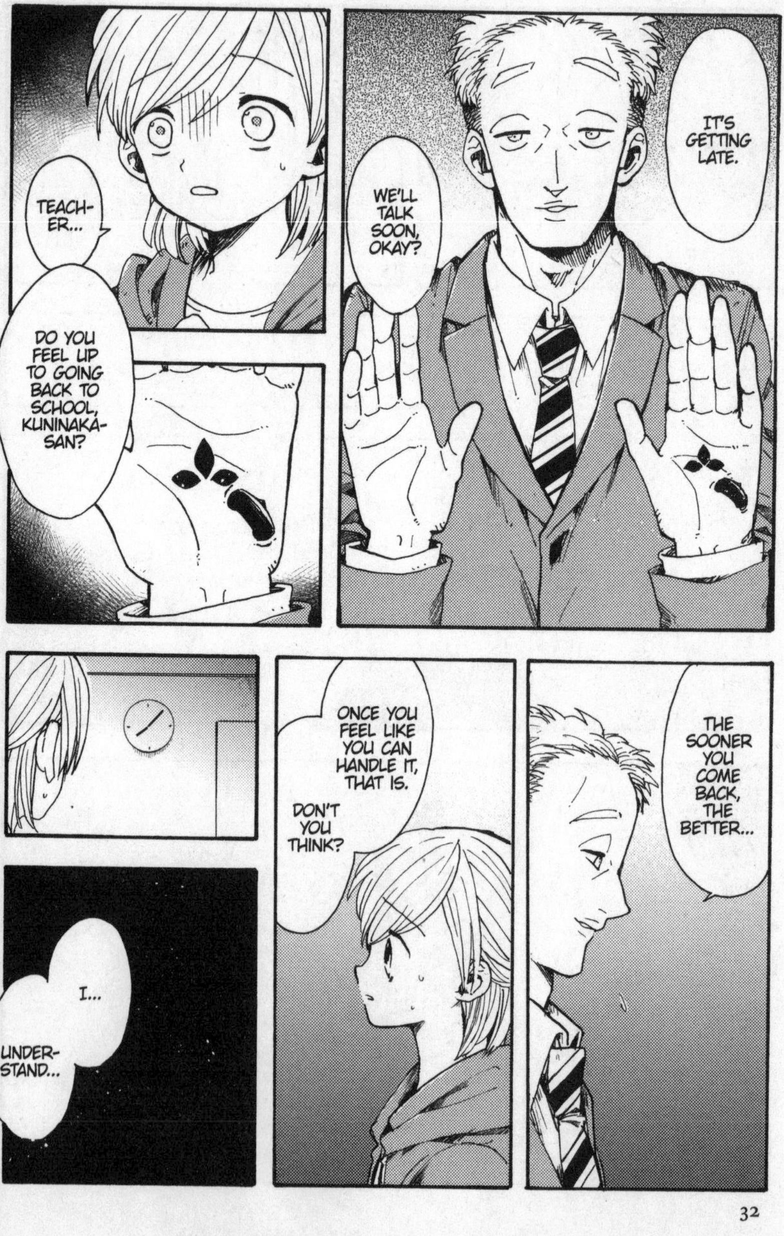
IT'S GETTING LATE.
WE'LL TALK SOON, OKAY?
TEACHER...
DO YOU FEEL UP TO GOING BACK TO SCHOOL, KUNINAKA-SAN?
THE SOONER YOU COME BACK, THE BETTER...
ONCE YOU FEEL LIKE YOU CAN HANDLE IT, THAT IS.
DON'T YOU THINK?
I...
UNDER-STAND...

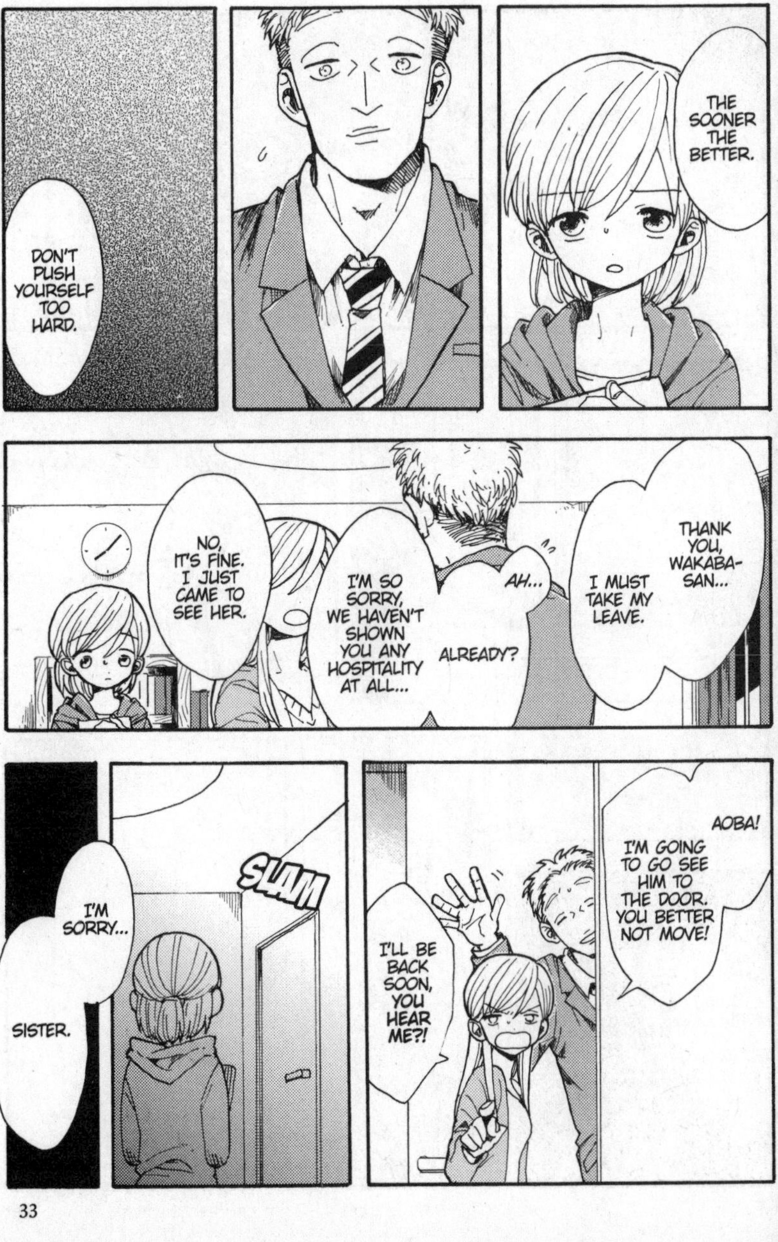
THE SOONER THE BETTER.
DON'T PUSH YOURSELF TOO HARD.
THANK YOU, WAKABA-SAN...
I MUST TAKE MY LEAVE.
AH...
ALREADY?
I'M SO SORRY, WE HAVEN'T SHOWN YOU ANY HOSPITALITY AT ALL...
NO, IT'S FINE. I JUST CAME TO SEE HER.
AOBA! I'M GOING TO GO SEE HIM TO THE DOOR. YOU BETTER NOT MOVE!
I'LL BE BACK SOON, YOU HEAR ME?!
SLAM
I'M SORRY...
SISTER.

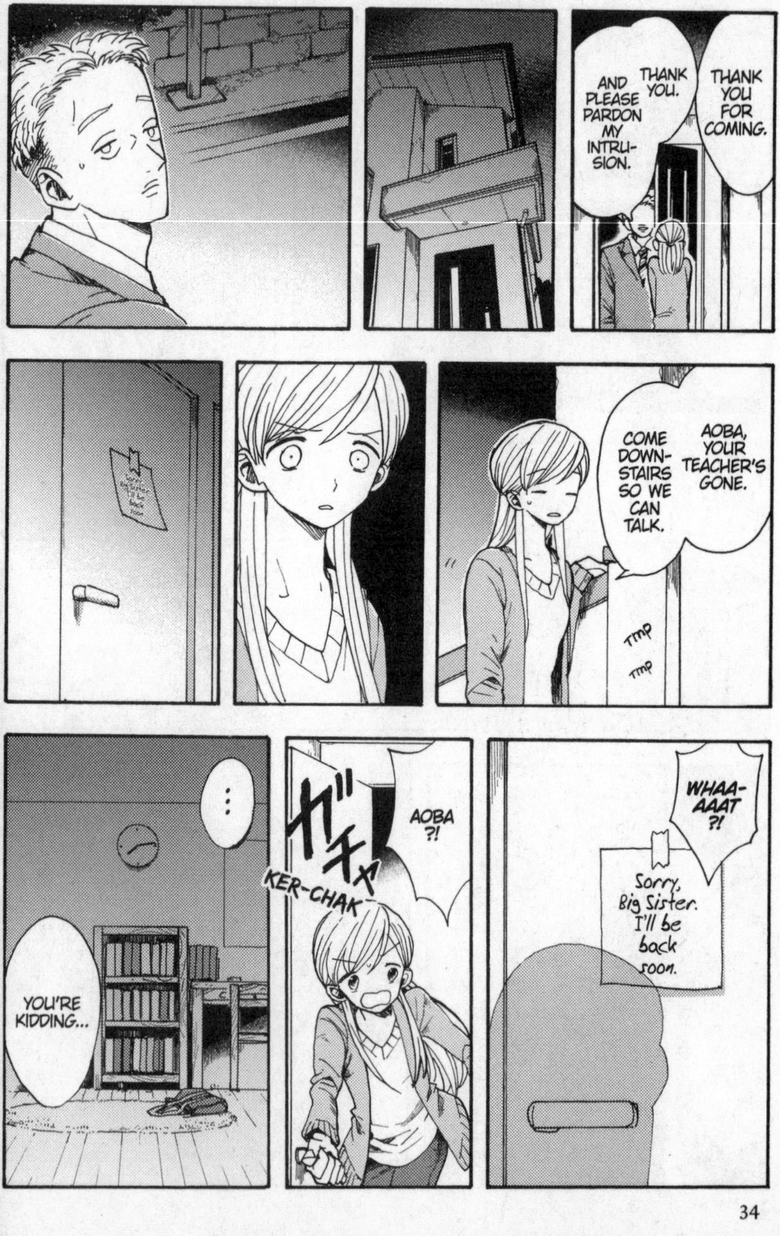
THANK YOU FOR COMING.
THANK YOU.
AND PLEASE PARDON MY INTRU-SION.
AOBA, YOUR TEACHER'S GONE.
COME DOWN-STAIRS SO WE CAN TALK.
TMP
TMP
WHAA-AAAT ?!
Sorry, Big Sister. I'll be back soon.
AOBA ?!
ガチャ
KER-CHAK
...
YOU'RE KIDDING...

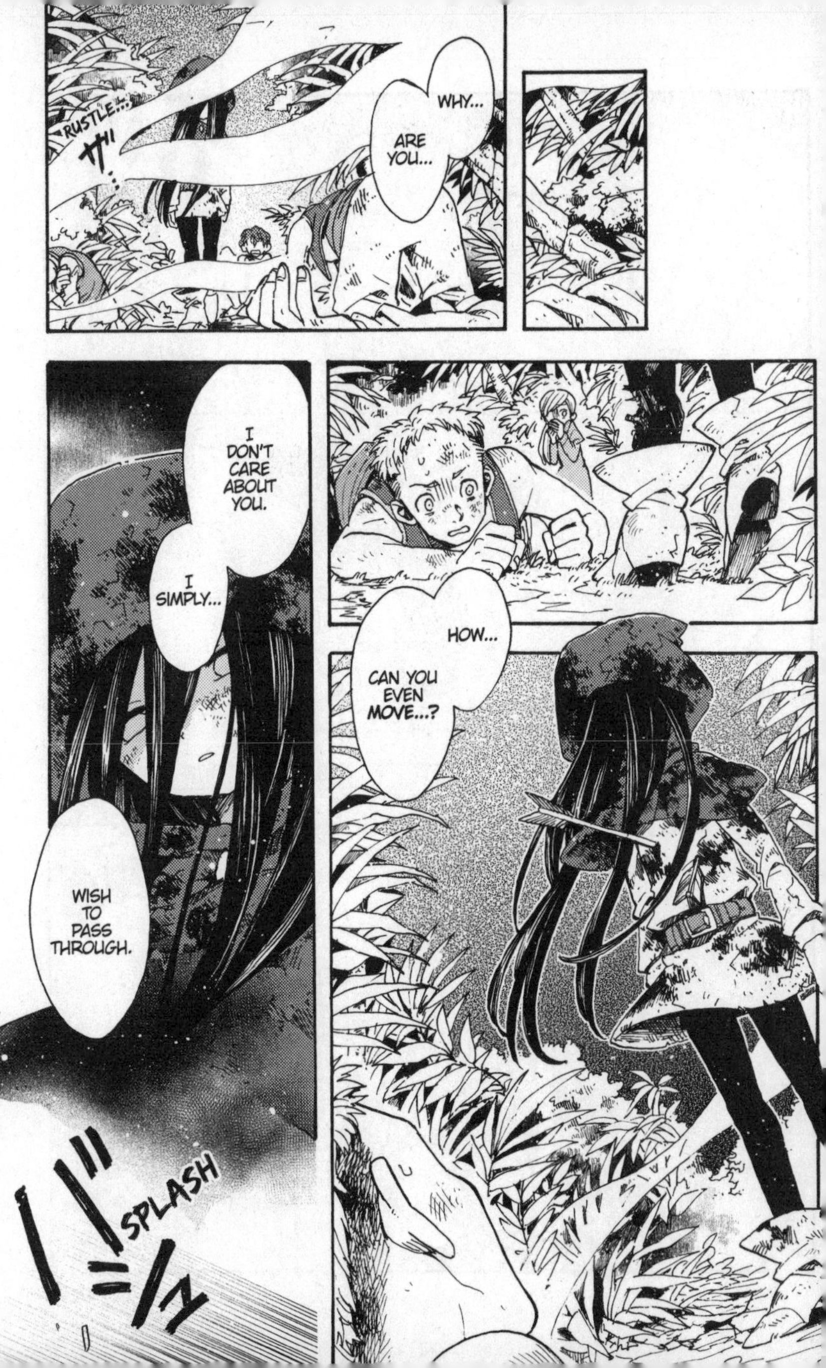
WHY...
ARE YOU...
RUSTLE...
HOW...
CAN YOU EVEN MOVE...?
I DON'T CARE ABOUT YOU.
I SIMPLY...
WISH TO PASS THROUGH.
SPLASH

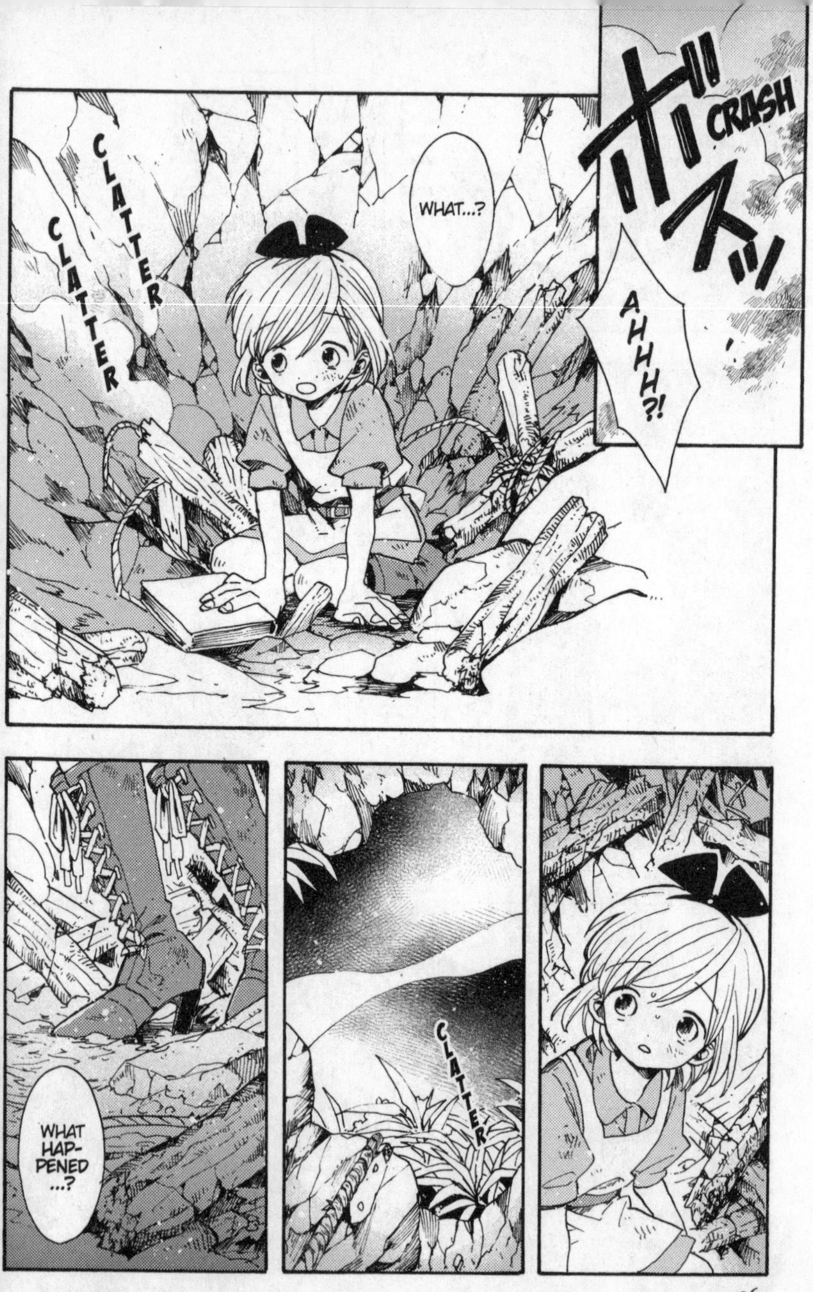
ボスッ
CRASH
AHHHH?!
WHAT...?
CLATTER
CLATTER
CLATTER
WHAT HAP-PENED ...?

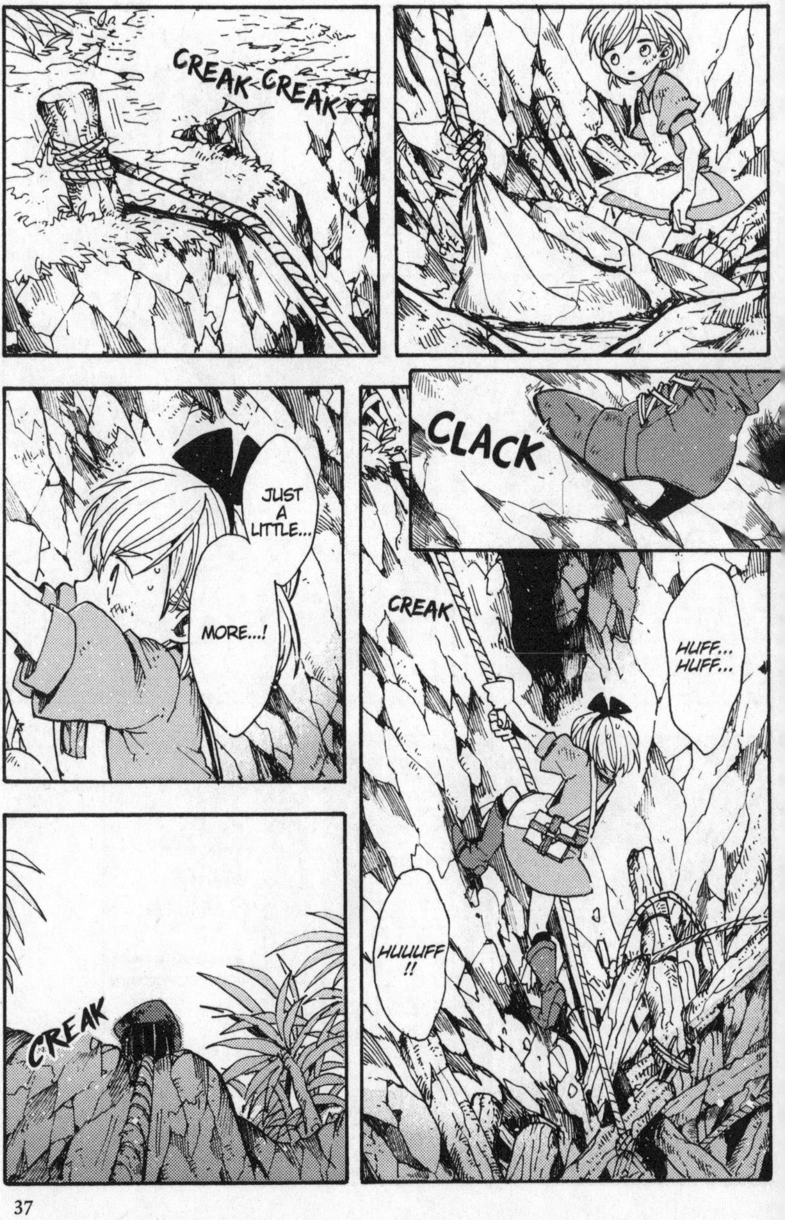
CREAK CREAK
CLACK
CREAK
HUFF... HUFF...
HUUUFF !!
JUST A LITTLE...
MORE...!
CREAK

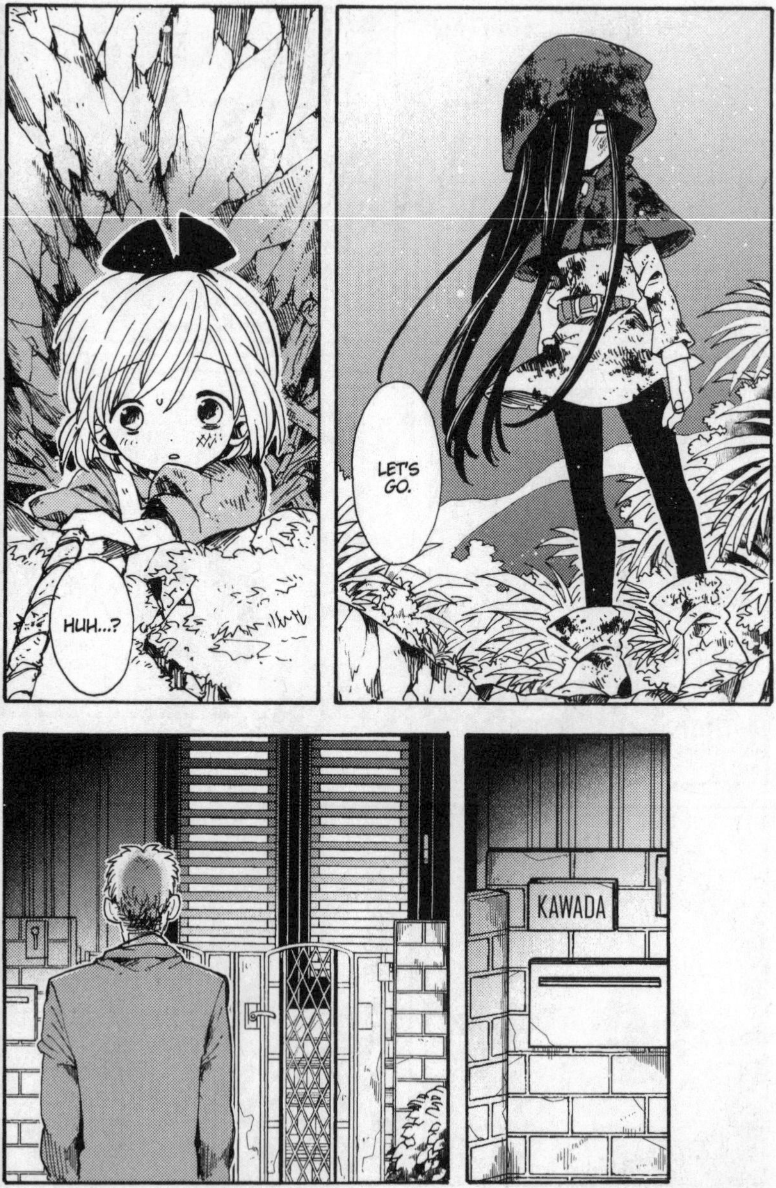
LET'S GO.
HUH...?
KAWADA

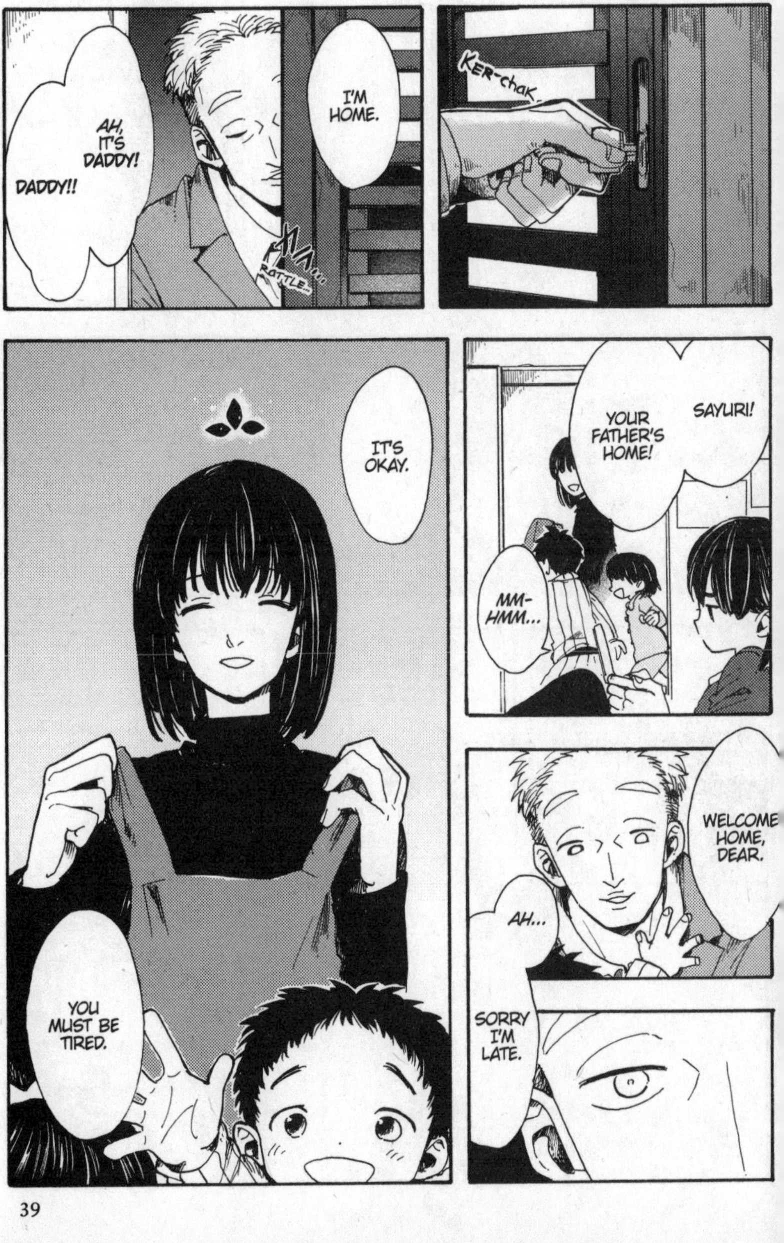
KER-chak
I'M HOME.
AH, IT'S DADDY!
DADDY!!
RATTLE...
SAYURI!
YOUR FATHER'S HOME!
MM-HMM...
WELCOME HOME, DEAR.
AH...
SORRY I'M LATE.
IT'S OKAY.
YOU MUST BE TIRED.

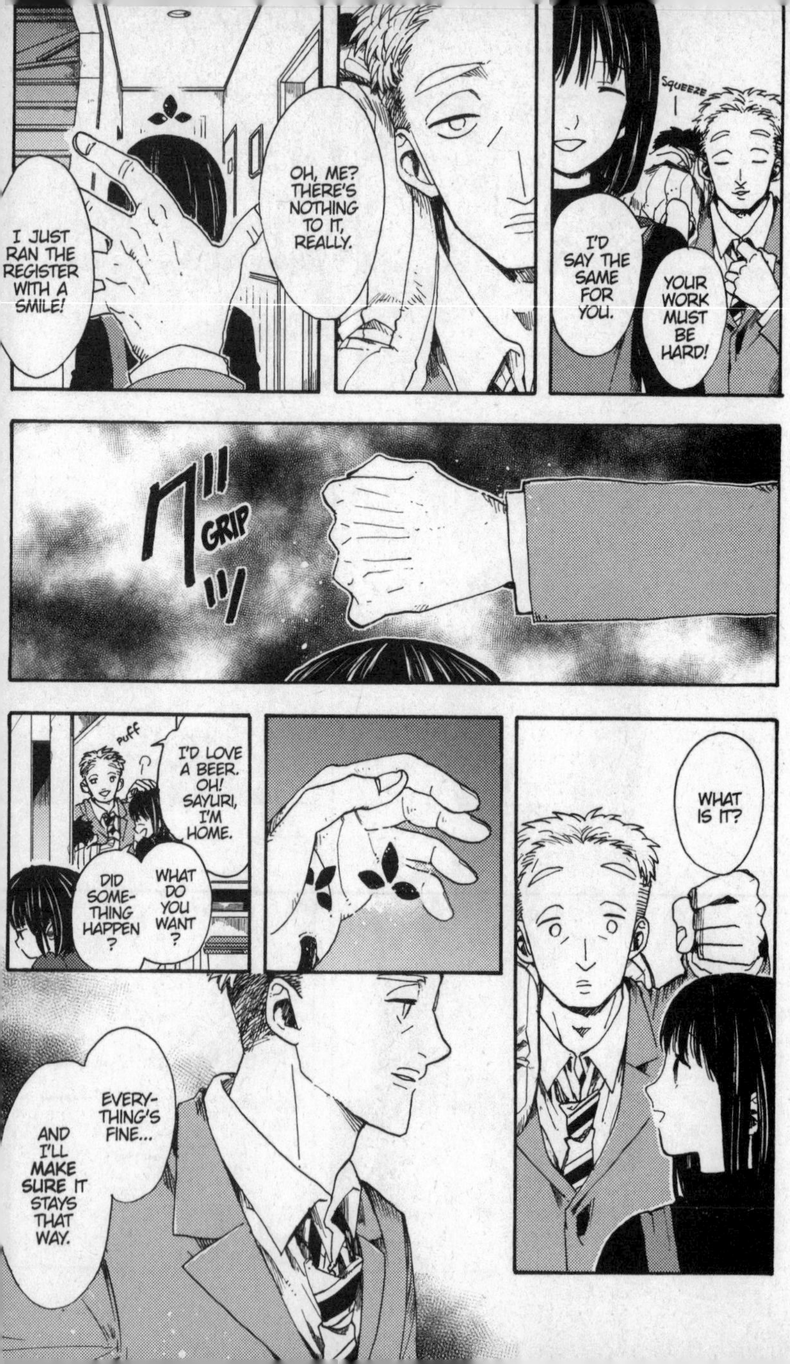
Squeeze
YOUR WORK MUST BE HARD!
I'D SAY THE SAME FOR YOU.
OH, ME? THERE'S NOTHING TO IT, REALLY.
I JUST RAN THE REGISTER WITH A SMILE!
GRIP
WHAT IS IT?
puff
I'D LOVE A BEER. OH! SAYURI, I'M HOME.
WHAT DO YOU WANT?
DID SOMETHING HAPPEN?
EVERYTHING'S FINE...
AND I'LL MAKE SURE IT STAYS THAT WAY.

FAIRY
TALE
BATTLE
ROYALE

FAIRY
TALE
BATTLE
ROYALE

Chapter 14: Second Coming

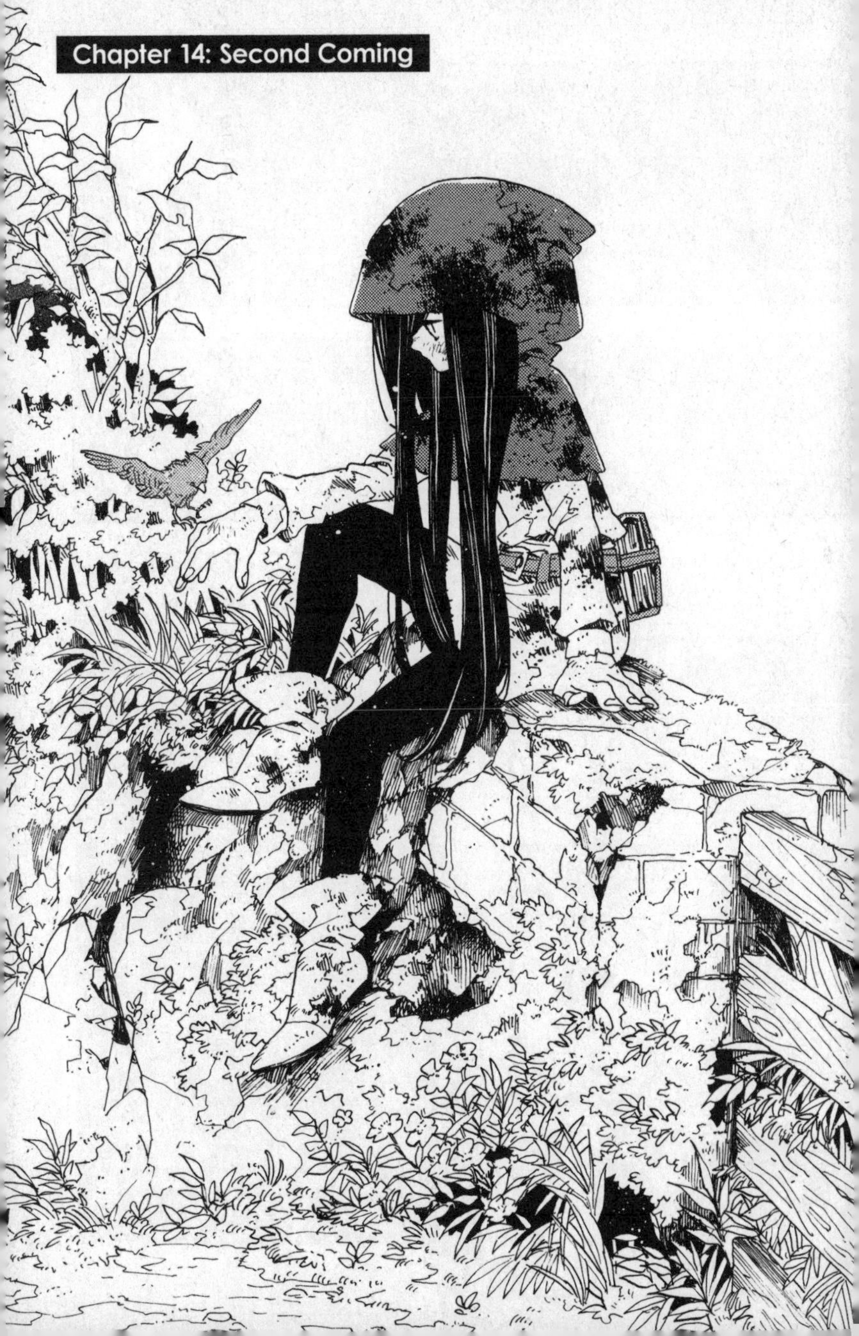

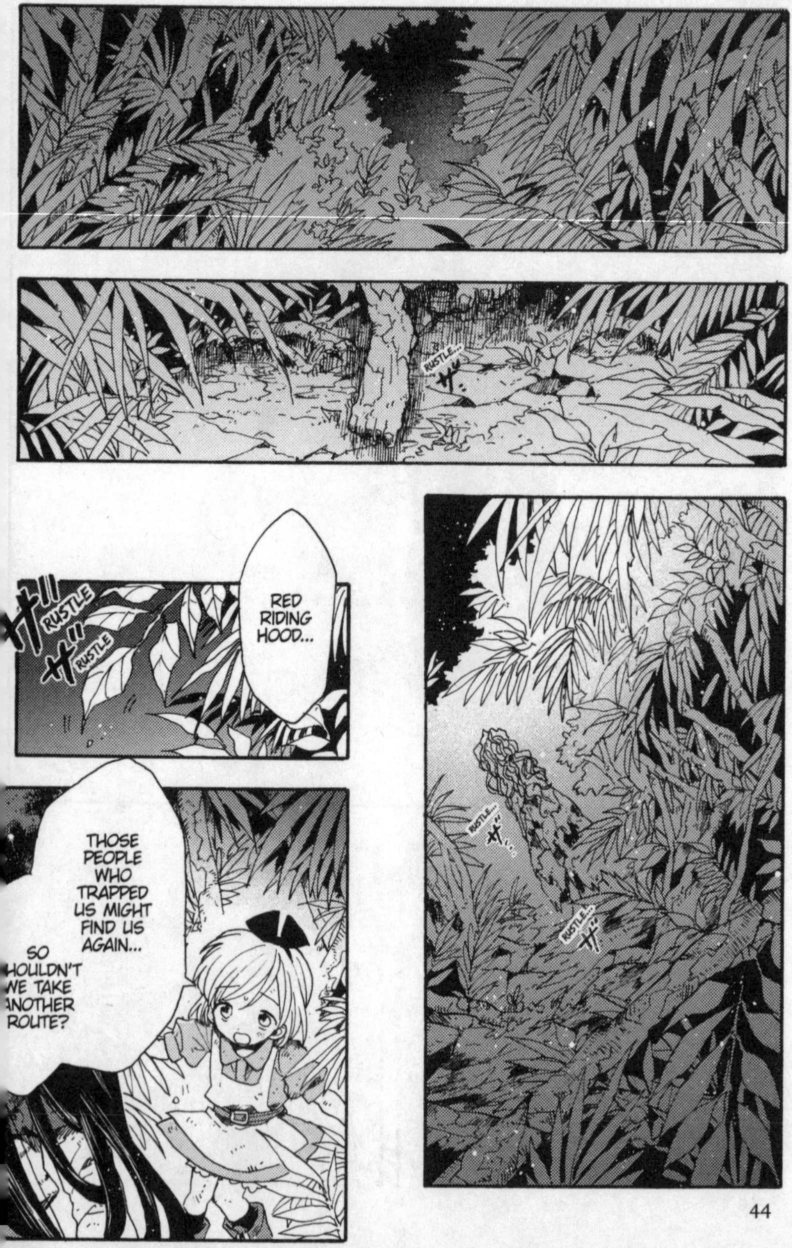
RUSTLE...
RUSTLE...
RUSTLE...
RUSTLE
RUSTLE
RED RIDING HOOD...
THOSE PEOPLE WHO TRAPPED US MIGHT FIND US AGAIN...
SO HOULDN'T WE TAKE ANOTHER ROUTE?

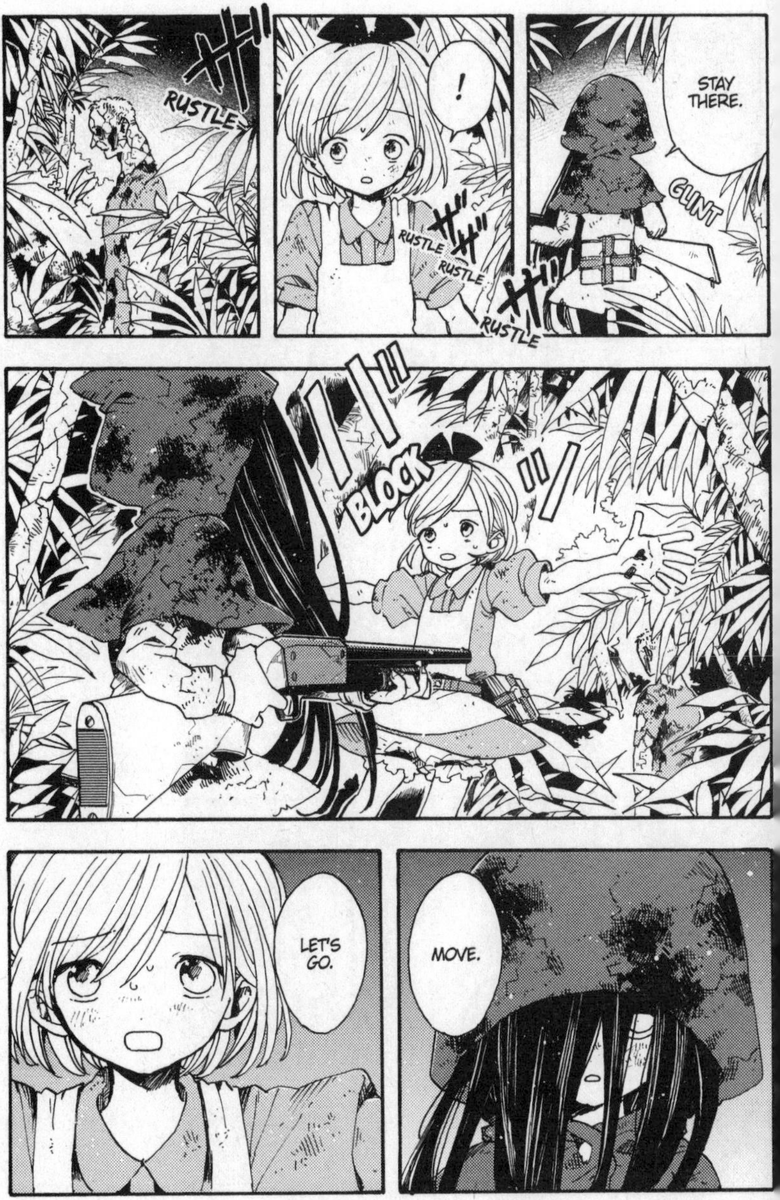

STAY THERE.
GLINT
RUSTLE
!
RUSTLE
RUSTLE
RUSTLE
BLOCK
MOVE.
LET'S GO.

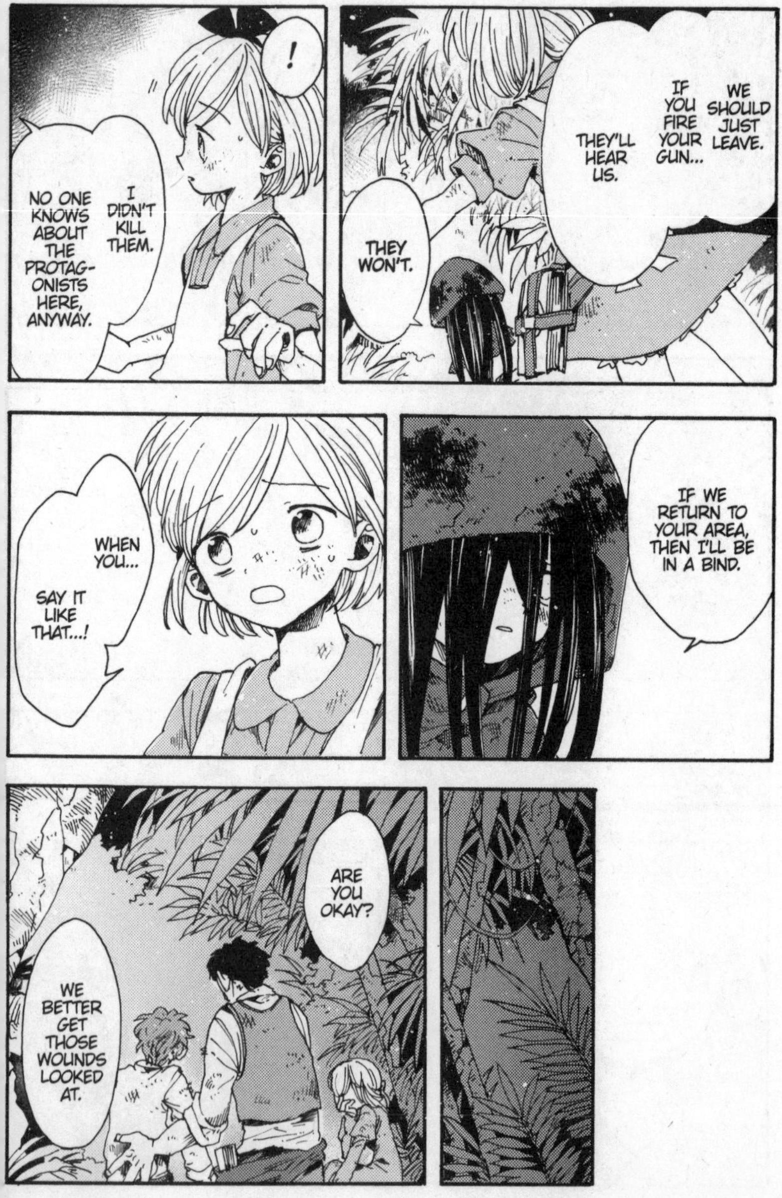
WE SHOULD JUST LEAVE.
IF YOU FIRE YOUR GUN...
THEY'LL HEAR US.
THEY WON'T.
!
I DIDN'T KILL THEM.
NO ONE KNOWS ABOUT THE PROTAGONISTS HERE, ANYWAY.
IF WE RETURN TO YOUR AREA, THEN I'LL BE IN A BIND.
WHEN YOU...
SAY IT LIKE THAT...!
ARE YOU OKAY?
WE BETTER GET THOSE WOUNDS LOOKED AT.

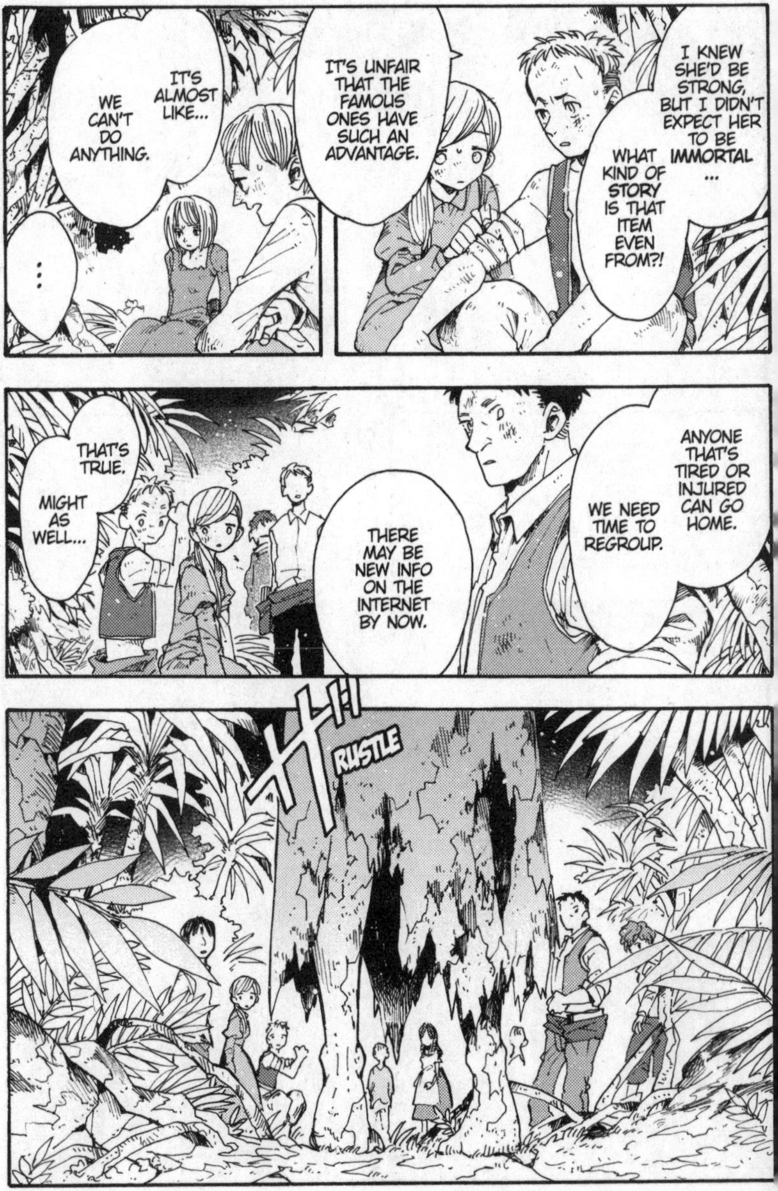
I KNEW SHE'D BE STRONG, BUT I DIDN'T EXPECT HER TO BE IMMORTAL...
WHAT KIND OF STORY IS THAT ITEM EVEN FROM?!
IT'S UNFAIR THAT THE FAMOUS ONES HAVE SUCH AN ADVANTAGE.
IT'S ALMOST LIKE...
WE CAN'T DO ANYTHING.
...
ANYONE THAT'S TIRED OR INJURED CAN GO HOME.
WE NEED TIME TO REGROUP.
THERE MAY BE NEW INFO ON THE INTERNET BY NOW.
THAT'S TRUE.
MIGHT AS WELL...
RUSTLE

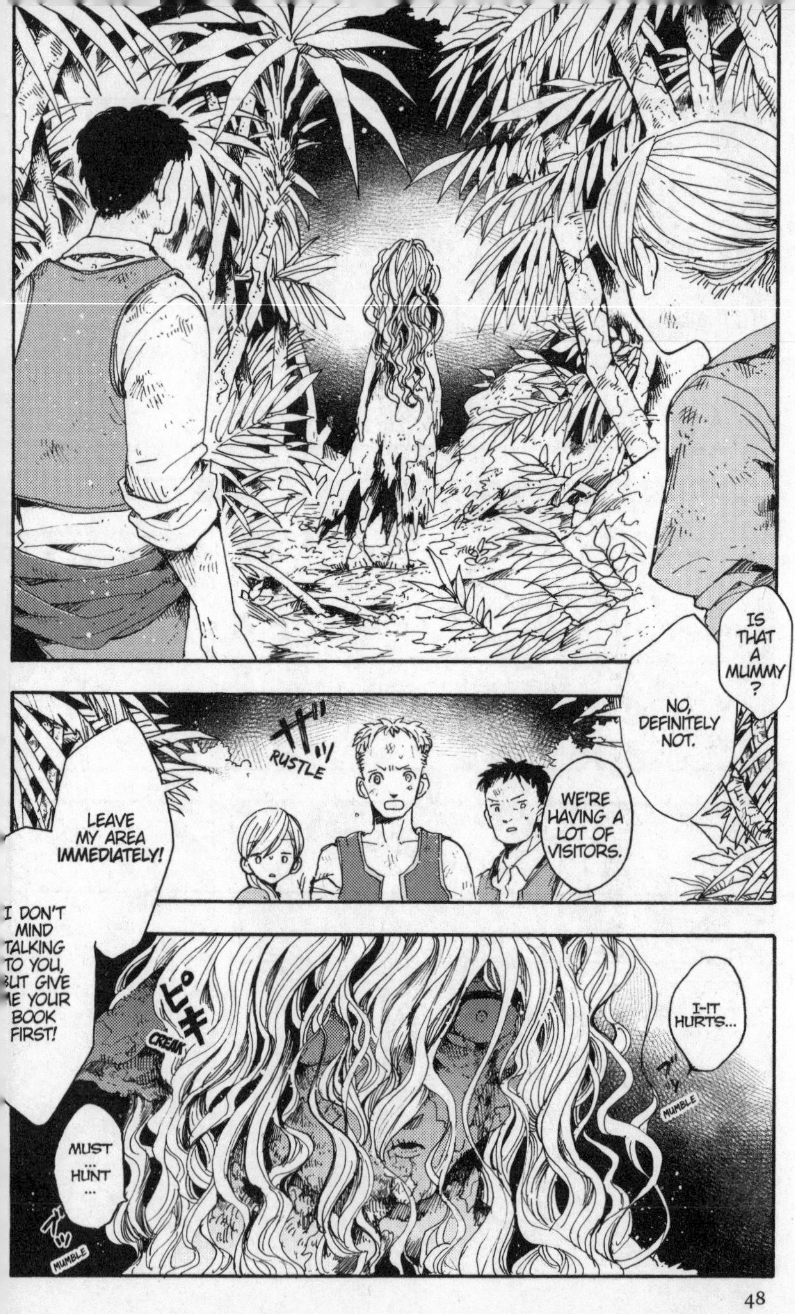
IS THAT A MUMMY?
NO, DEFINITELY NOT.
WE'RE HAVING A LOT OF VISITORS.
RUSTLE
LEAVE MY AREA IMMEDIATELY!
I DON'T MIND TALKING TO YOU, BUT GIVE ME YOUR BOOK FIRST!
I-IT HURTS...
MUMBLE
CREAK
MUST ... HUNT ...
MUMBLE

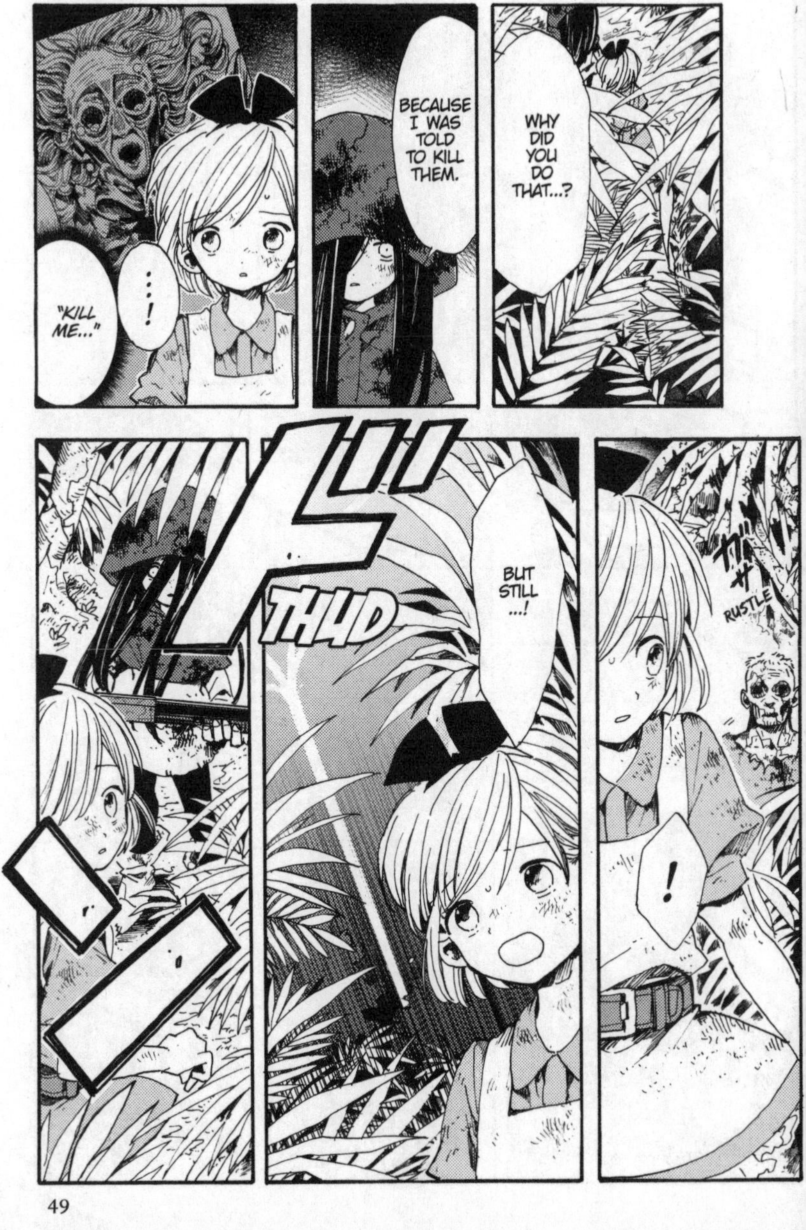
WHY DID YOU DO THAT...?
BECAUSE I WAS TOLD TO KILL THEM.
...!
"KILL ME..."
RUSTLE
!
BUT STILL ...!
THUD

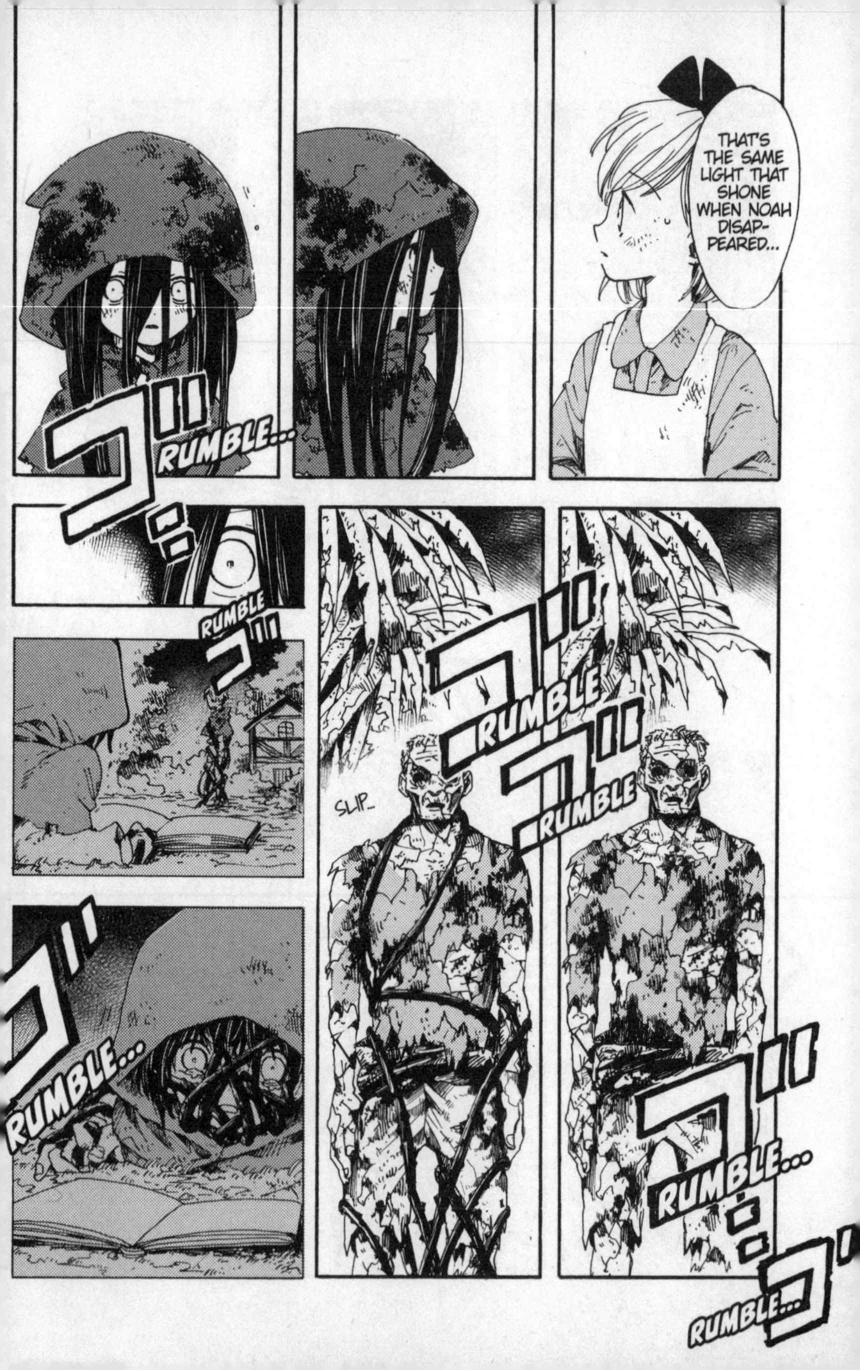
THAT'S THE SAME LIGHT THAT SHONE WHEN NOAH DISAP-PEARED...
RUMBLE...
RUMBLE...
RUMBLE...
RUMBLE
RUMBLE
SLIP...
RUMBLE
RUMBLE...

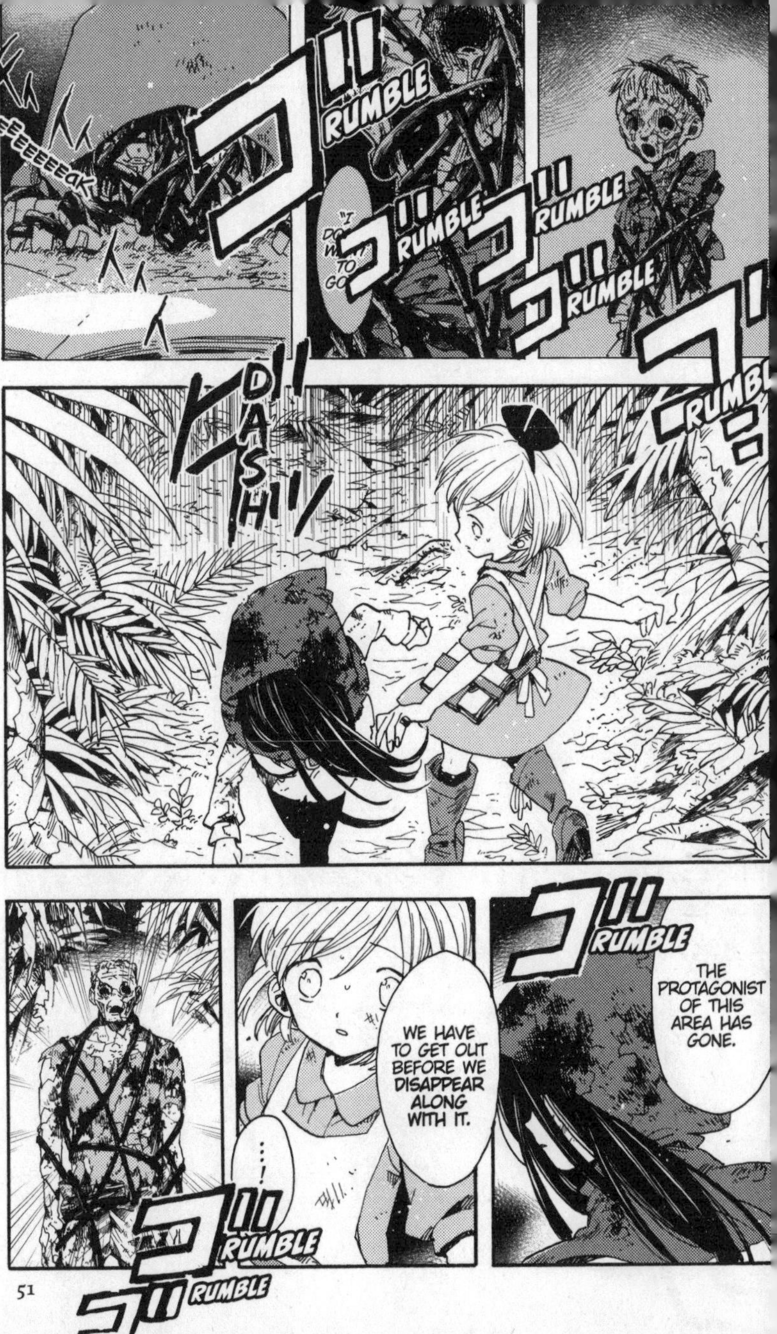
RUMBLE
RUMBLE
RUMBLE
RUMBLE
"I DO... TO GO
RUMBLE
CREEEEEEEEAK
RUMBLE
DASH
RUMBLE
THE PROTAGONIST OF THIS AREA HAS GONE.
WE HAVE TO GET OUT BEFORE WE DISAPPEAR ALONG WITH IT.
...!
RUMBLE
RUMBLE

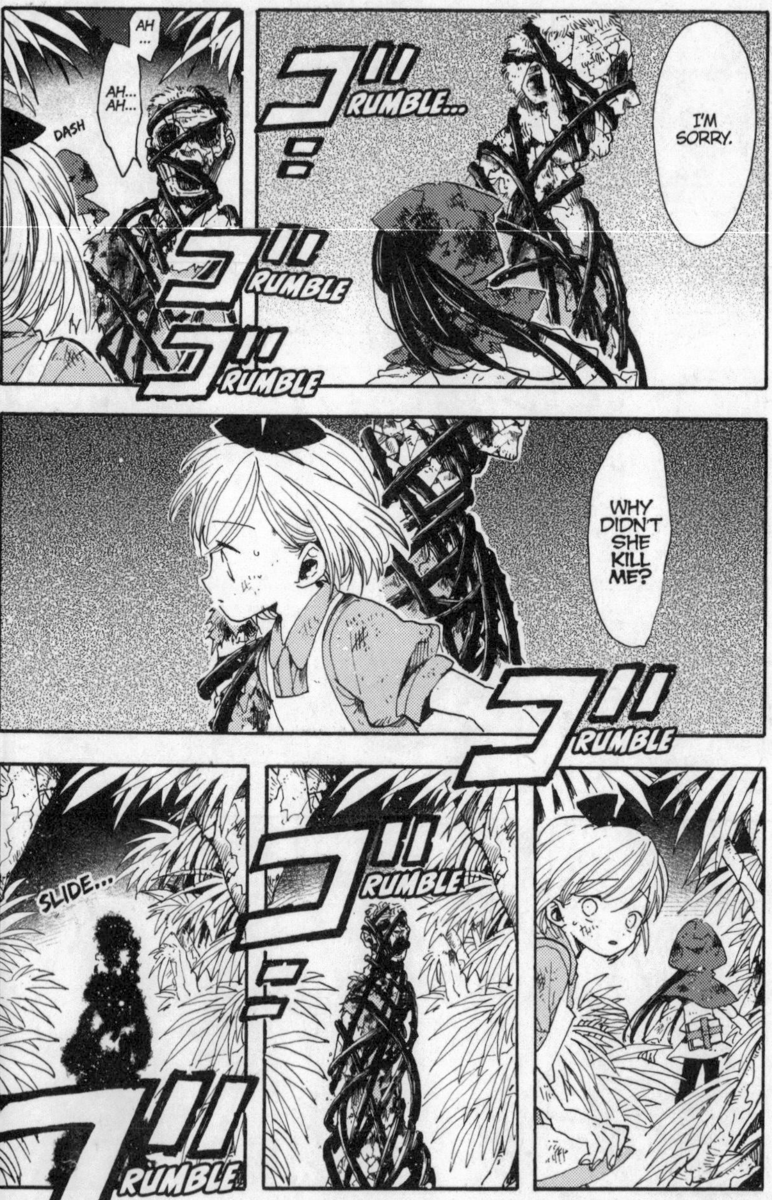

RUMBLE...
I'M SORRY.
AH ...
AH... AH...
DASH
RUMBLE
RUMBLE
WHY DIDN'T SHE KILL ME?
RUMBLE
RUMBLE
SLIDE...
RUMBLE

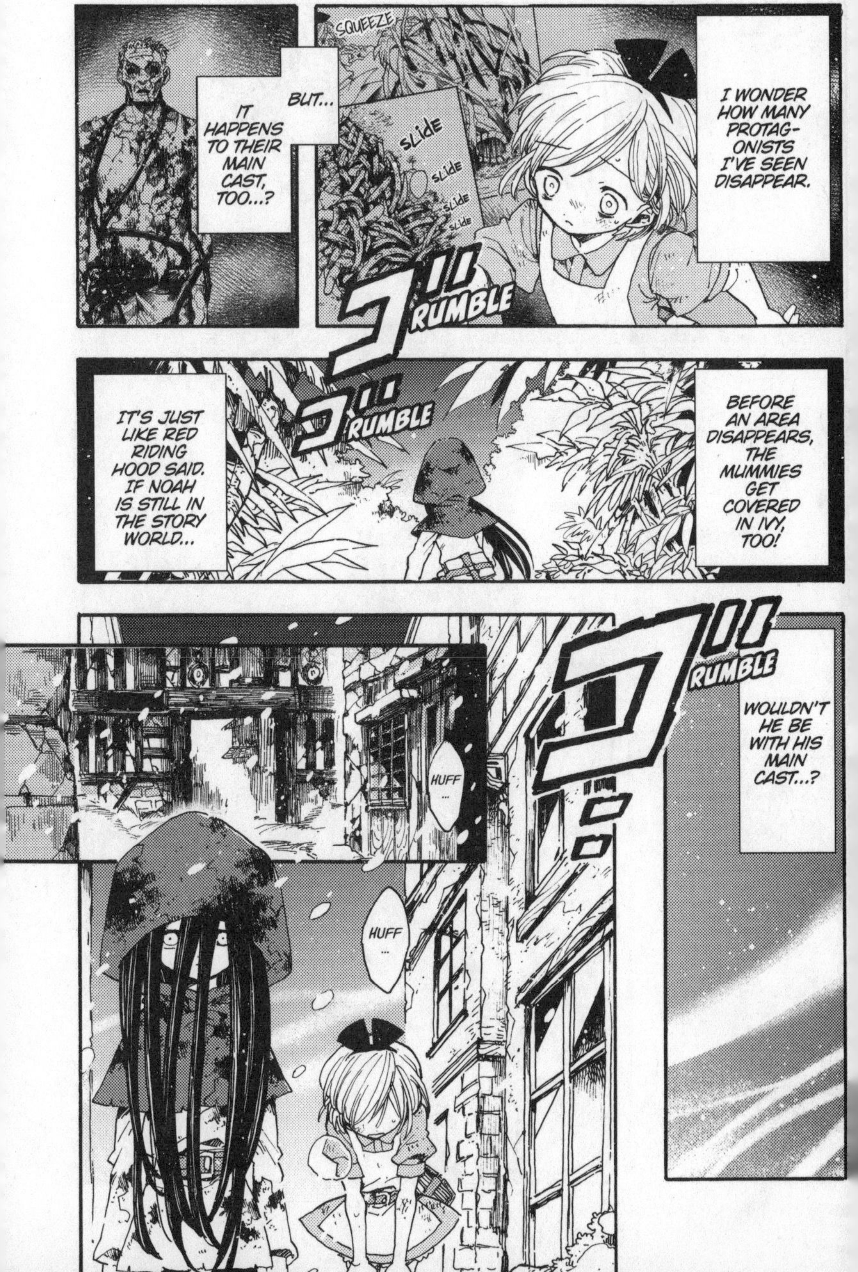
I WONDER HOW MANY PROTAG-ONISTS I'VE SEEN DISAPPEAR.
SQUEEZE
SLIDE
SLIDE
SLIDE
SLIDE
RUMBLE
BUT...
IT HAPPENS TO THEIR MAIN CAST, TOO...?
BEFORE AN AREA DISAPPEARS, THE MUMMIES GET COVERED IN IVY, TOO!
RUMBLE
IT'S JUST LIKE RED RIDING HOOD SAID. IF NOAH IS STILL IN THE STORY WORLD...
RUMBLE
WOULDN'T HE BE WITH HIS MAIN CAST...?
HUFF...
HUFF...

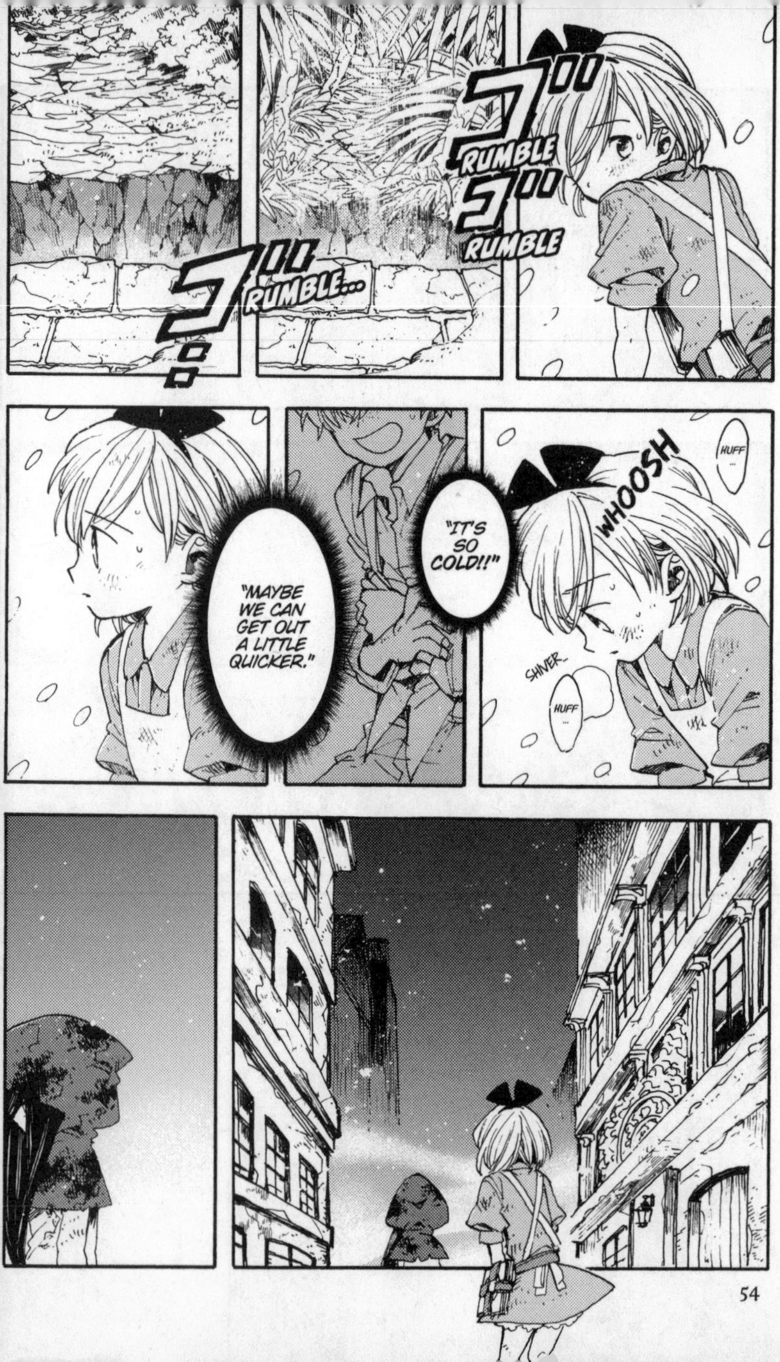
RUMBLE
RUMBLE
RUMBLE...
HUFF...
WHOOSH
SHIVER...
HUFF...
"IT'S SO COLD!!"
"MAYBE WE CAN GET OUT A LITTLE QUICKER."

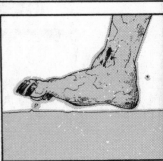

PLOD...

PLOD...

I
WANT
TO
GO
HOME
...

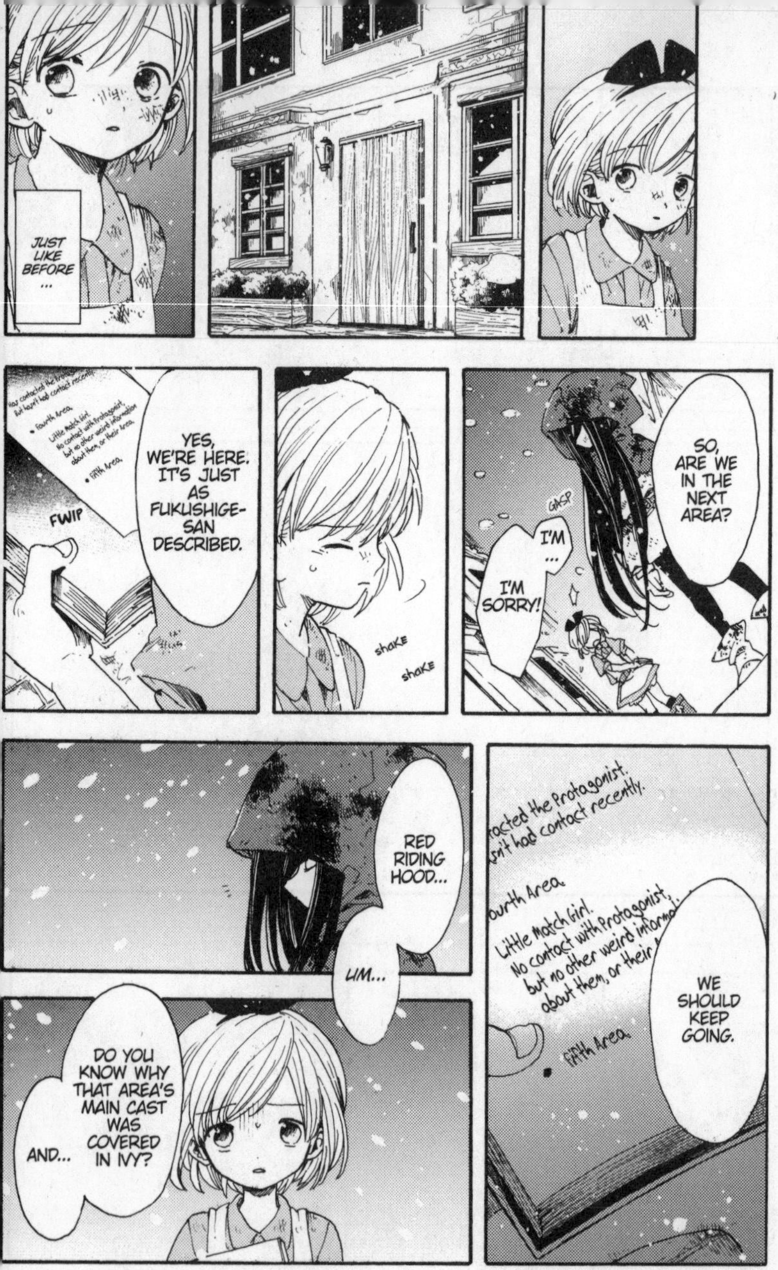
JUST LIKE BEFORE ...
SO, ARE WE IN THE NEXT AREA?
GASP
I'M ...
I'M SORRY!
shake
shake
Has contacted the Protagonist. But hasn't had contact recently.
Fourth Area.
Little Match Girl. No contact with Protagonist, but no other weird information about them, or their Area.
Fifth Area.
YES, WE'RE HERE. IT'S JUST AS FUKUSHIGE-SAN DESCRIBED.
FWIP
WE SHOULD KEEP GOING.
RED RIDING HOOD...
UM...
DO YOU KNOW WHY THAT AREA'S MAIN CAST WAS COVERED IN IVY?
AND...

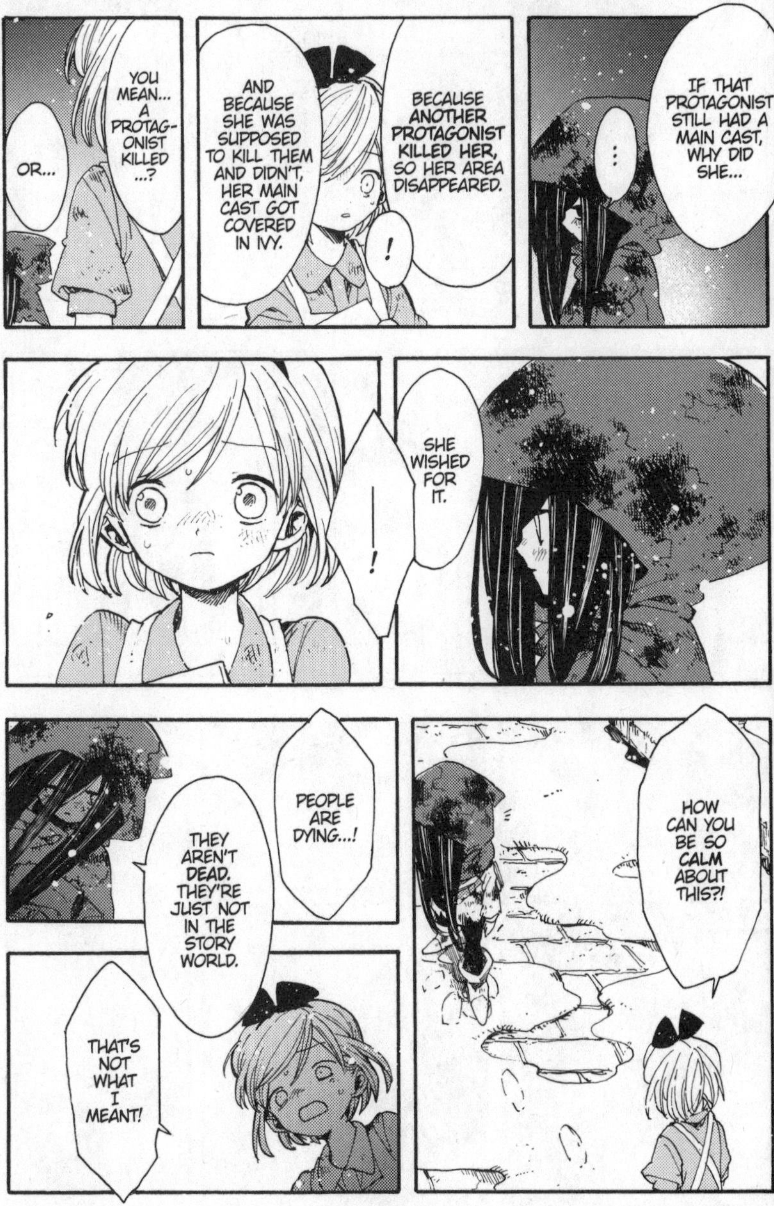
IF THAT PROTAGONIST STILL HAD A MAIN CAST, WHY DID SHE...
...
BECAUSE ANOTHER PROTAGONIST KILLED HER, SO HER AREA DISAPPEARED.
!
AND BECAUSE SHE WAS SUPPOSED TO KILL THEM AND DIDN'T, HER MAIN CAST GOT COVERED IN IVY.
YOU MEAN... A PROTAG-ONIST KILLED ...?
OR...
SHE WISHED FOR IT.
—!
HOW CAN YOU BE SO CALM ABOUT THIS?!
PEOPLE ARE DYING...!
THEY AREN'T DEAD. THEY'RE JUST NOT IN THE STORY WORLD.
THAT'S NOT WHAT I MEANT!

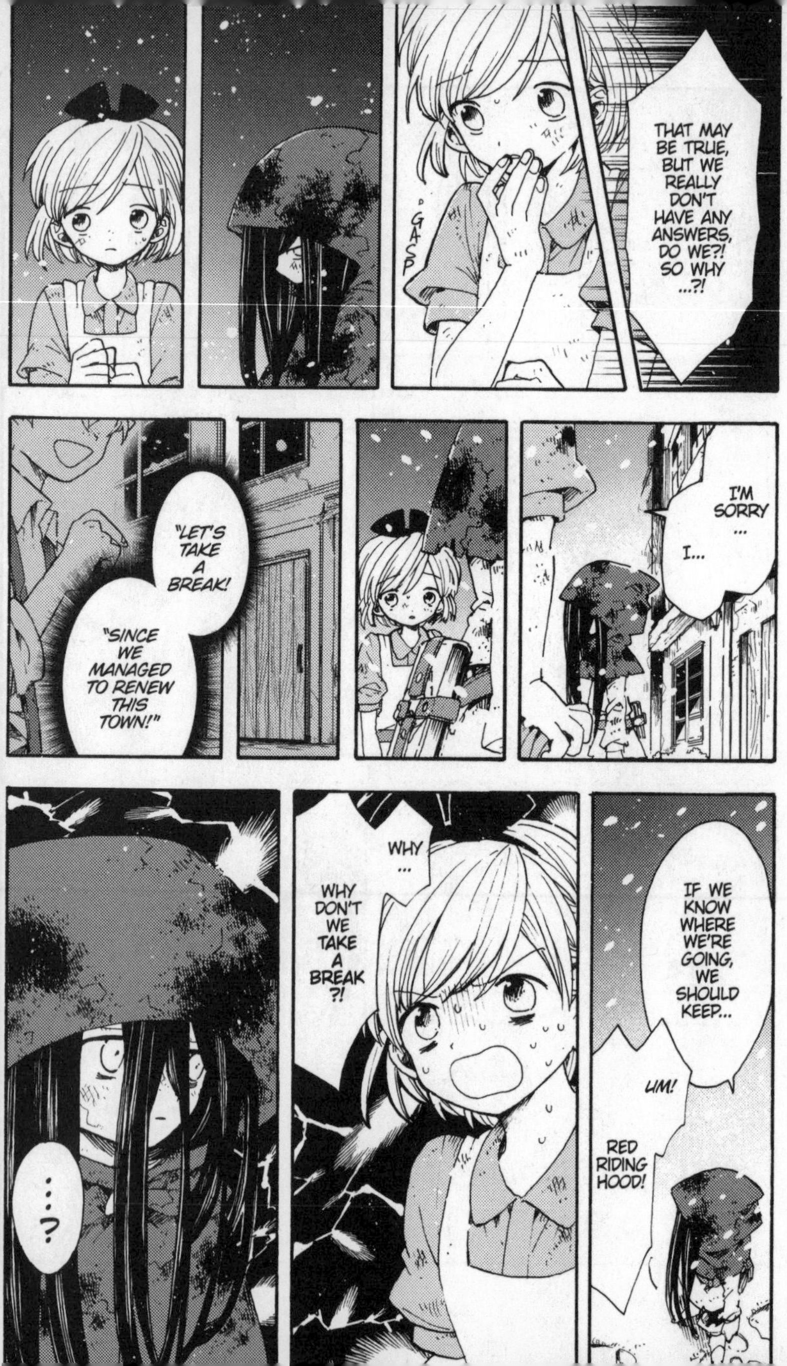
GASP
THAT MAY BE TRUE, BUT WE REALLY DON'T HAVE ANY ANSWERS, DO WE?! SO WHY ...?!
I'M SORRY ... I...
"LET'S TAKE A BREAK!
"SINCE WE MANAGED TO RENEW THIS TOWN!"
IF WE KNOW WHERE WE'RE GOING, WE SHOULD KEEP...
UM!
RED RIDING HOOD!
WHY ...
WHY DON'T WE TAKE A BREAK ?!
...?

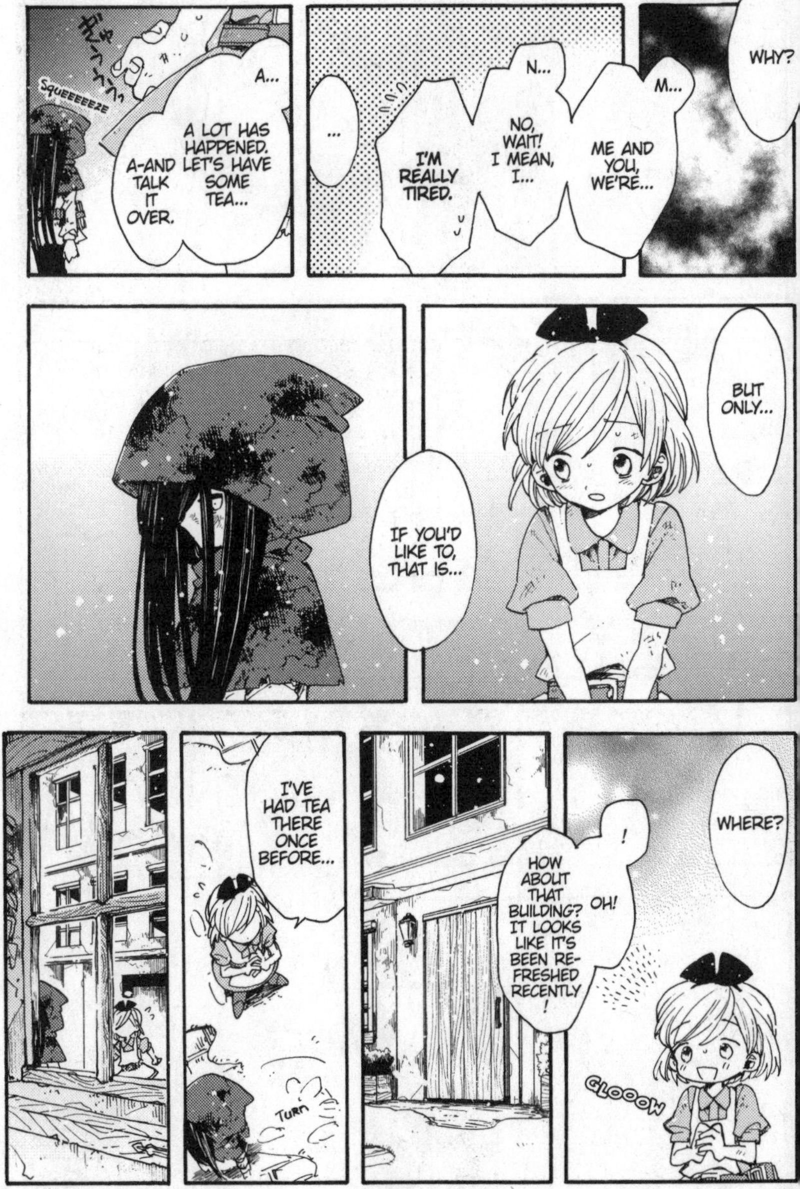
WHY?
M...
N...
ME AND YOU, WE'RE...
NO, WAIT! I MEAN, I...
I'M REALLY TIRED.
...
A...
A LOT HAS HAPPENED. LET'S HAVE SOME TEA...
A-AND TALK IT OVER.
Squeeeeeze
BUT ONLY...
IF YOU'D LIKE TO, THAT IS...
WHERE?
GLOOOW
!
OH!
HOW ABOUT THAT BUILDING? IT LOOKS LIKE IT'S BEEN RE-FRESHED RECENTLY!
I'VE HAD TEA THERE ONCE BEFORE...
Turn

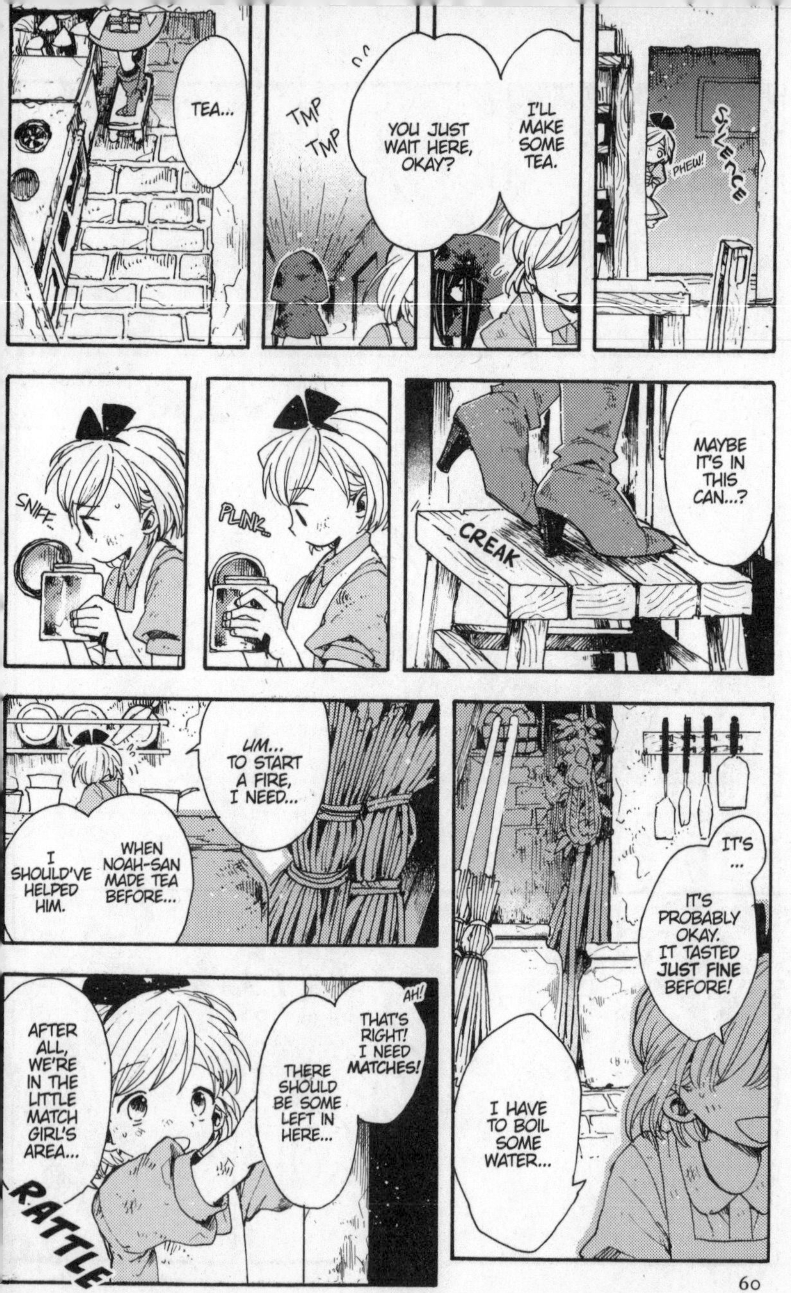
SILENCE
PHEW!
I'LL MAKE SOME TEA.
YOU JUST WAIT HERE, OKAY?
TMP TMP
TEA...
MAYBE IT'S IN THIS CAN...?
CREAK
PLINK...
SNIFF...
IT'S ... IT'S PROBABLY OKAY. IT TASTED JUST FINE BEFORE!
I HAVE TO BOIL SOME WATER...
UM... TO START A FIRE, I NEED...
WHEN NOAH-SAN MADE TEA BEFORE...
I SHOULD'VE HELPED HIM.
AH!
THAT'S RIGHT! I NEED MATCHES!
THERE SHOULD BE SOME LEFT IN HERE...
AFTER ALL, WE'RE IN THE LITTLE MATCH GIRL'S AREA...
RATTLE

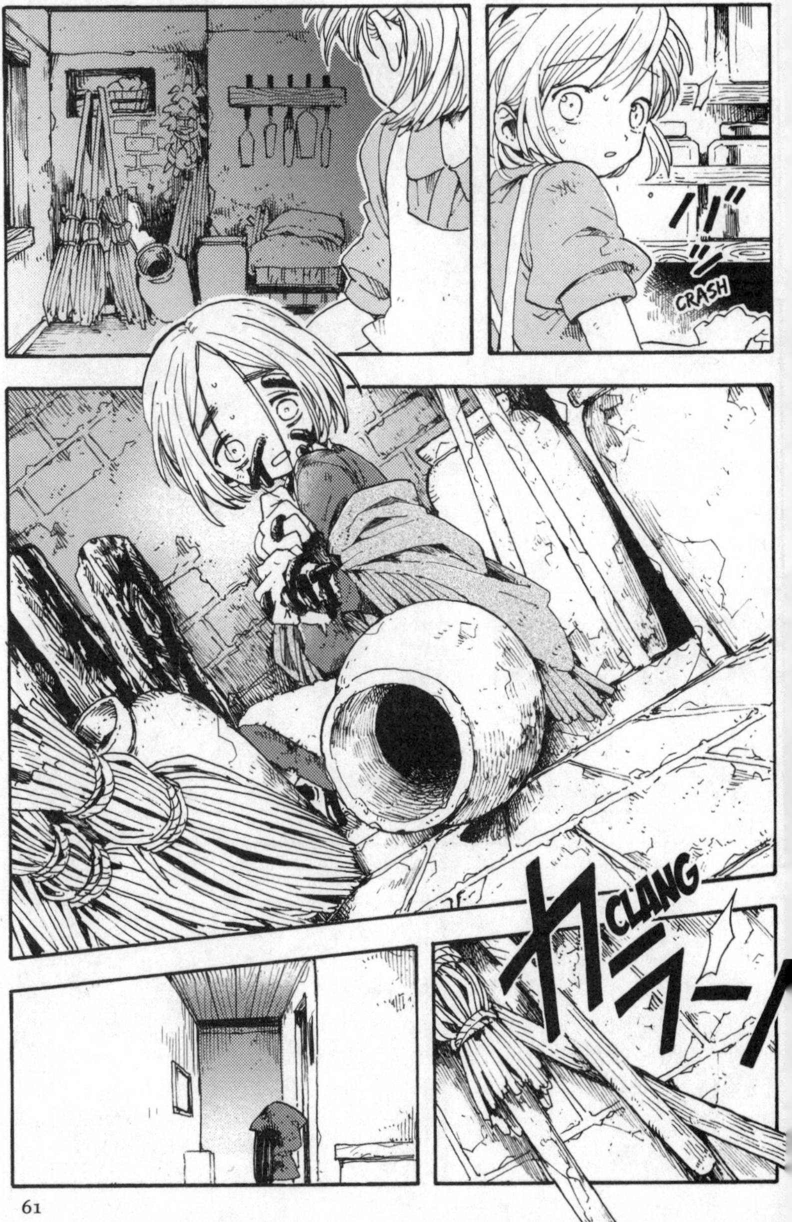
CRASH
CLANG

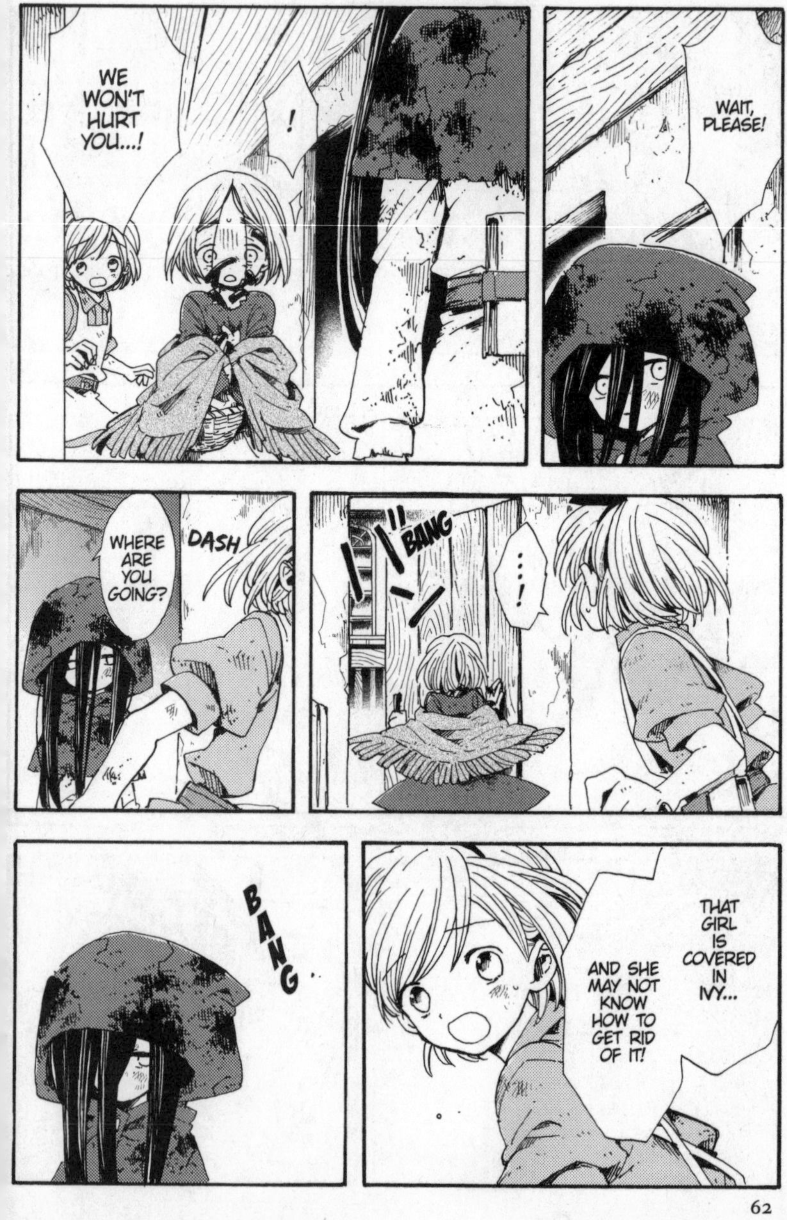
WAIT, PLEASE!
WE WON'T HURT YOU...!
!
BANG
...!
DASH
WHERE ARE YOU GOING?
THAT GIRL IS COVERED IN IVY...
AND SHE MAY NOT KNOW HOW TO GET RID OF IT!
BANG

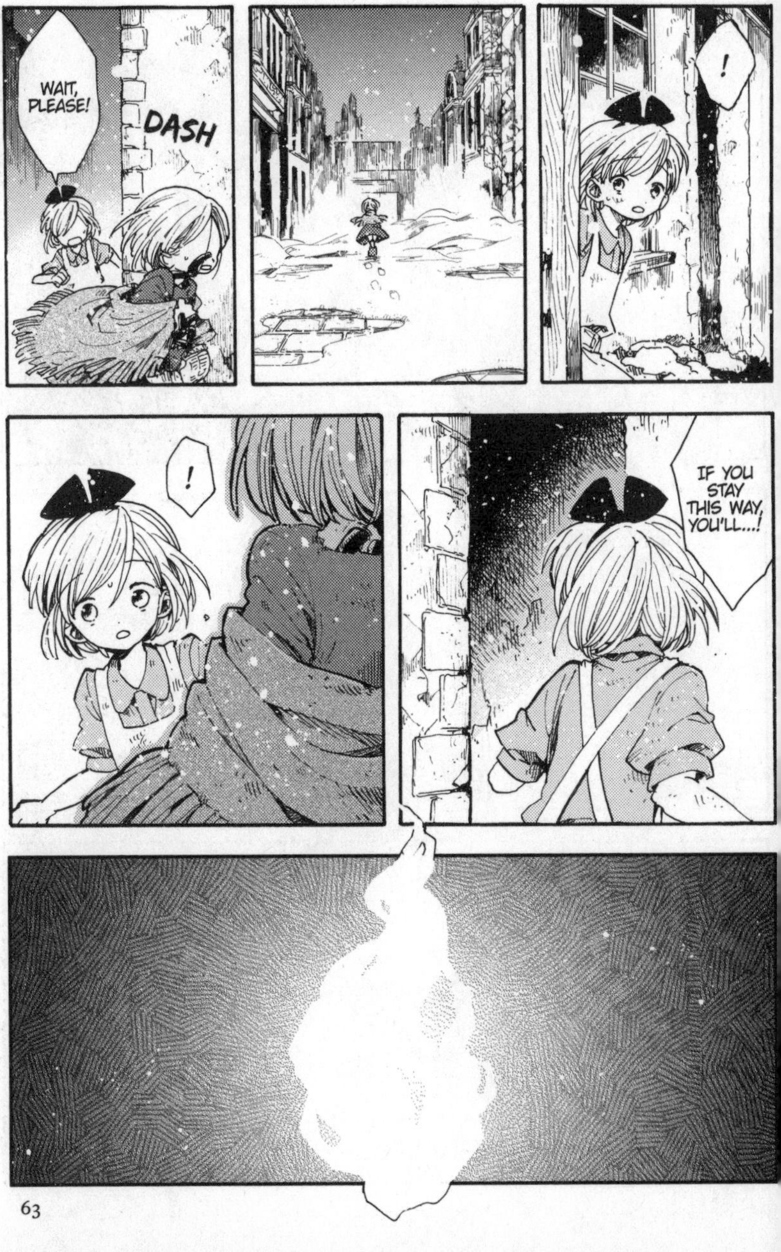
!
WAIT, PLEASE!
DASH
IF YOU STAY THIS WAY, YOU'LL...!
!

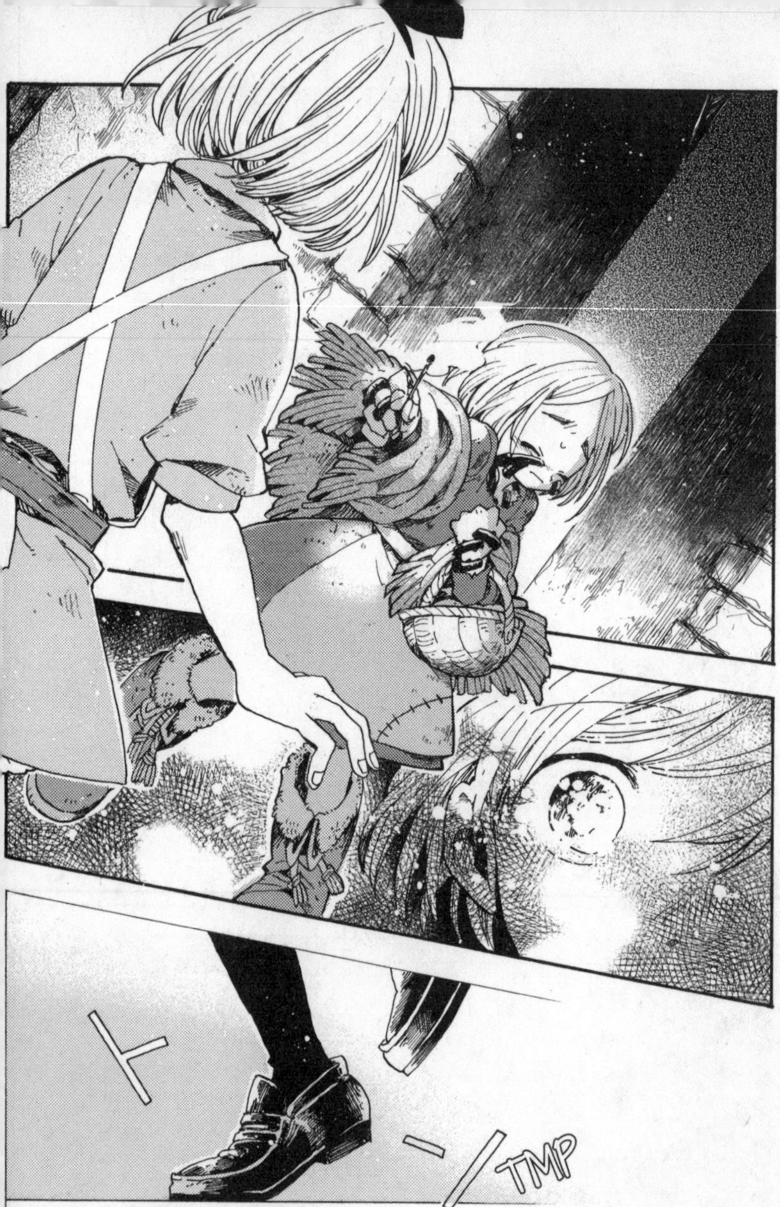
TMP

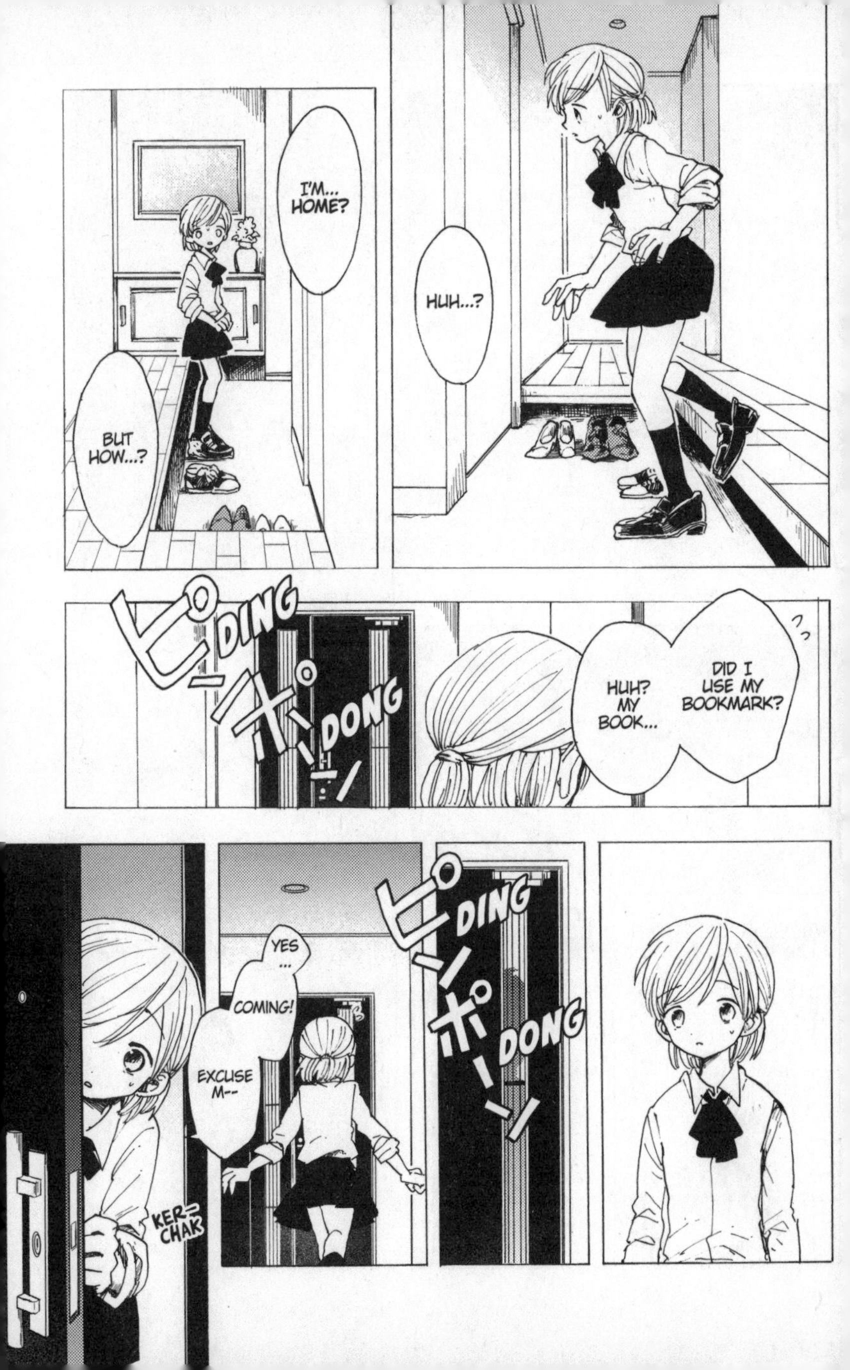
HUH...?
I'M... HOME?
BUT HOW...?
DID I USE MY BOOKMARK?
HUH? MY BOOK...
ピーDING
ポーンDONG
ピーDING
ポーンDONG
YES ...
COMING!
EXCUSE M--
KER-CHAK

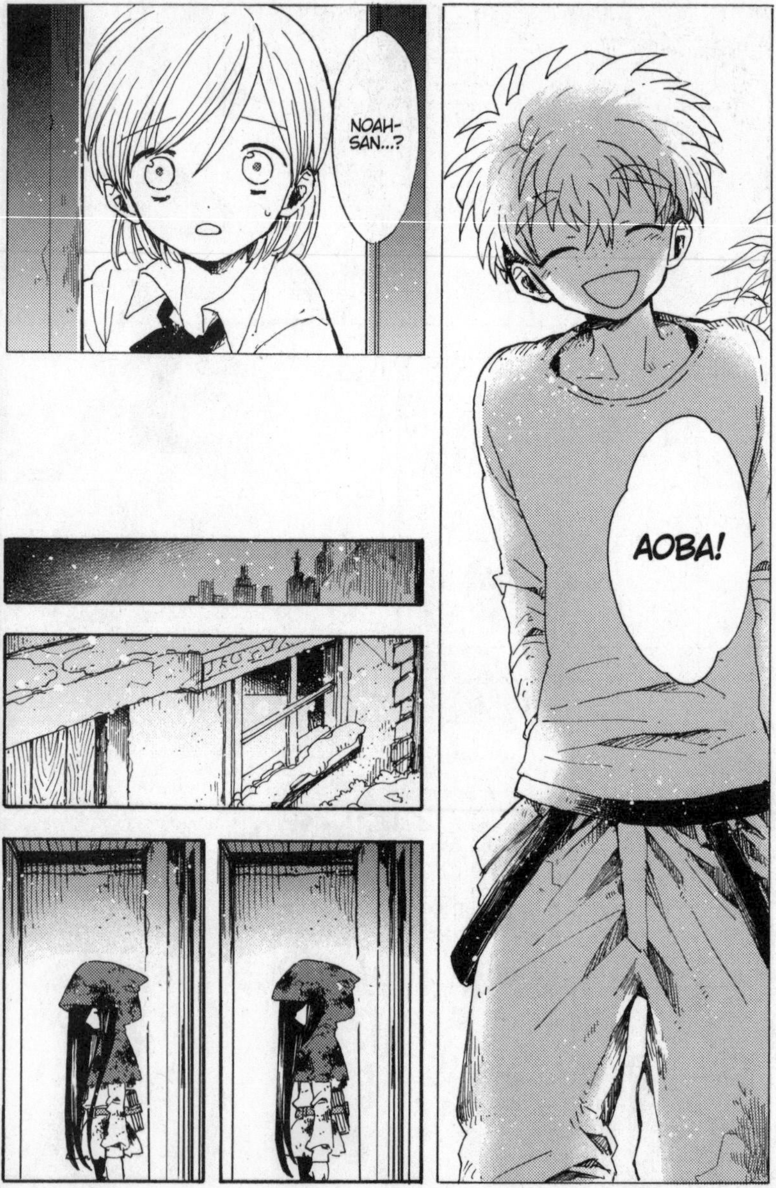
AOBA!
NOAH-SAN...?

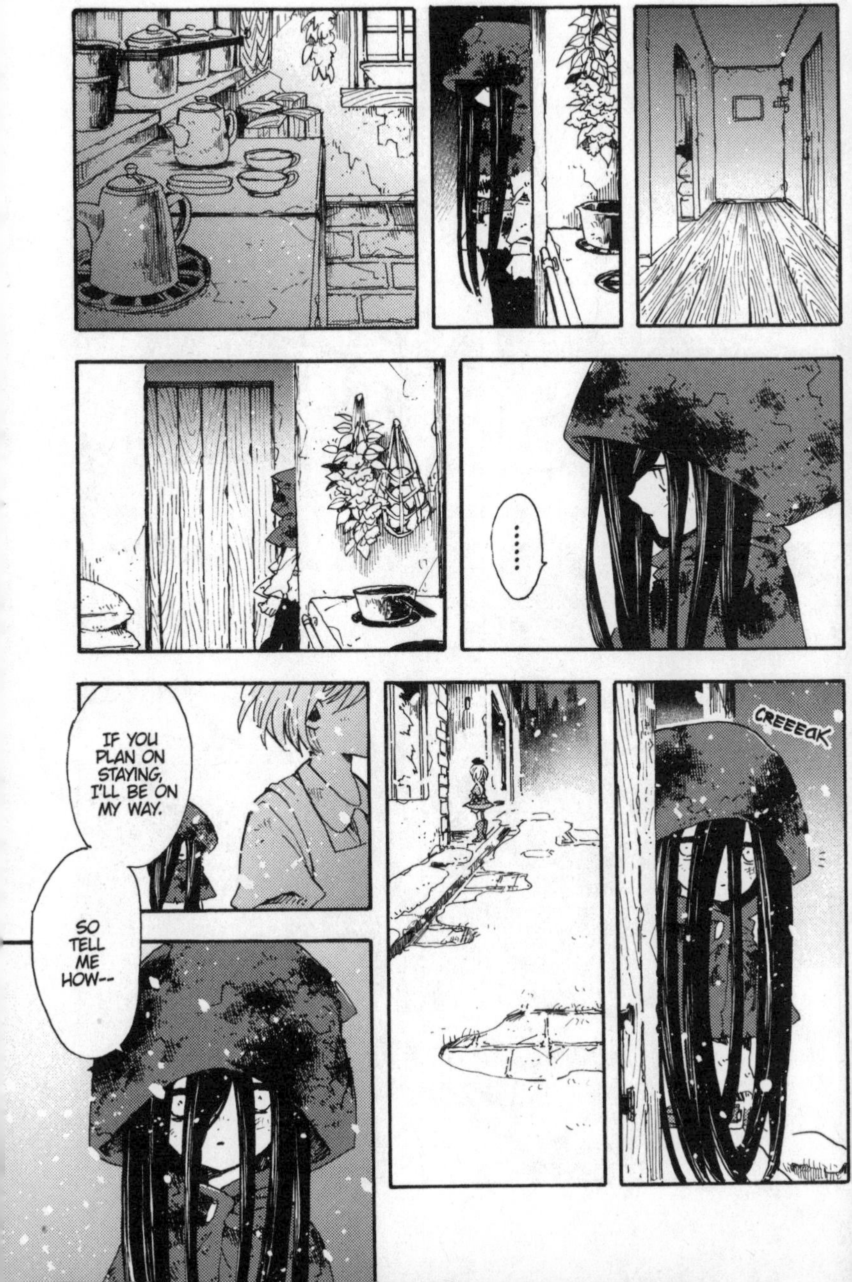
......
CREEEAK
IF YOU PLAN ON STAYING, I'LL BE ON MY WAY.
SO TELL ME HOW--

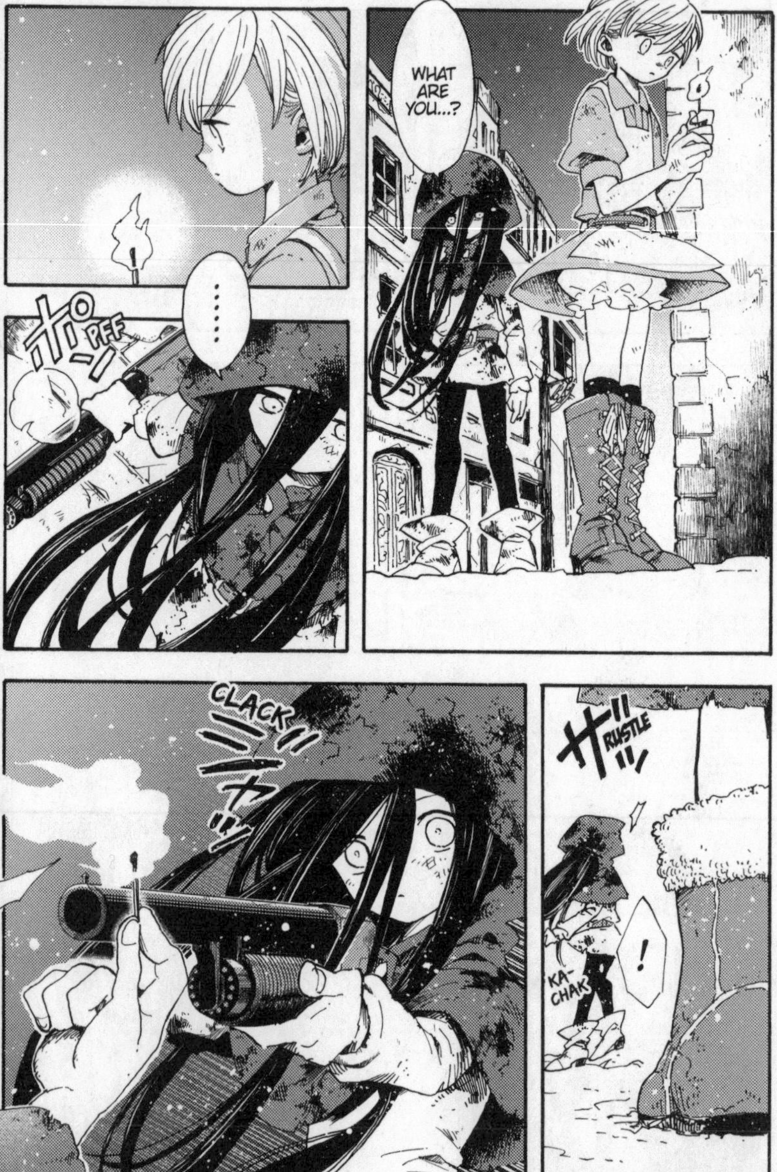
WHAT ARE YOU...?
......
PFF
RUSTLE
!
KA-CHAK
CLACK

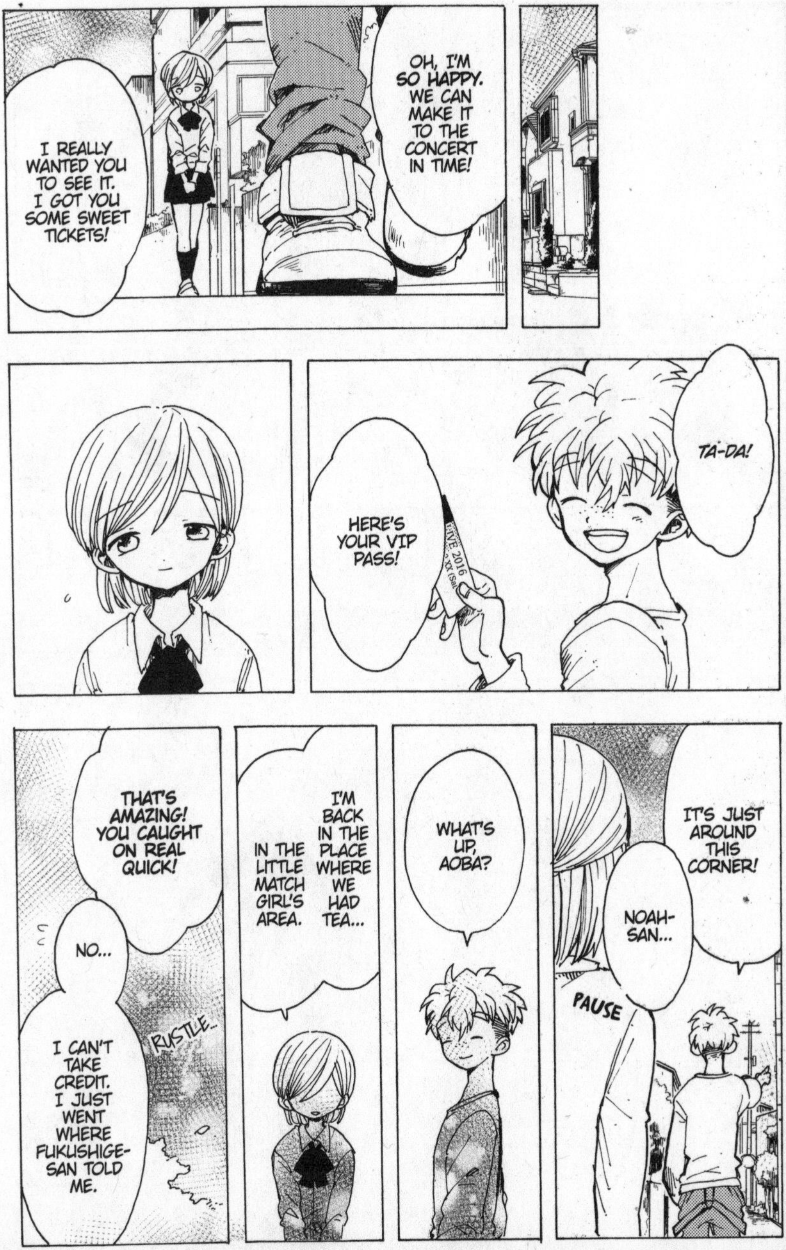
OH, I'M SO HAPPY. WE CAN MAKE IT TO THE CONCERT IN TIME!
I REALLY WANTED YOU TO SEE IT. I GOT YOU SOME SWEET TICKETS!
TA-DA!
HERE'S YOUR VIP PASS!
IT'S JUST AROUND THIS CORNER!
NOAH-SAN...
PAUSE
WHAT'S UP, AOBA?
I'M BACK IN THE PLACE WHERE WE HAD TEA...
IN THE LITTLE MATCH GIRL'S AREA.
THAT'S AMAZING! YOU CAUGHT ON REAL QUICK!
NO...
RUSTLE..
I CAN'T TAKE CREDIT. I JUST WENT WHERE FUKUSHIGE-SAN TOLD ME.

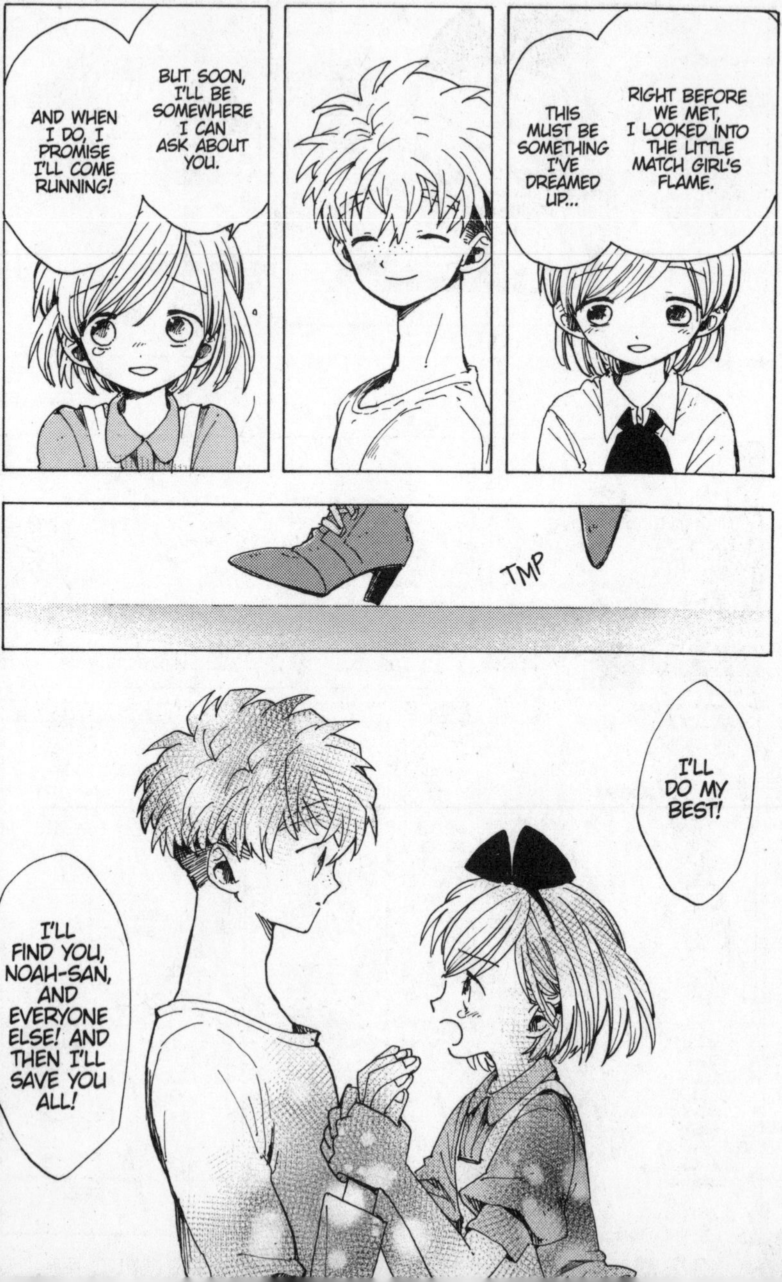
RIGHT BEFORE WE MET, I LOOKED INTO THE LITTLE MATCH GIRL'S FLAME.
THIS MUST BE SOMETHING I'VE DREAMED UP...
BUT SOON, I'LL BE SOMEWHERE I CAN ASK ABOUT YOU.
AND WHEN I DO, I PROMISE I'LL COME RUNNING!
TMP
I'LL DO MY BEST!
I'LL FIND YOU, NOAH-SAN, AND EVERYONE ELSE! AND THEN I'LL SAVE YOU ALL!

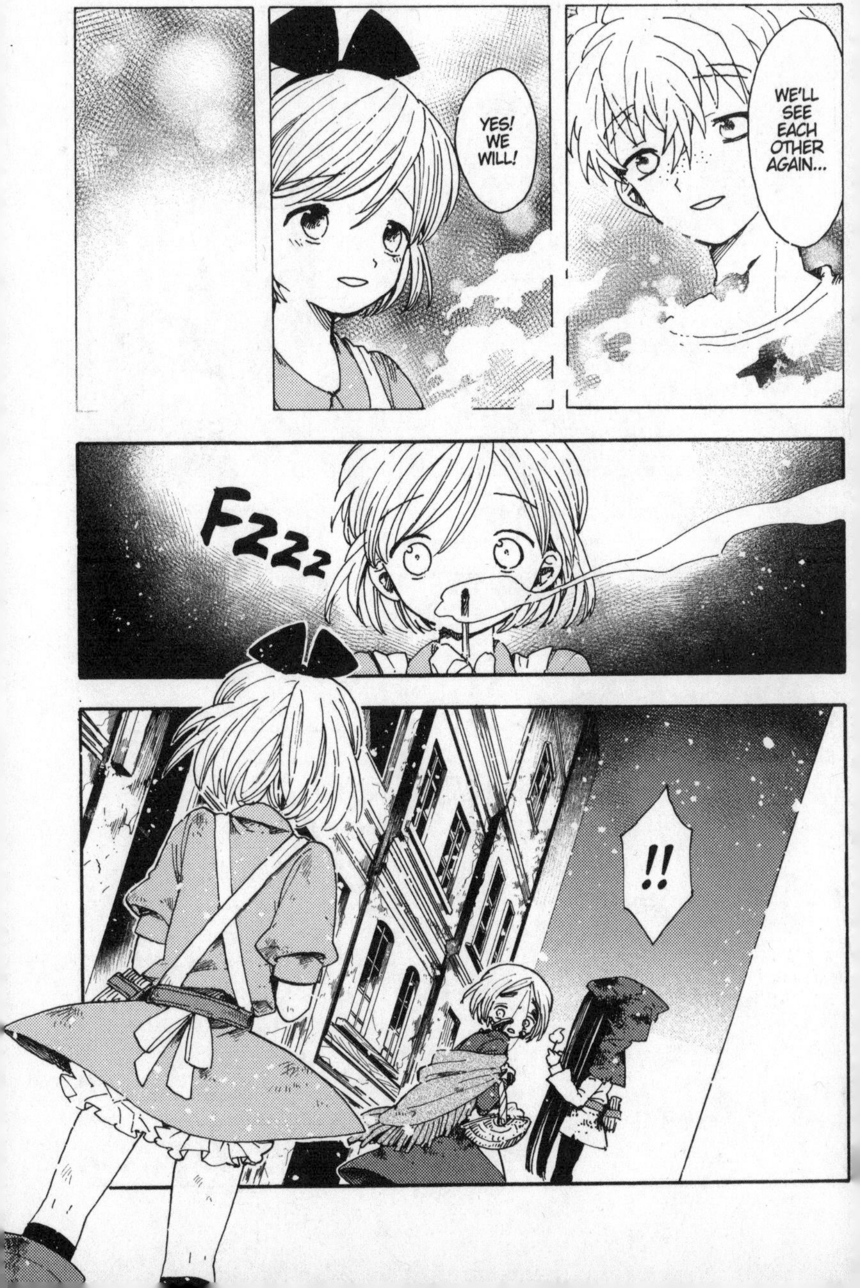
WE'LL SEE EACH OTHER AGAIN...
YES! WE WILL!
FZZZ
!!

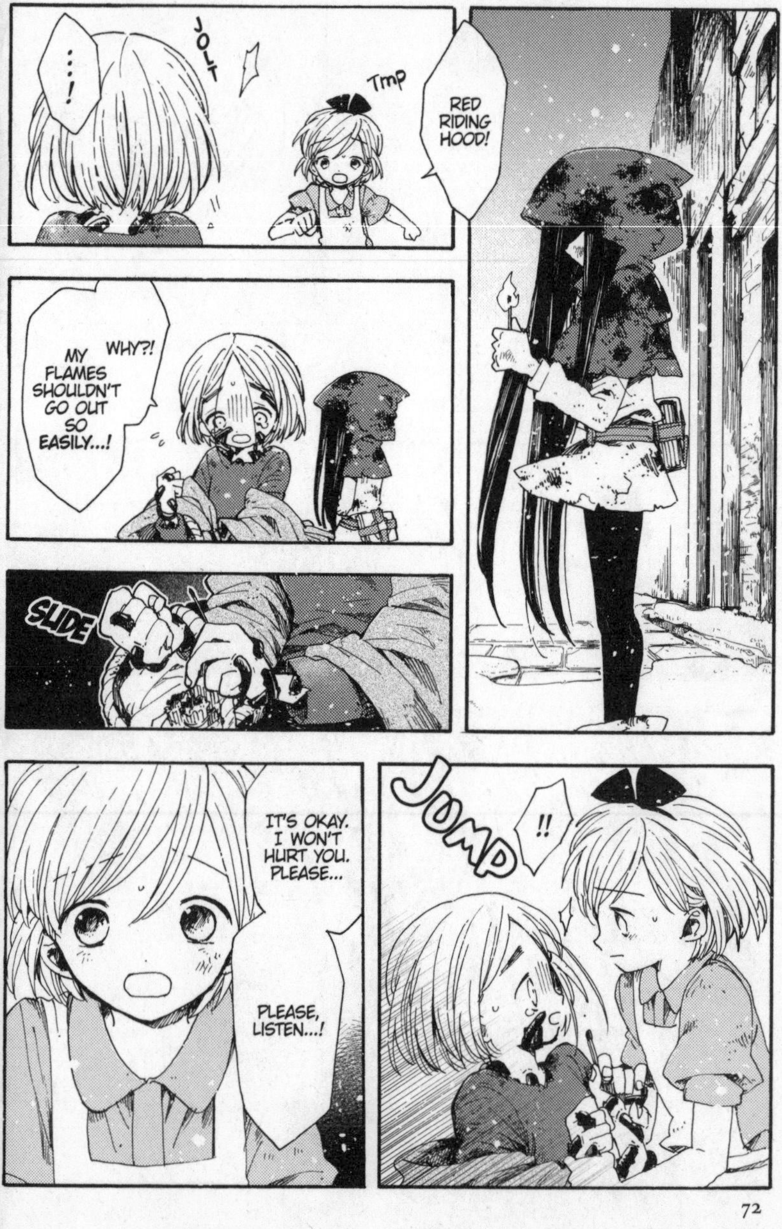
RED RIDING HOOD!
...!
JOLT
Tmp
MY FLAMES SHOULDN'T GO OUT SO EASILY...!
WHY?!
SLIDE
JUMP
!!
IT'S OKAY. I WON'T HURT YOU. PLEASE...
PLEASE, LISTEN...!

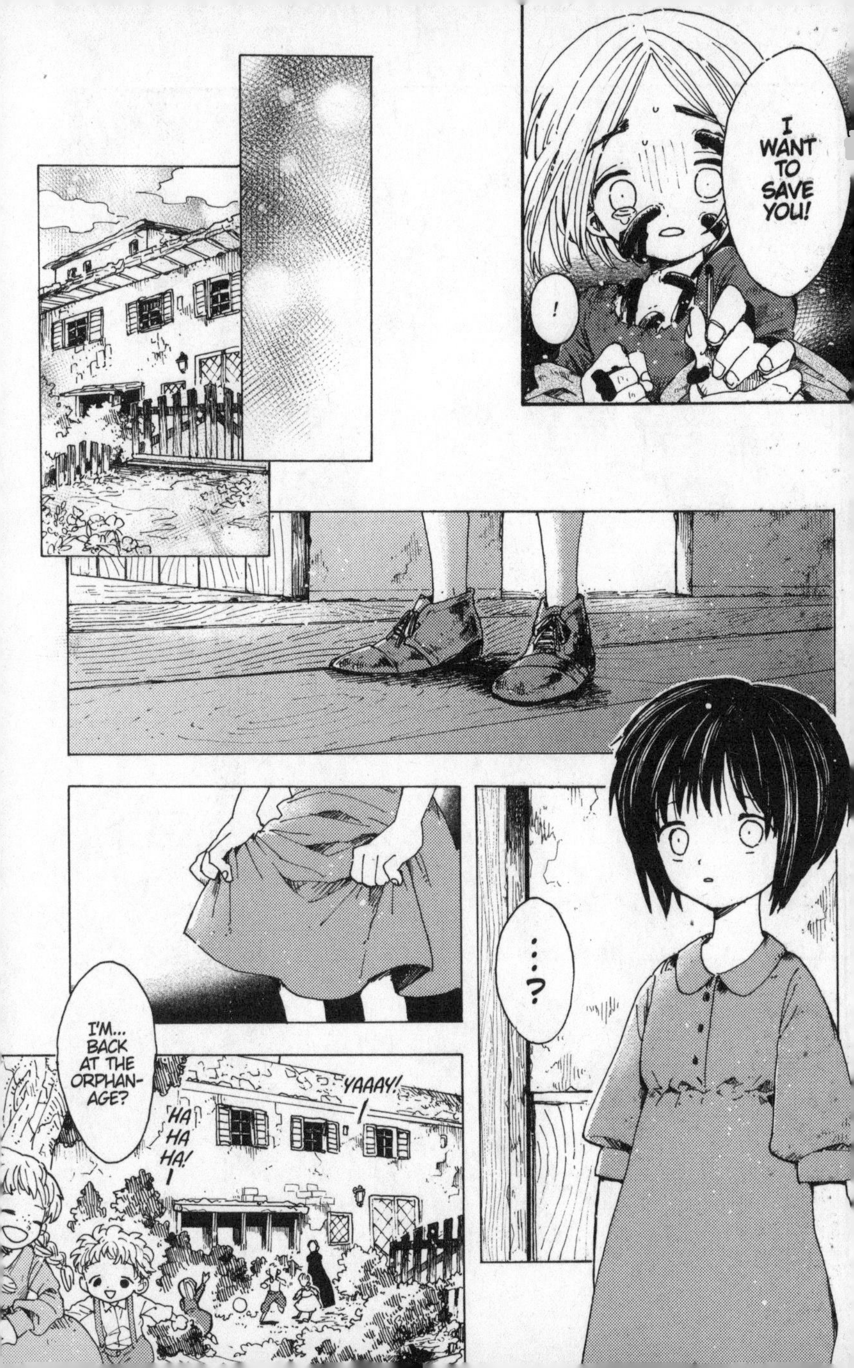
I WANT TO SAVE YOU!
!
...?
I'M... BACK AT THE ORPHANAGE?
YAAAY!
HA HA HA!

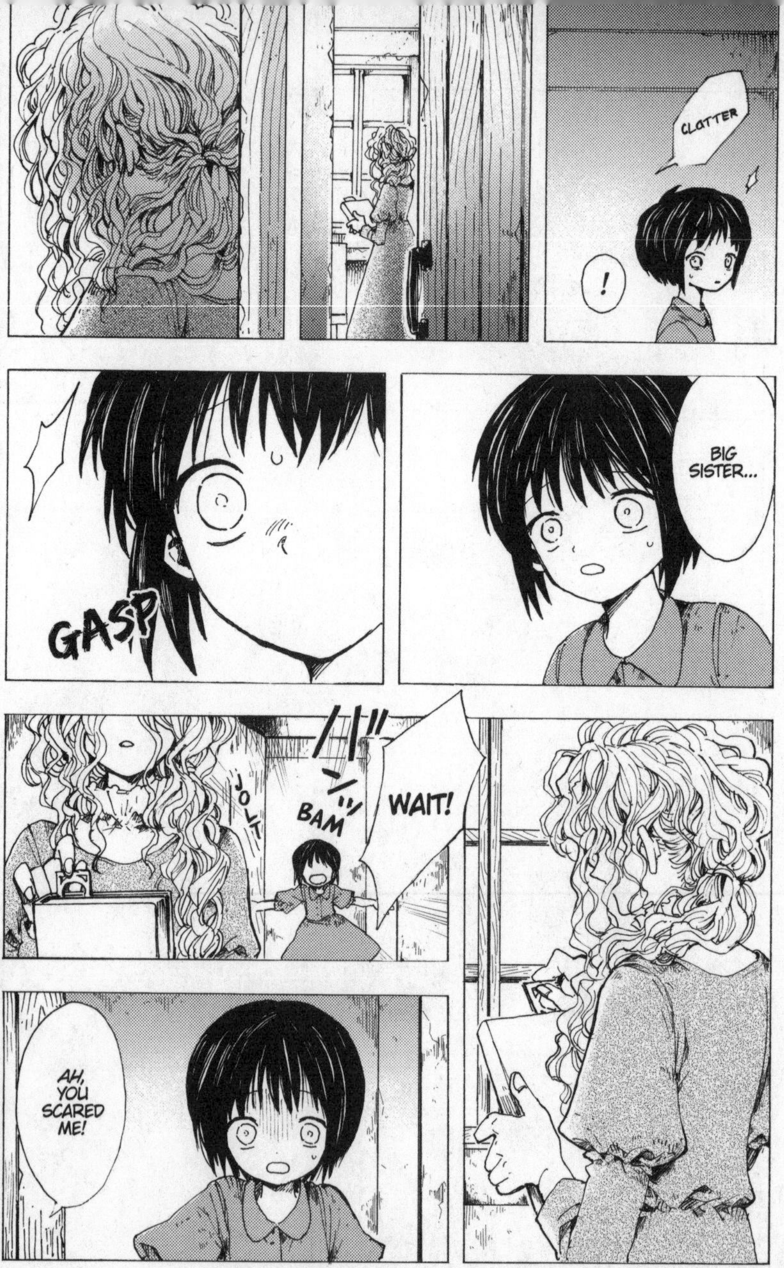
CLATTER
!
BIG SISTER...
GASP
WAIT!
BAM
JOLT
AH, YOU SCARED ME!

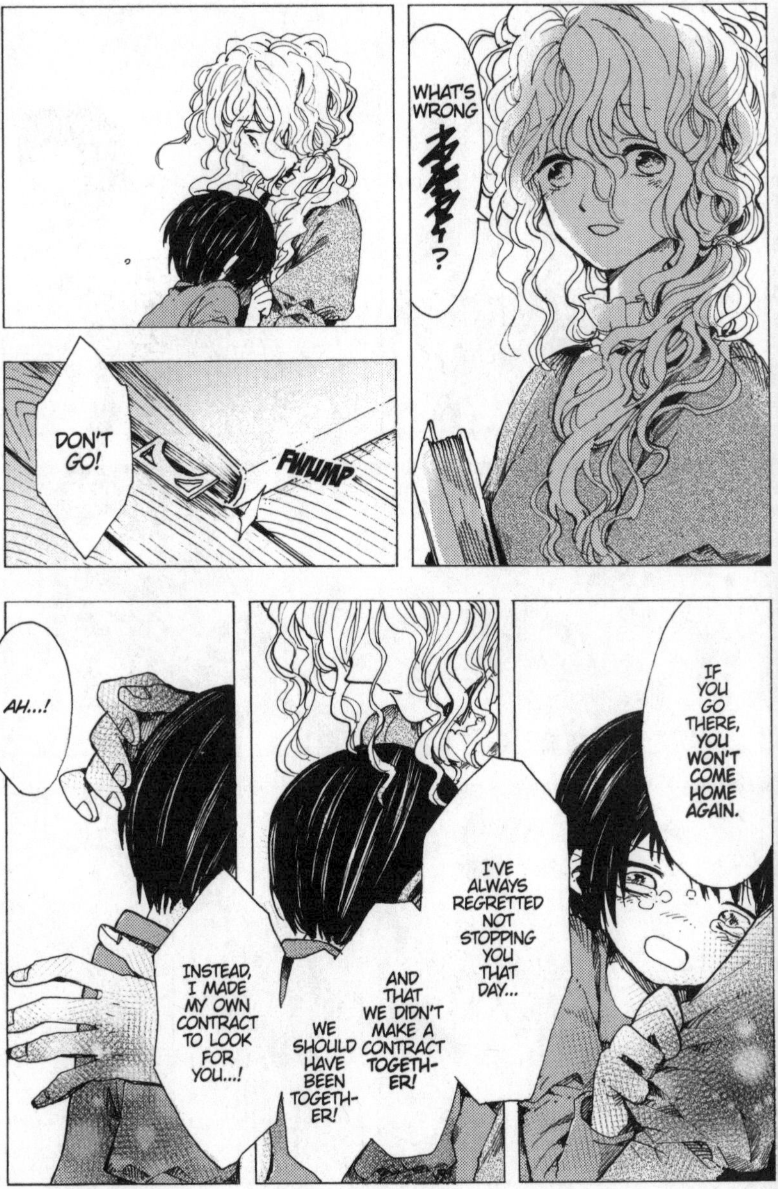
WHAT'S WRONG ?
DON'T GO!
FWUMP
IF YOU GO THERE, YOU WON'T COME HOME AGAIN.
I'VE ALWAYS REGRETTED NOT STOPPING YOU THAT DAY...
AND THAT WE DIDN'T MAKE A CONTRACT TOGETH-ER!
WE SHOULD HAVE BEEN TOGETH-ER!
INSTEAD, I MADE MY OWN CONTRACT TO LOOK FOR YOU...!
AH...!

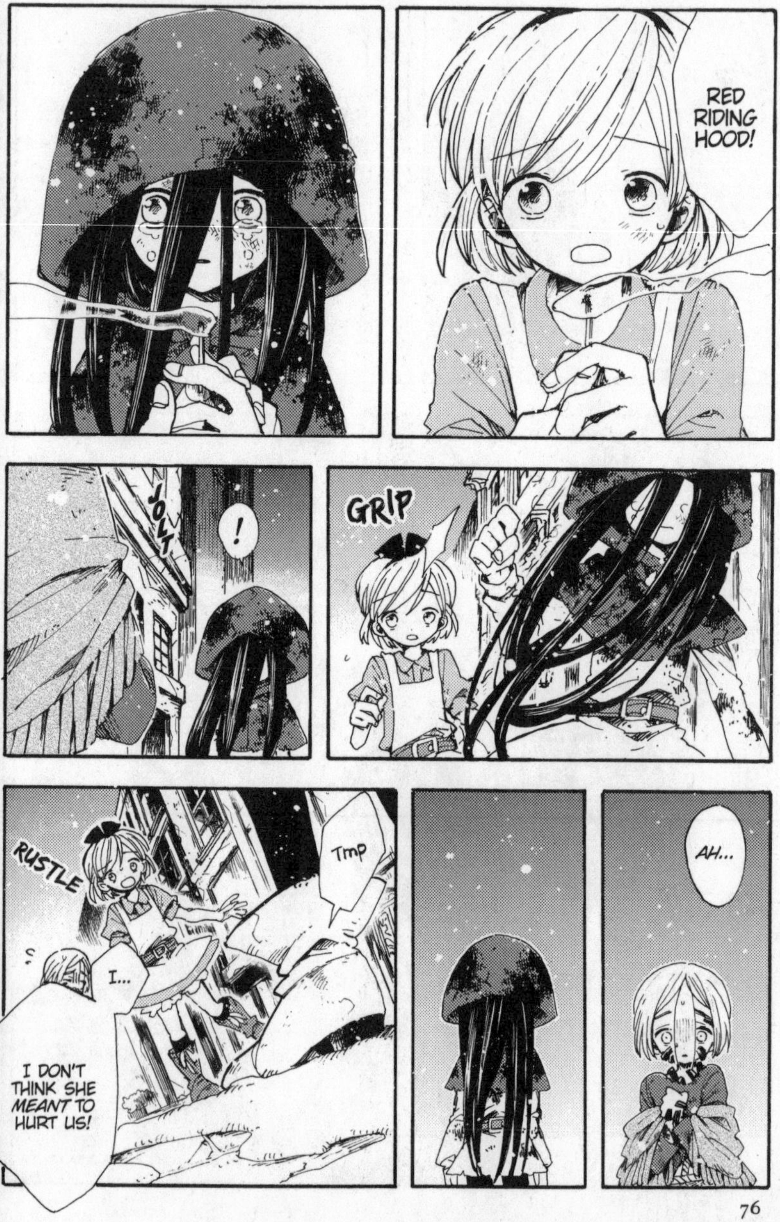
RED RIDING HOOD!
GRIP
JOLT
!
AH...
Tmp
RUSTLE
I...
I DON'T THINK SHE *MEANT* TO HURT US!

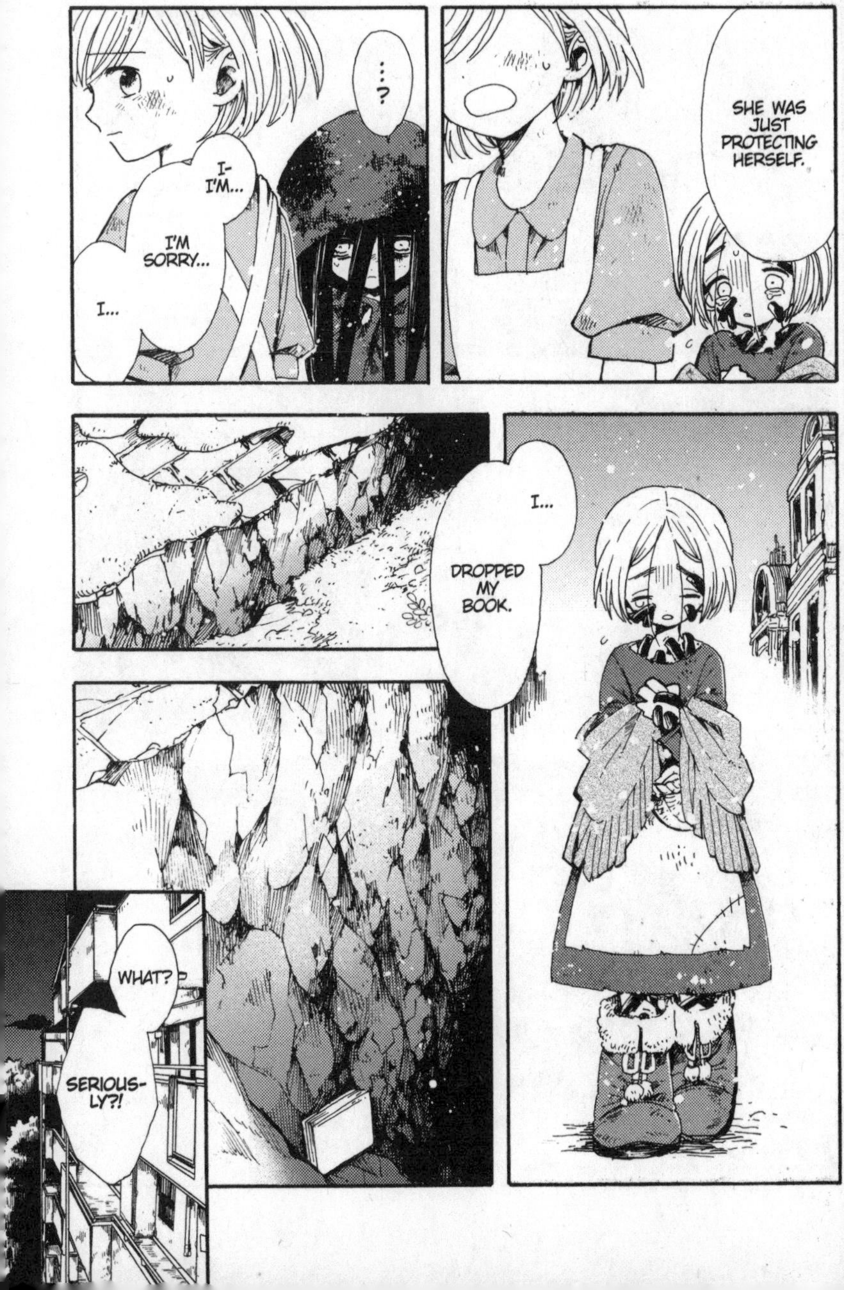
SHE WAS JUST PROTECTING HERSELF.
...?
I- I'M...
I'M SORRY...
I...
I...
DROPPED MY BOOK.
WHAT?
SERIOUS-LY?!

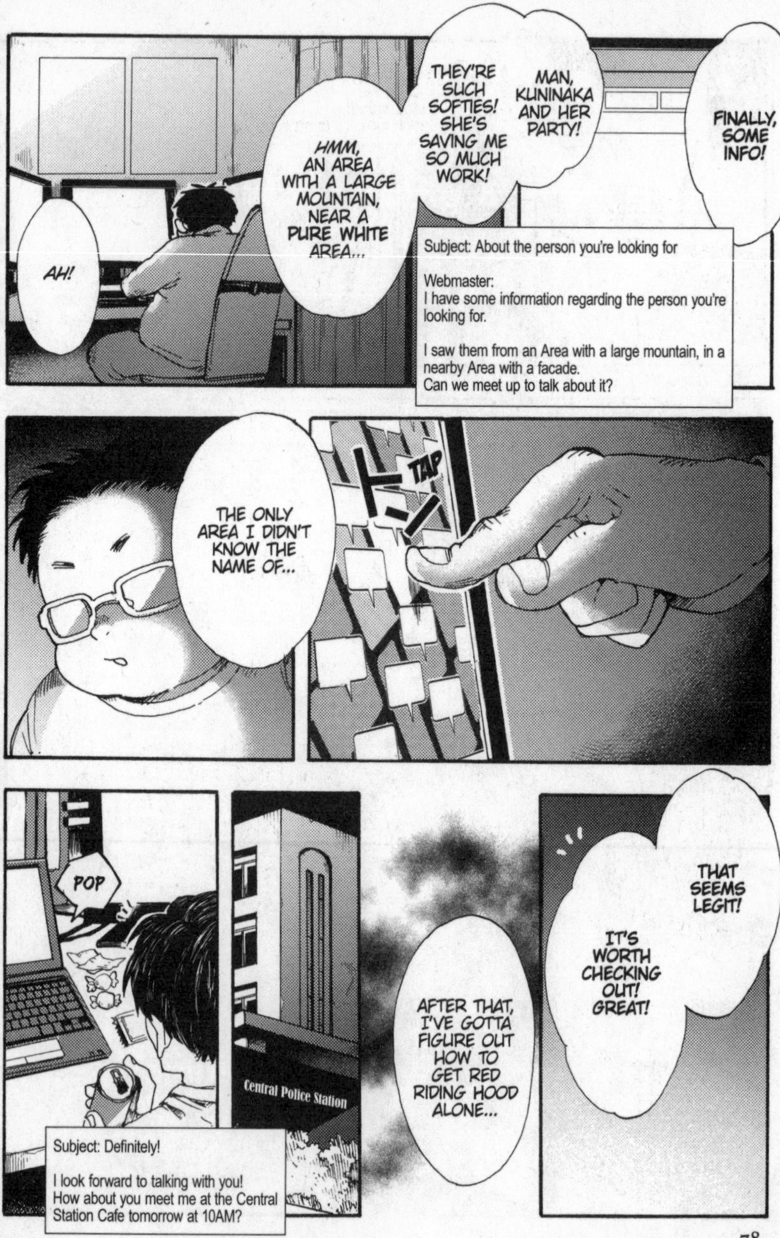
FINALLY, SOME INFO!
Subject: About the person you're looking for
Webmaster:
I have some information regarding the person you're looking for.
I saw them from an Area with a large mountain, in a nearby Area with a facade.
Can we meet up to talk about it?
MAN, KUNINAKA AND HER PARTY!
THEY'RE SUCH SOFTIES! SHE'S SAVING ME SO MUCH WORK!
HMM, AN AREA WITH A LARGE MOUNTAIN, NEAR A PURE WHITE AREA...
AH!
TAP
THE ONLY AREA I DIDN'T KNOW THE NAME OF...
THAT SEEMS LEGIT!
IT'S WORTH CHECKING OUT! GREAT!
AFTER THAT, I'VE GOTTA FIGURE OUT HOW TO GET RED RIDING HOOD ALONE...
Central Police Station
POP
Subject: Definitely!
I look forward to talking with you!
How about you meet me at the Central Station Cafe tomorrow at 10AM?

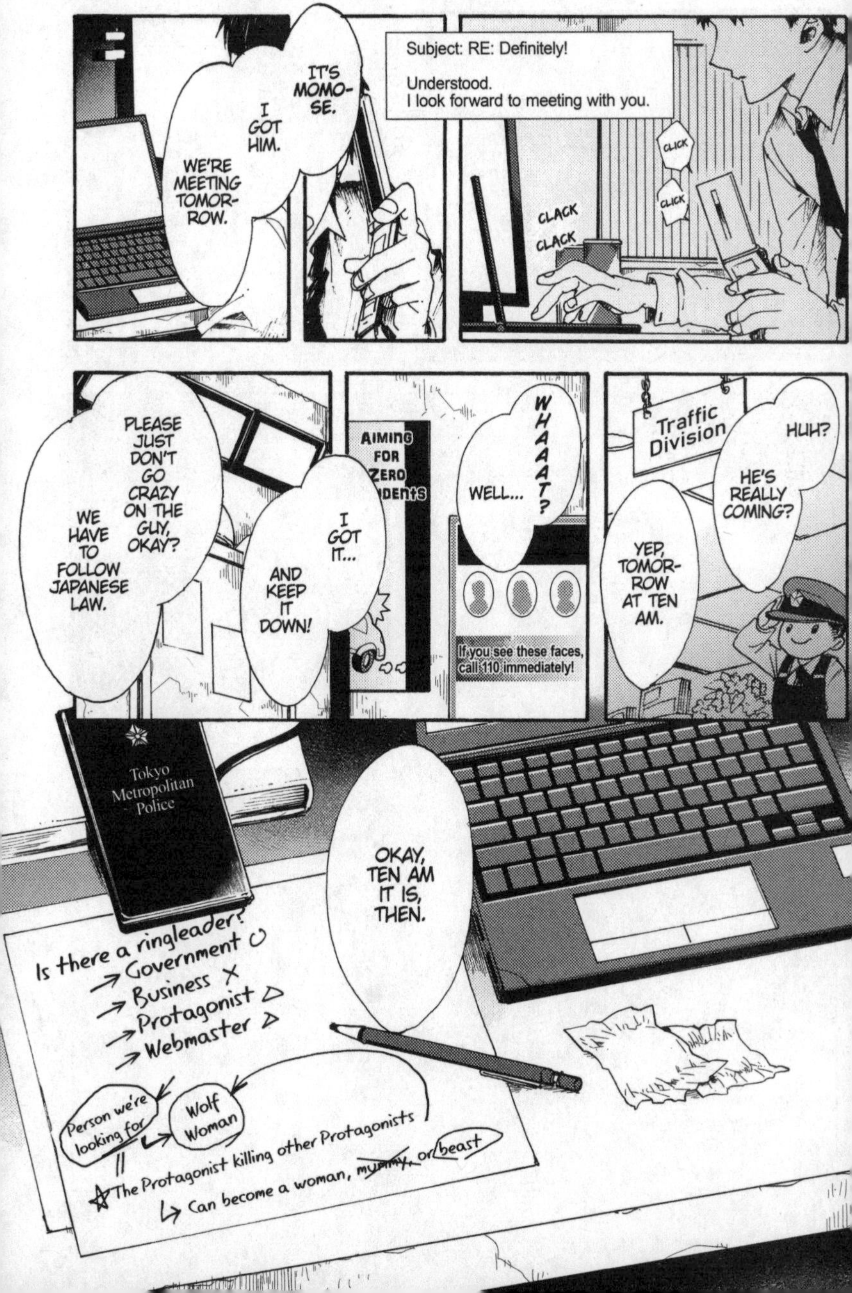
Subject: RE: Definitely!
Understood.
I look forward to meeting with you.
CLICK
CLICK
CLACK
CLACK
IT'S MOMO-SE.
I GOT HIM.
WE'RE MEETING TOMOR-ROW.
Traffic Division
HUH?
HE'S REALLY COMING?
YEP, TOMOR-ROW AT TEN AM.
WHAAAT?
WELL...
AIMING FOR ZERO
If you see these faces, call 110 immediately!
I GOT IT...
AND KEEP IT DOWN!
PLEASE JUST DON'T GO CRAZY ON THE GUY, OKAY?
WE HAVE TO FOLLOW JAPANESE LAW.
Tokyo Metropolitan Police
OKAY, TEN AM IT IS, THEN.
Is there a ringleader?
→ Government ○
→ Business ×
→ Protagonist △
→ Webmaster △
Person we're looking for
Wolf Woman
The Protagonist killing other Protagonists
Can become a woman, mummy, or beast

FAIRY
TALE
BATTLE
ROYALE

Chapter 15: Old Tales

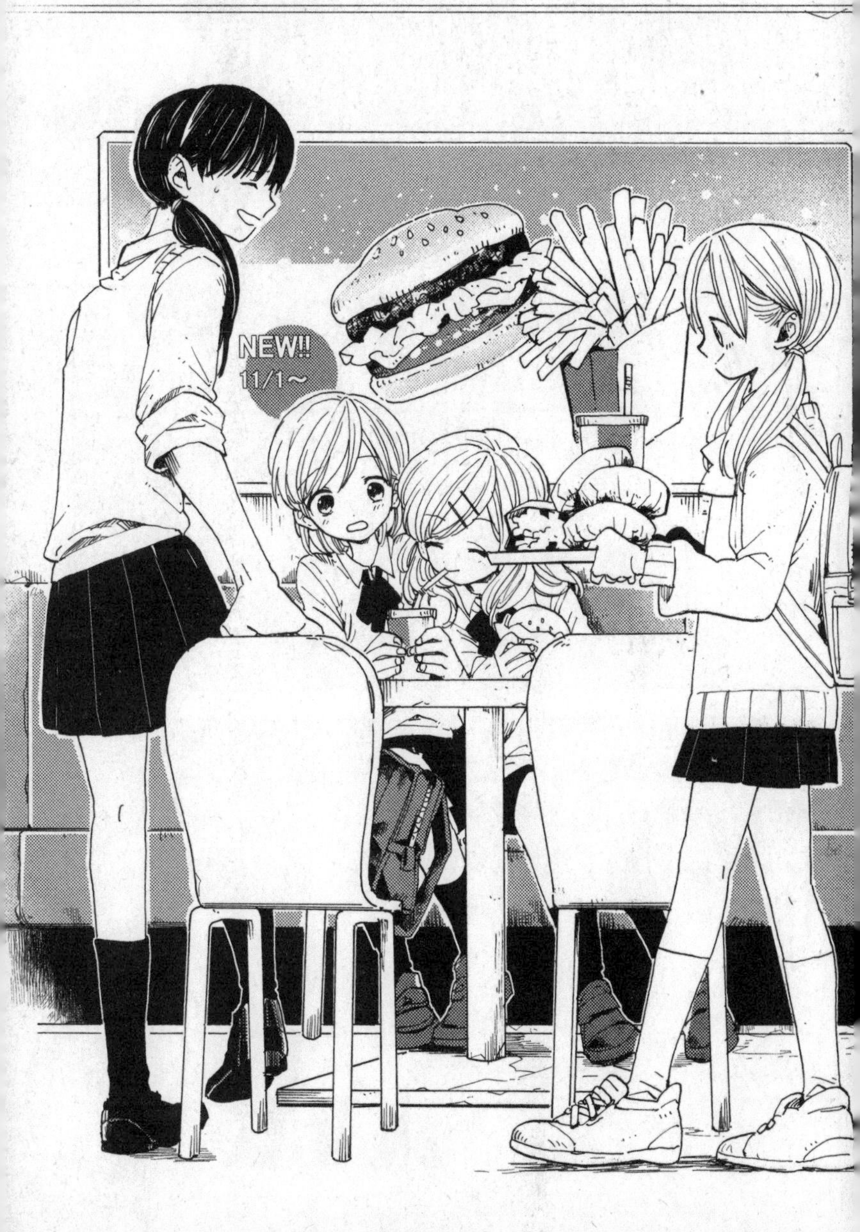
NEW!!
11/1～

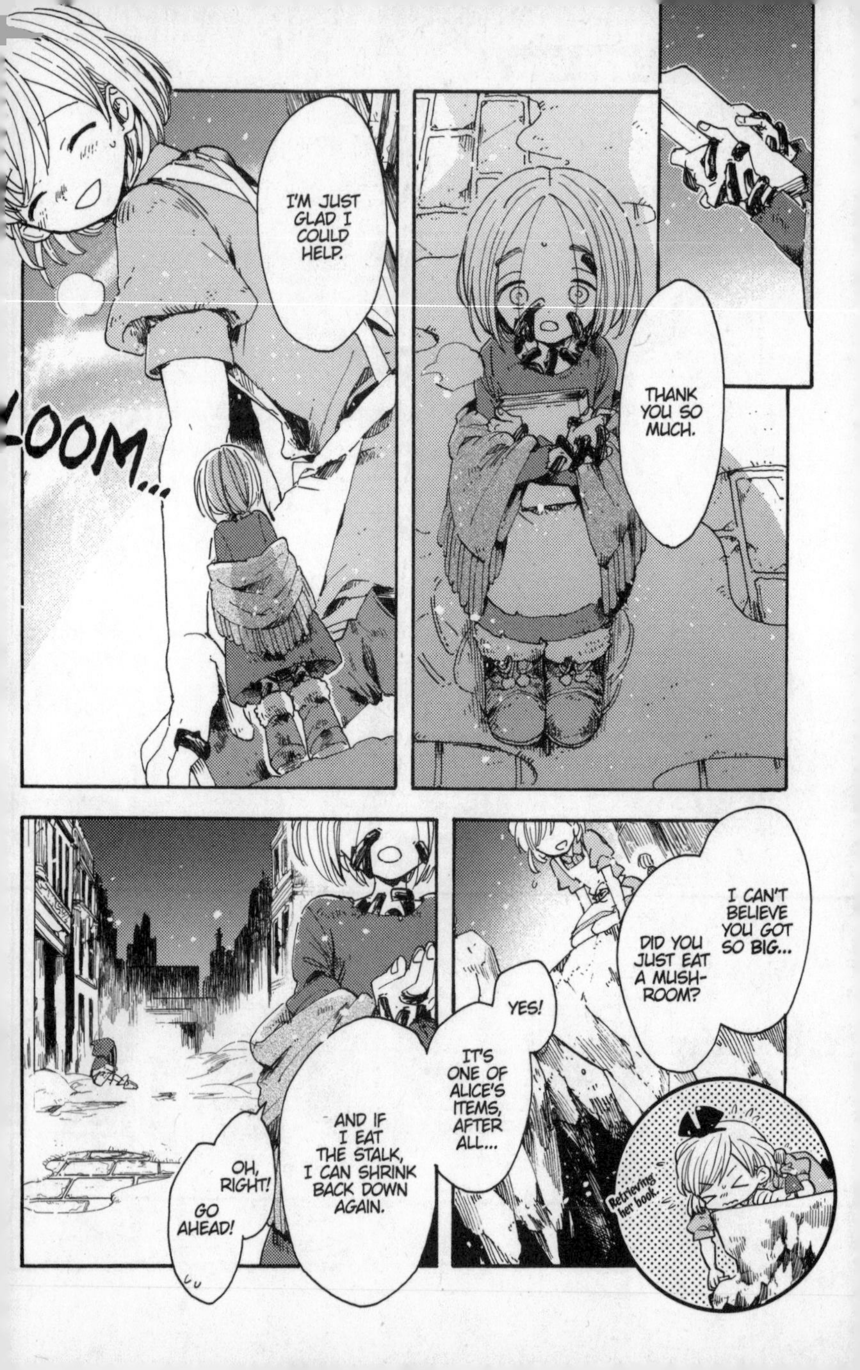
THANK YOU SO MUCH.
I'M JUST GLAD I COULD HELP.
LOOM...
I CAN'T BELIEVE YOU GOT SO BIG...
DID YOU JUST EAT A MUSH-ROOM?
YES!
IT'S ONE OF ALICE'S ITEMS, AFTER ALL...
Retrieving her book.
AND IF I EAT THE STALK, I CAN SHRINK BACK DOWN AGAIN.
OH, RIGHT!
GO AHEAD!

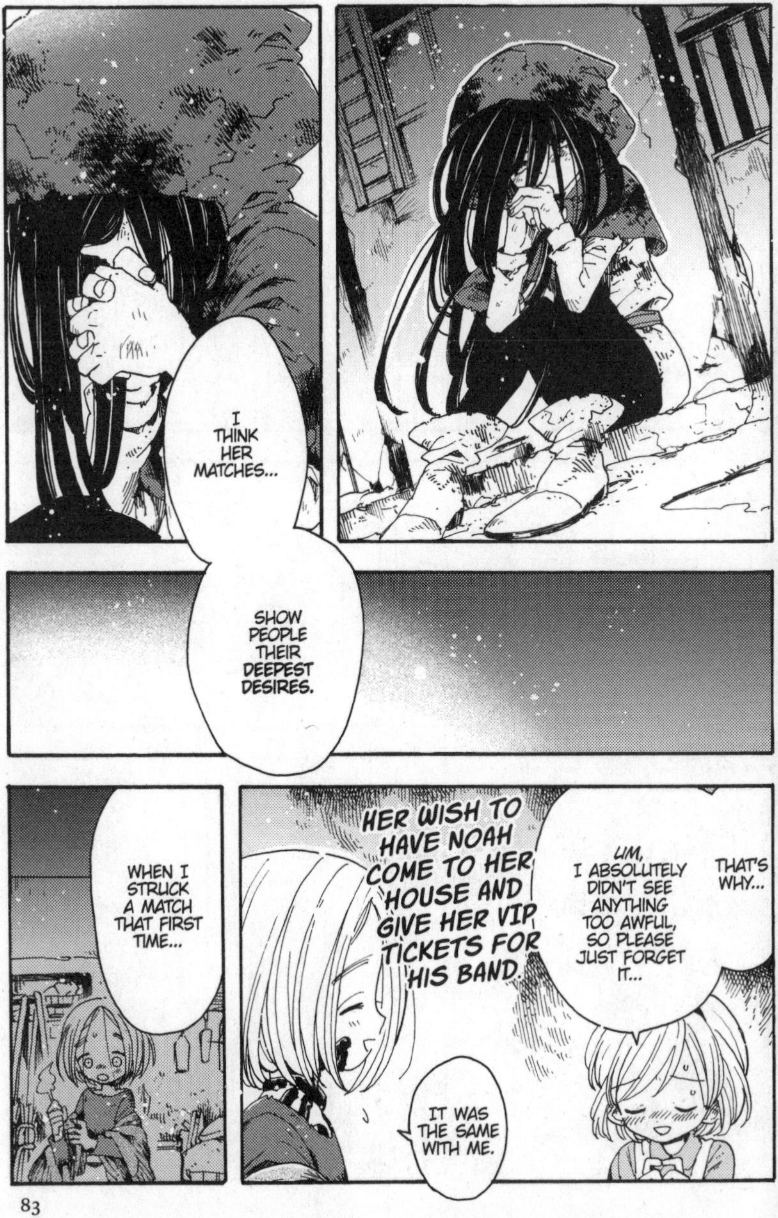
I THINK HER MATCHES...
SHOW PEOPLE THEIR DEEPEST DESIRES.
THAT'S WHY...
UM, I ABSOLUTELY DIDN'T SEE ANYTHING TOO AWFUL, SO PLEASE JUST FORGET IT...
HER WISH TO HAVE NOAH COME TO HER HOUSE AND GIVE HER VIP TICKETS FOR HIS BAND.
IT WAS THE SAME WITH ME.
WHEN I STRUCK A MATCH THAT FIRST TIME...

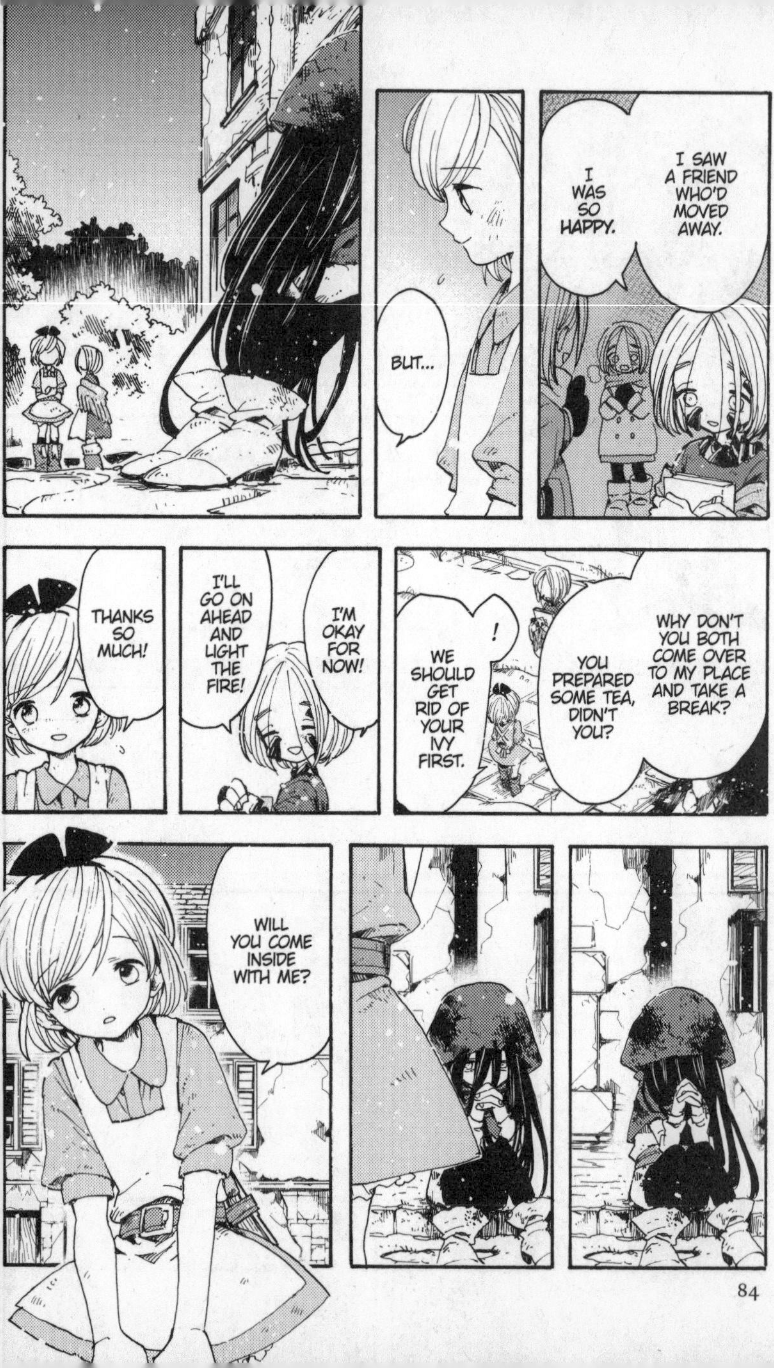
I SAW A FRIEND WHO'D MOVED AWAY.
I WAS SO HAPPY.
BUT...
WHY DON'T YOU BOTH COME OVER TO MY PLACE AND TAKE A BREAK?
YOU PREPARED SOME TEA, DIDN'T YOU?
!
WE SHOULD GET RID OF YOUR IVY FIRST.
I'M OKAY FOR NOW!
I'LL GO ON AHEAD AND LIGHT THE FIRE!
THANKS SO MUCH!
WILL YOU COME INSIDE WITH ME?

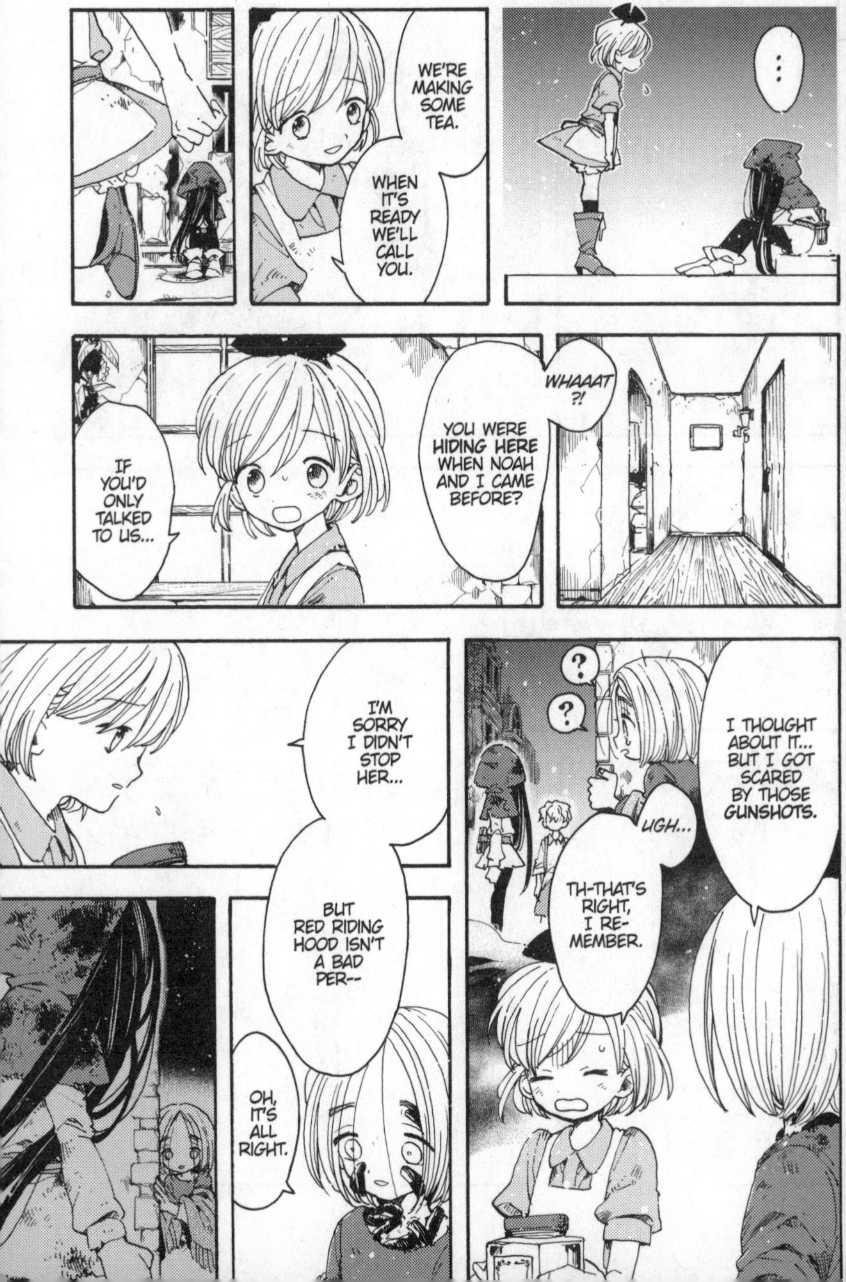
...
WE'RE MAKING SOME TEA.
WHEN IT'S READY WE'LL CALL YOU.
WHAAAT?!
YOU WERE HIDING HERE WHEN NOAH AND I CAME BEFORE?
IF YOU'D ONLY TALKED TO US...
?
?
I THOUGHT ABOUT IT... BUT I GOT SCARED BY THOSE GUNSHOTS.
UGH...
TH-THAT'S RIGHT, I RE-MEMBER.
I'M SORRY I DIDN'T STOP HER...
BUT RED RIDING HOOD ISN'T A BAD PER--
OH, IT'S ALL RIGHT.

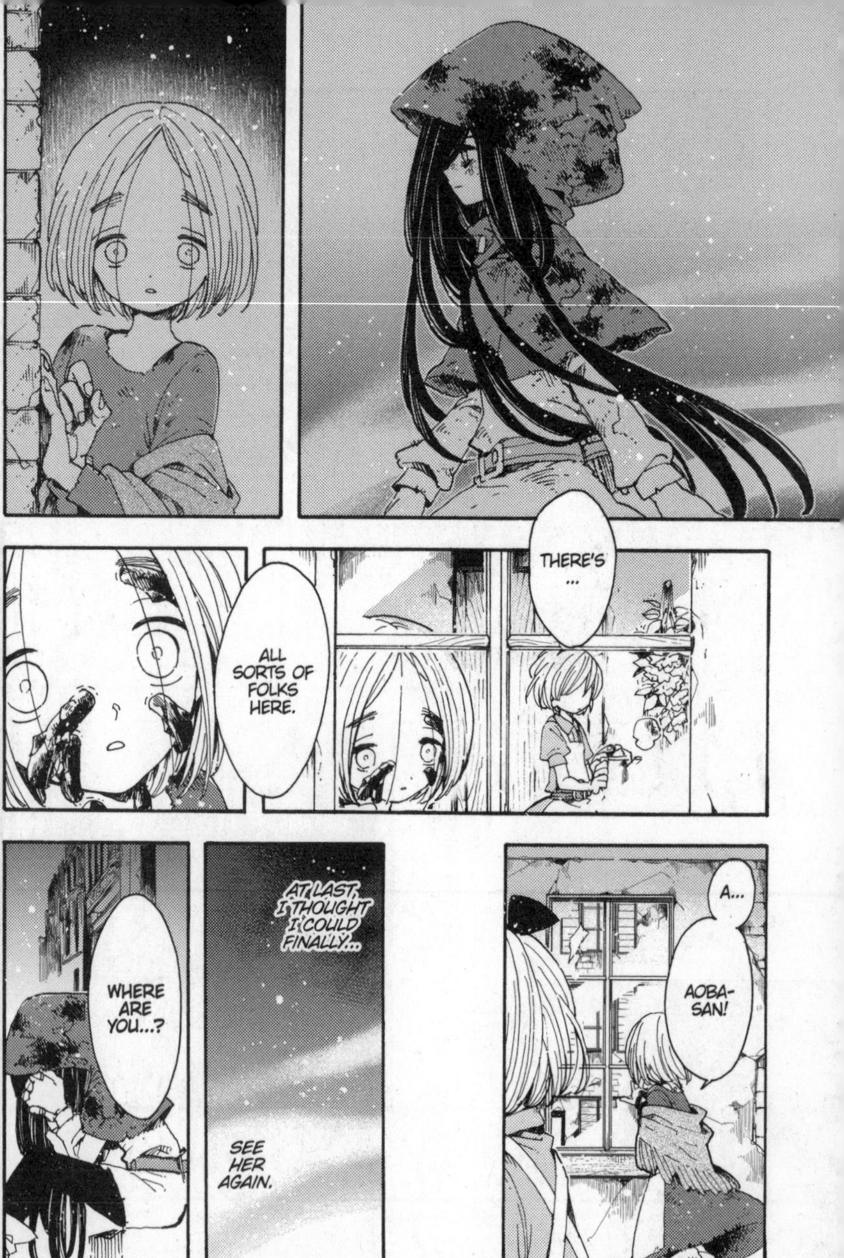
THERE'S ...
ALL SORTS OF FOLKS HERE.
A...
AOBA-SAN!
AT LAST, I THOUGHT I COULD FINALLY...
SEE HER AGAIN.
WHERE ARE YOU...?

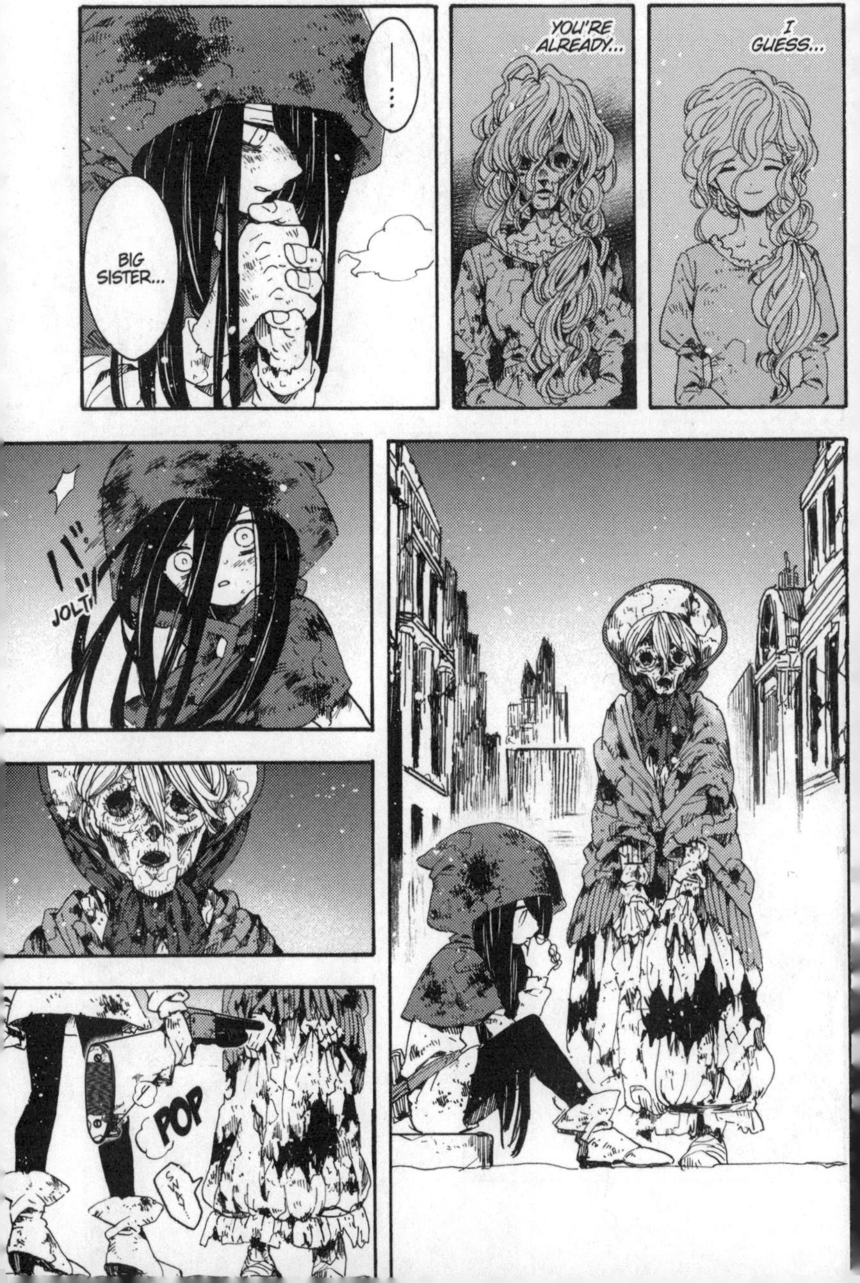
I GUESS...
YOU'RE ALREADY...
—...
BIG SISTER...
JOLT
POP
SWAY...

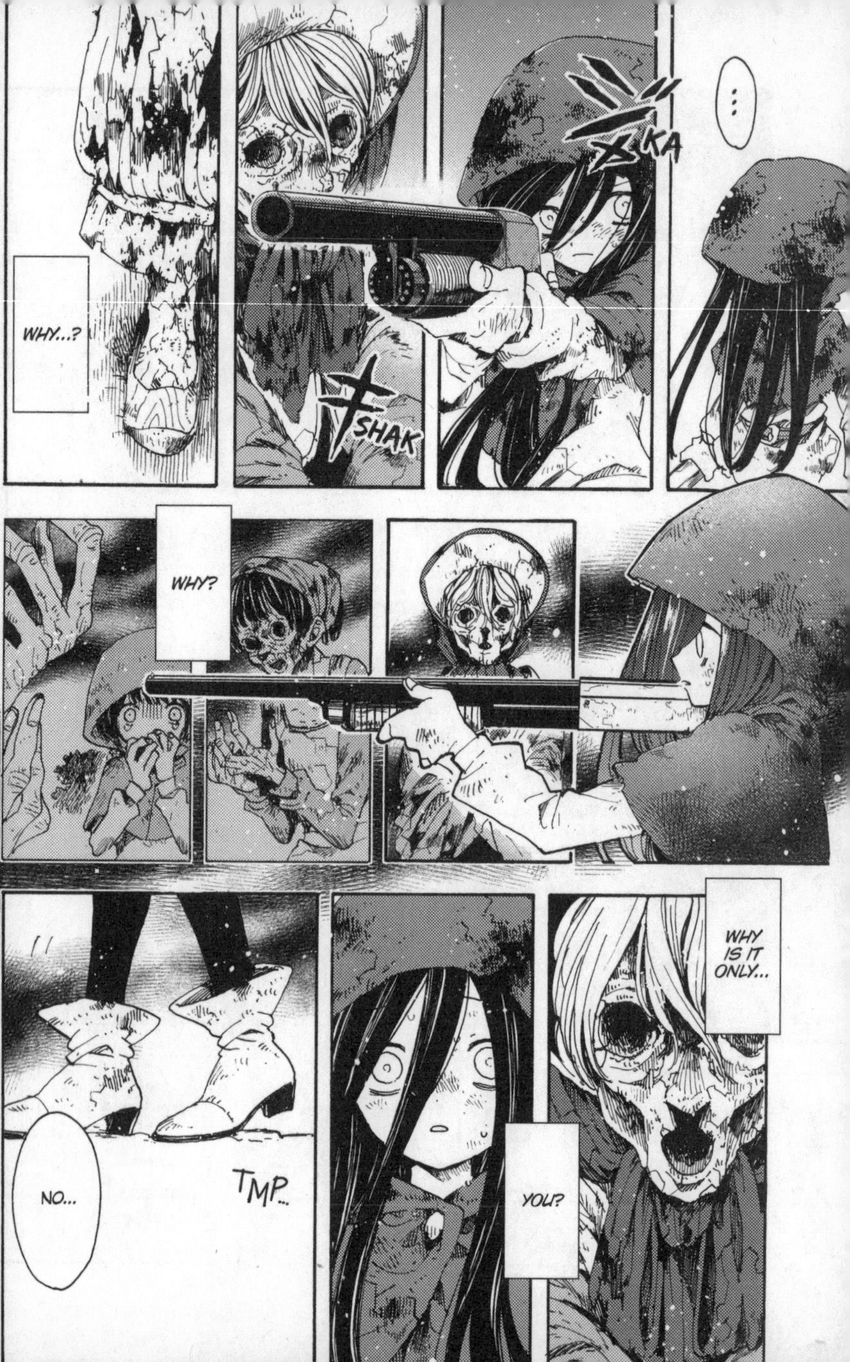

...
KA
SHAK
WHY...?
WHY?
WHY IS IT ONLY...
YOU?
TMP...
NO...

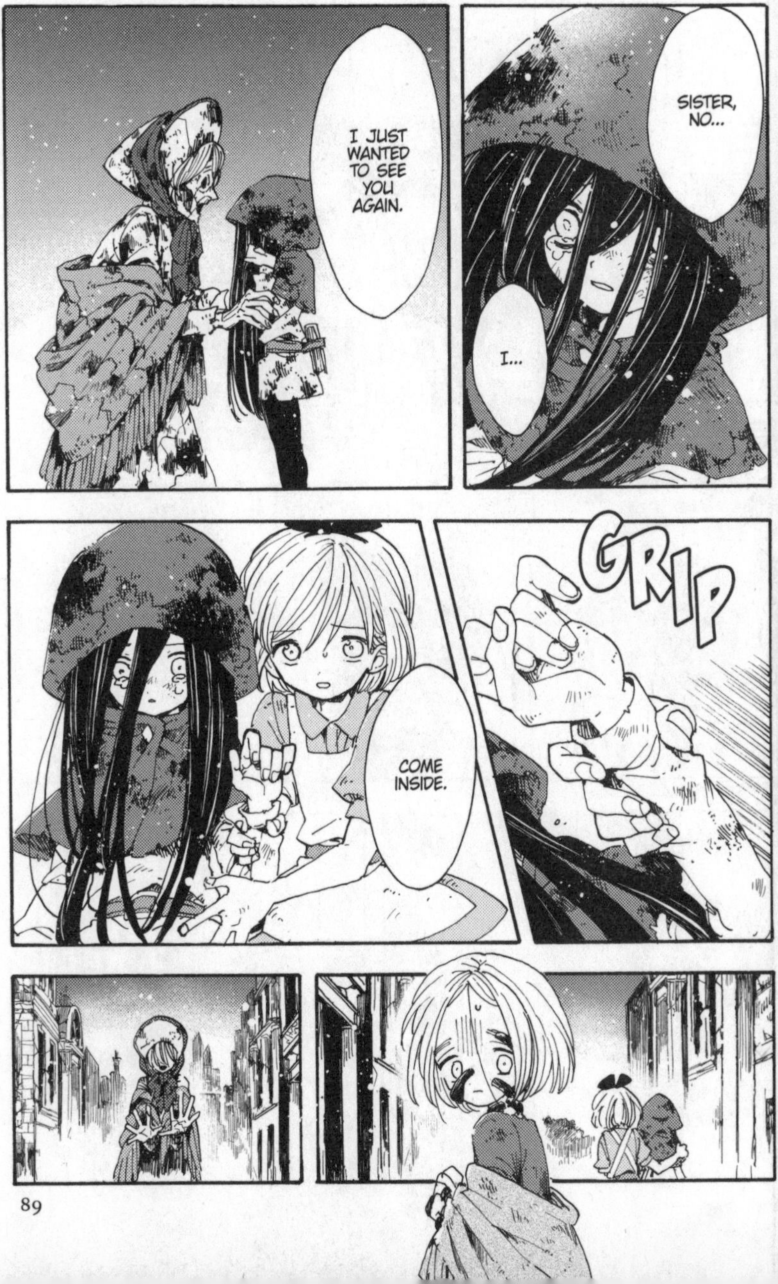
SISTER, NO...
I...
I JUST WANTED TO SEE YOU AGAIN.
GRIP
COME INSIDE.

HERE YOU ARE.

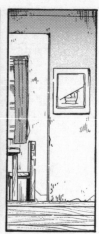

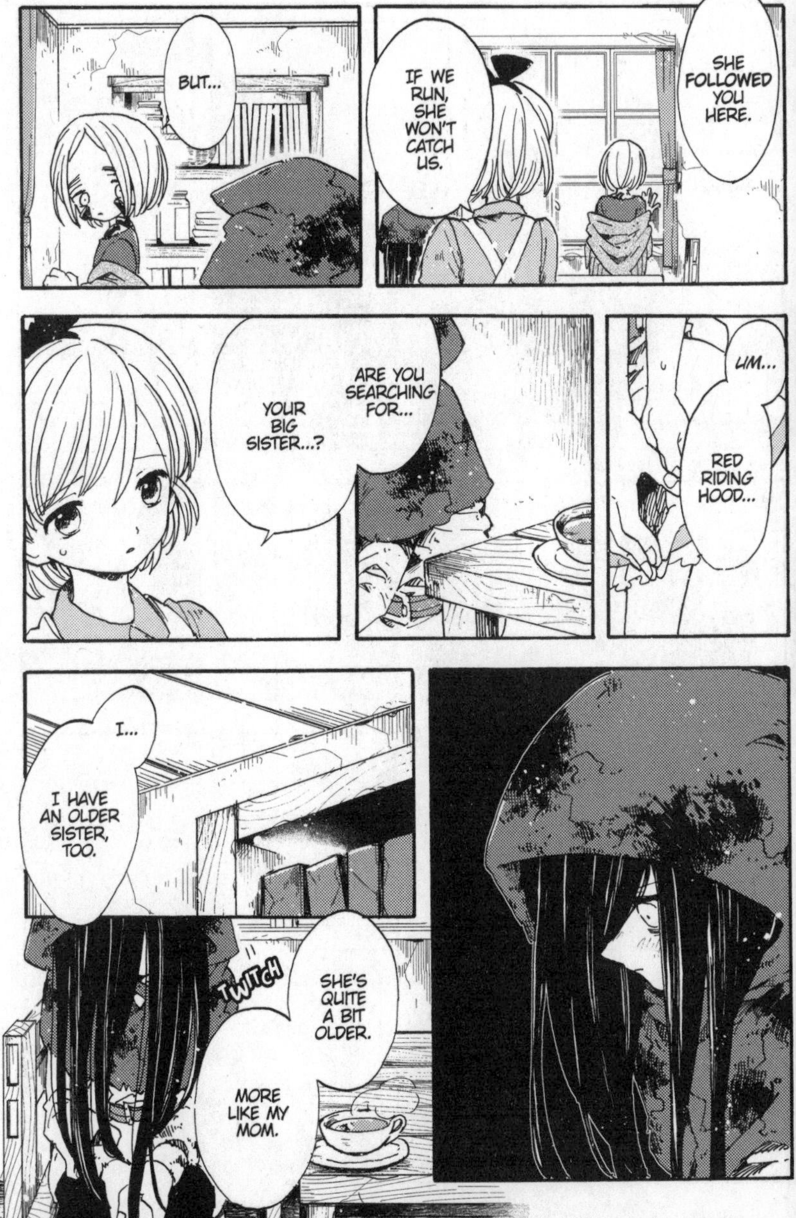
SHE FOLLOWED YOU HERE.
IF WE RUN, SHE WON'T CATCH US.
BUT...
UM...
RED RIDING HOOD...
ARE YOU SEARCHING FOR...
YOUR BIG SISTER...?
I...
I HAVE AN OLDER SISTER, TOO.
TWITCH
SHE'S QUITE A BIT OLDER.
MORE LIKE MY MOM.

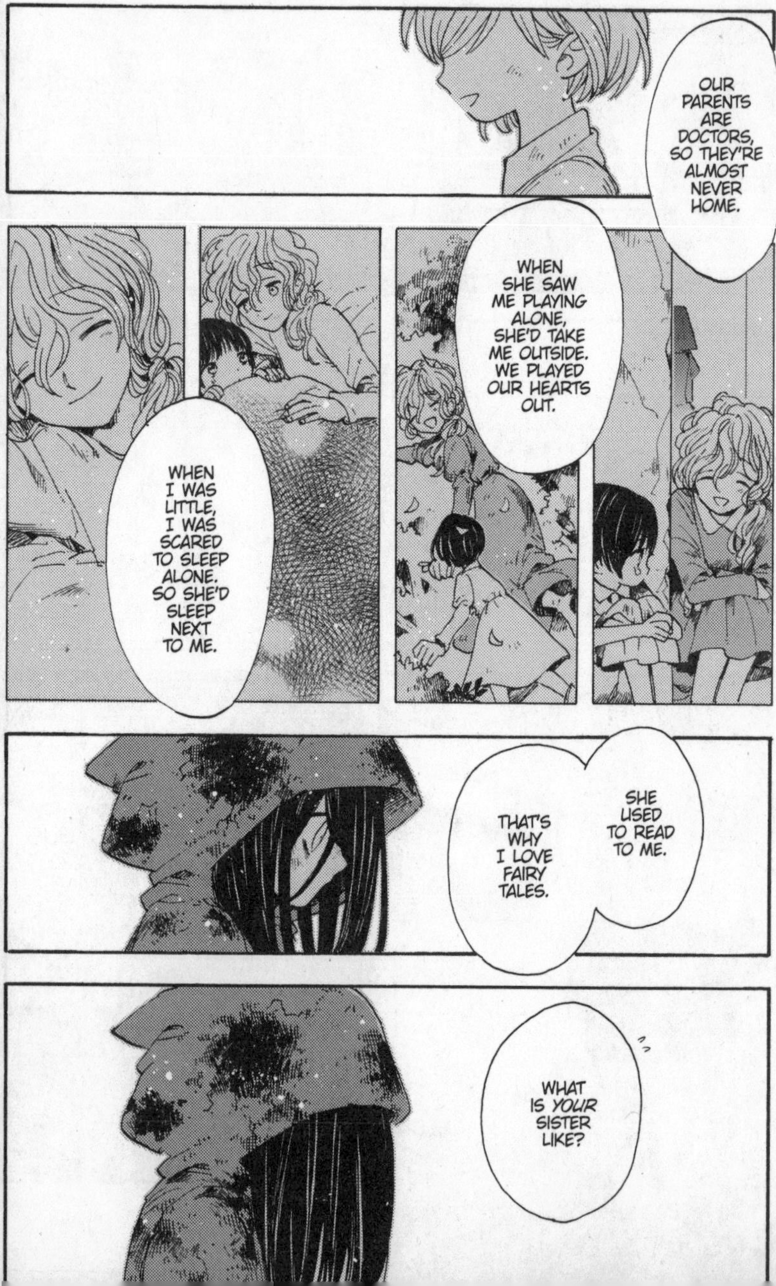
OUR PARENTS ARE DOCTORS, SO THEY'RE ALMOST NEVER HOME.
WHEN SHE SAW ME PLAYING ALONE, SHE'D TAKE ME OUTSIDE. WE PLAYED OUR HEARTS OUT.
WHEN I WAS LITTLE, I WAS SCARED TO SLEEP ALONE. SO SHE'D SLEEP NEXT TO ME.
SHE USED TO READ TO ME.
THAT'S WHY I LOVE FAIRY TALES.
WHAT IS *YOUR* SISTER LIKE?

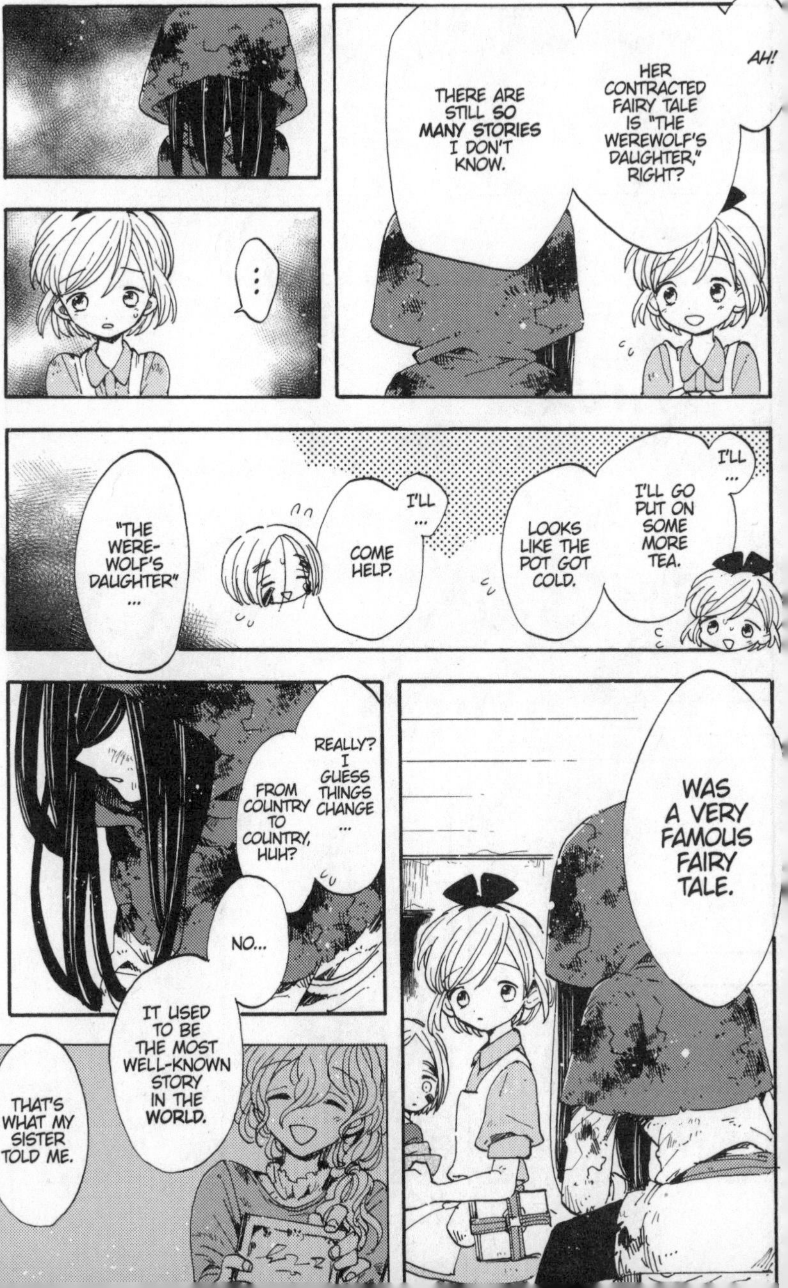
AH!
HER CONTRACTED FAIRY TALE IS "THE WEREWOLF'S DAUGHTER," RIGHT?
THERE ARE STILL SO MANY STORIES I DON'T KNOW.
...
I'LL ...
I'LL GO PUT ON SOME MORE TEA.
LOOKS LIKE THE POT GOT COLD.
I'LL ...
COME HELP.
"THE WERE-WOLF'S DAUGHTER" ...
WAS A VERY FAMOUS FAIRY TALE.
REALLY? I GUESS THINGS CHANGE ...
FROM COUNTRY TO COUNTRY, HUH?
NO...
IT USED TO BE THE MOST WELL-KNOWN STORY IN THE WORLD.
THAT'S WHAT MY SISTER TOLD ME.

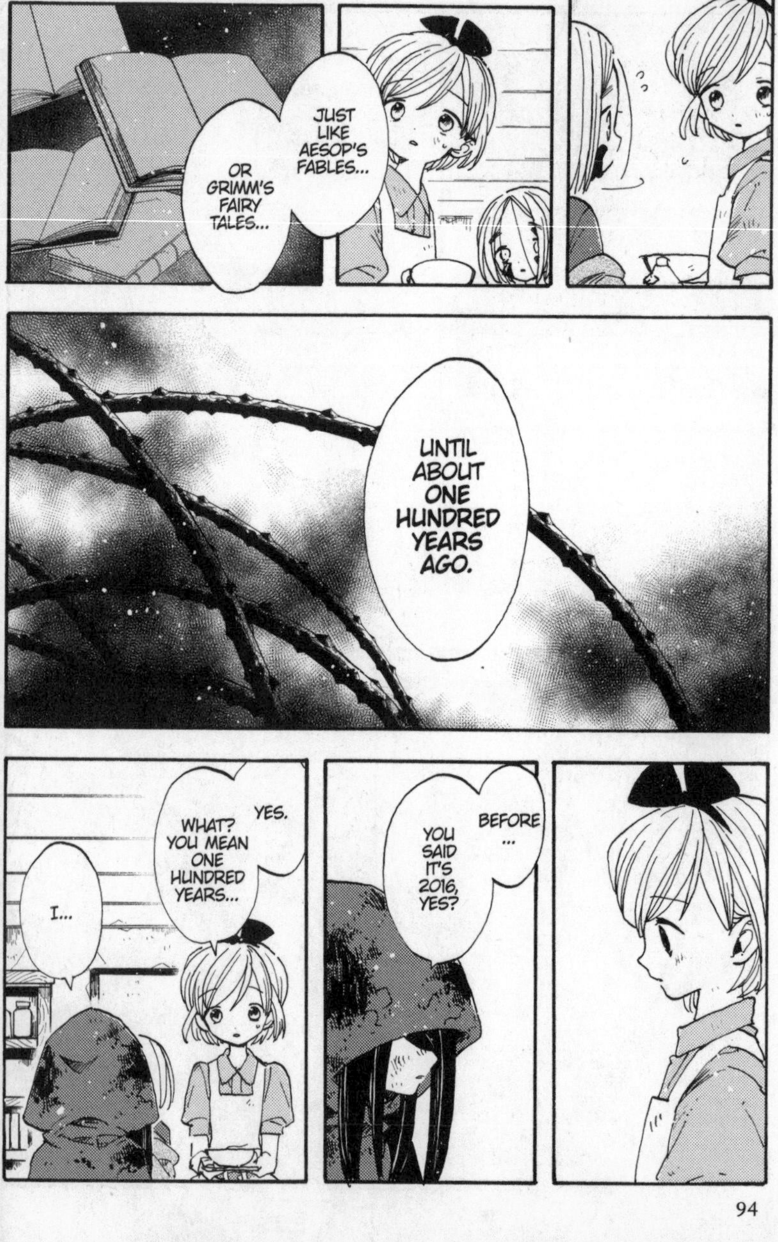
JUST LIKE AESOP'S FABLES...
OR GRIMM'S FAIRY TALES...
UNTIL ABOUT ONE HUNDRED YEARS AGO.
BEFORE ...
YOU SAID IT'S 2016, YES?
YES.
WHAT? YOU MEAN ONE HUNDRED YEARS...
I...

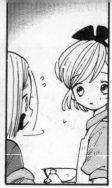

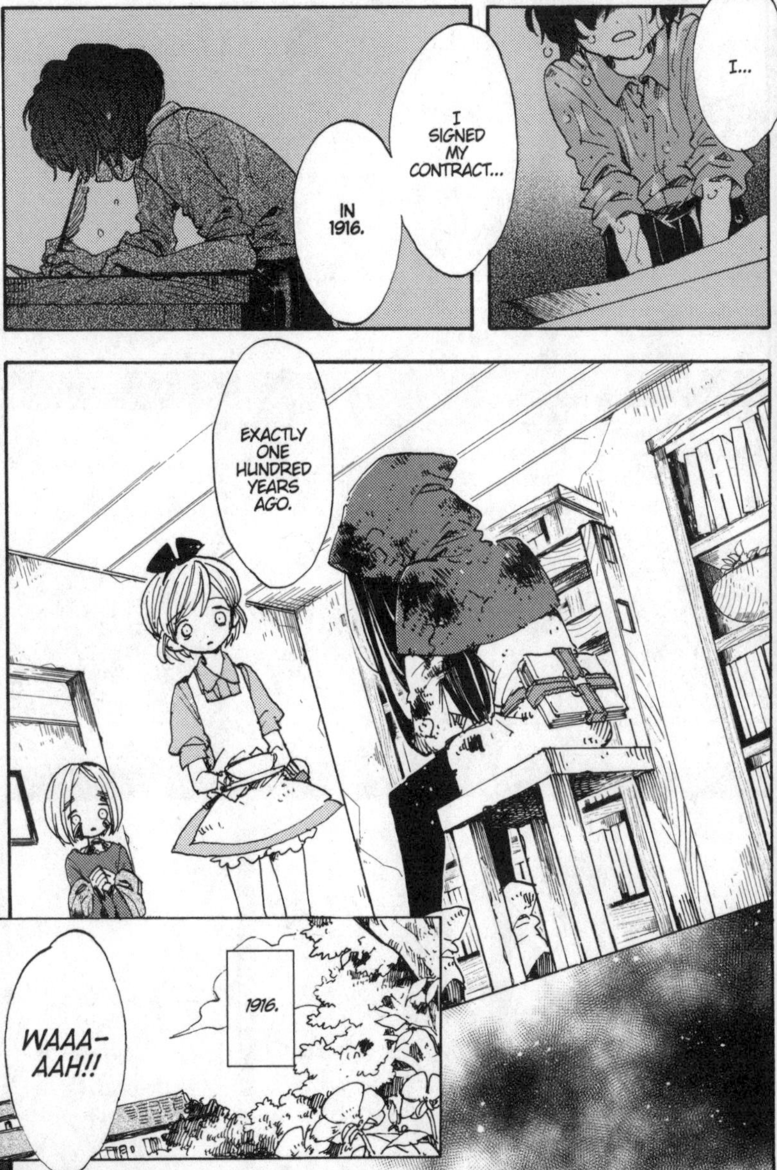
I...
I SIGNED MY CONTRACT...
IN 1916.
EXACTLY ONE HUNDRED YEARS AGO.
1916.
WAAA-AAH!!

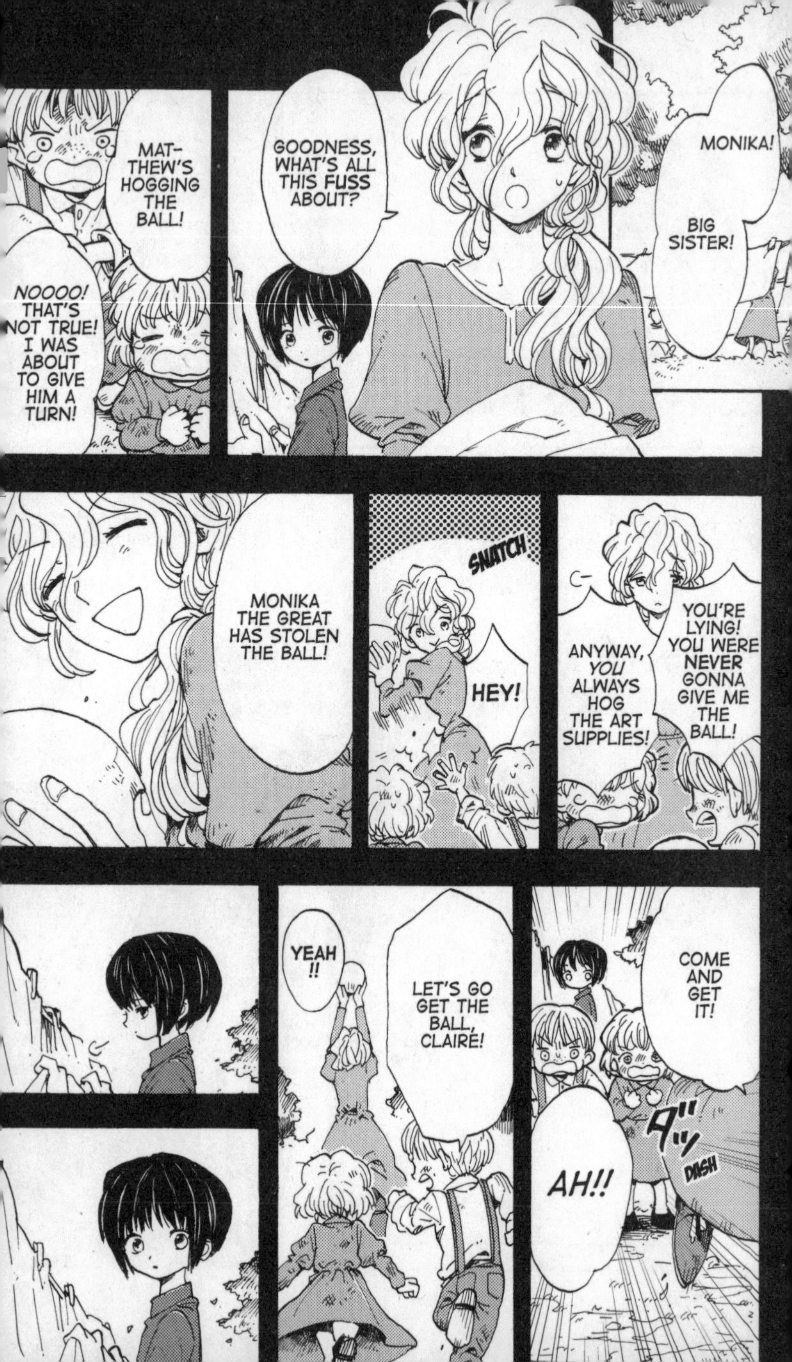
MONIKA!
BIG SISTER!
GOODNESS, WHAT'S ALL THIS FUSS ABOUT?
MAT-THEW'S HOGGING THE BALL!
NOOOO! THAT'S NOT TRUE! I WAS ABOUT TO GIVE HIM A TURN!
YOU'RE LYING! YOU WERE NEVER GONNA GIVE ME THE BALL!
ANYWAY, YOU ALWAYS HOG THE ART SUPPLIES!
SNATCH
HEY!
MONIKA THE GREAT HAS STOLEN THE BALL!
COME AND GET IT!
ダッ
DASH
AH!!
LET'S GO GET THE BALL, CLAIRE!
YEAH !!

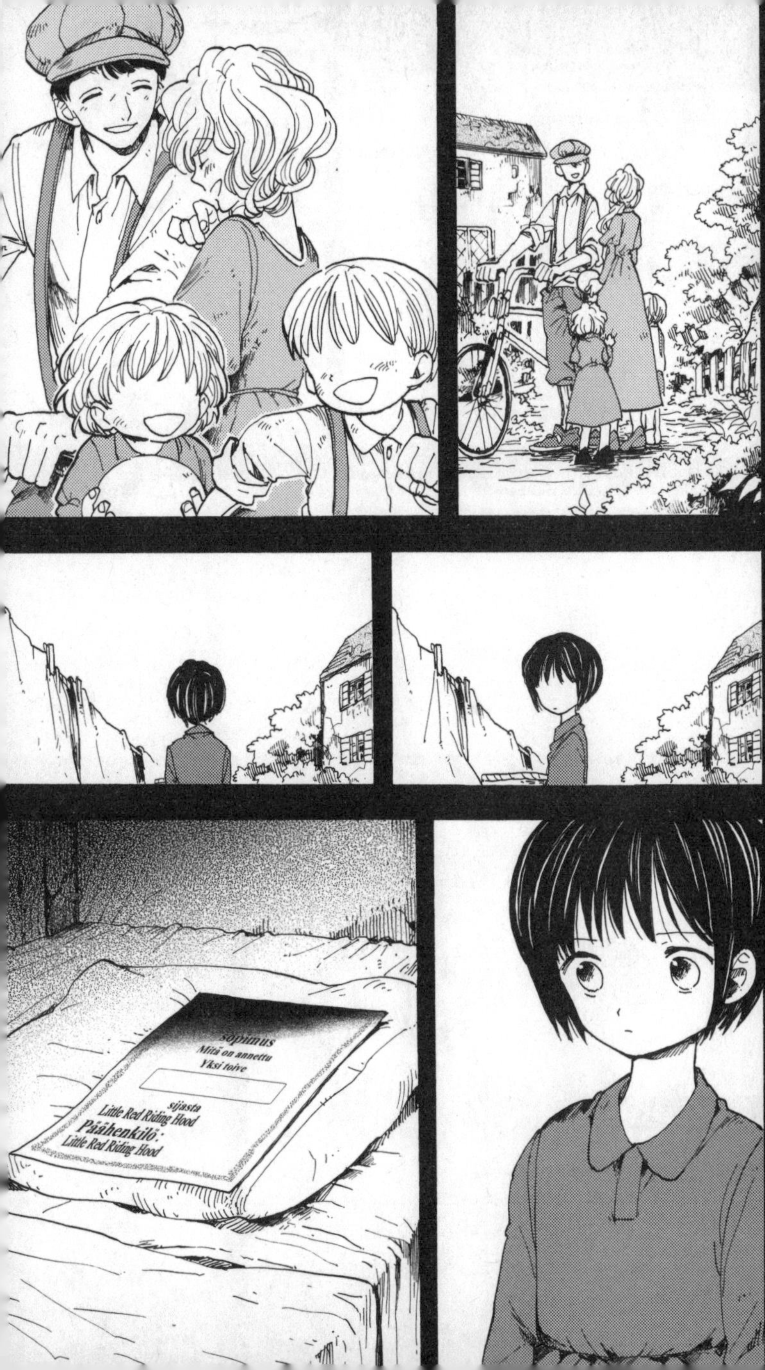
sopimus
Mitä on annettu
Yksi toive
sijasta
Little Red Riding Hood
Päähenkilö:
Little Red Riding Hood

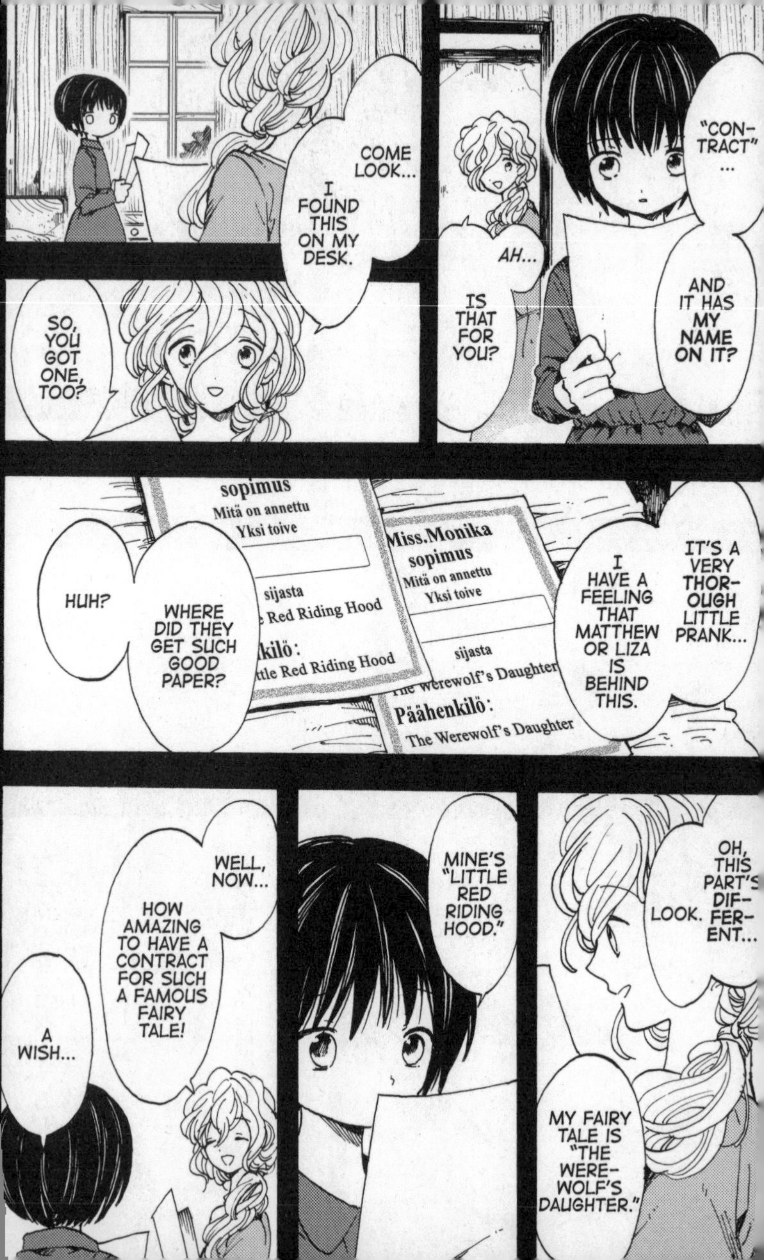
"CON-TRACT"...
AND IT HAS MY NAME ON IT?
AH...
IS THAT FOR YOU?
COME LOOK...
I FOUND THIS ON MY DESK.
SO, YOU GOT ONE, TOO?
IT'S A VERY THOR-OUGH LITTLE PRANK...
I HAVE A FEELING THAT MATTHEW OR LIZA IS BEHIND THIS.
Miss.Monika
sopimus
Mitä on annettu
Yksi toive
sijasta
The Werewolf's Daughter
Päähenkilö:
The Werewolf's Daughter
sopimus
Mitä on annettu
Yksi toive
sijasta
WHERE DID THEY GET SUCH GOOD PAPER?
HUH?
OH, THIS PART'S DIF-FER-ENT...
LOOK.
MY FAIRY TALE IS "THE WERE-WOLF'S DAUGHTER."
MINE'S "LITTLE RED RIDING HOOD."
WELL, NOW...
HOW AMAZING TO HAVE A CONTRACT FOR SUCH A FAMOUS FAIRY TALE!
A WISH...

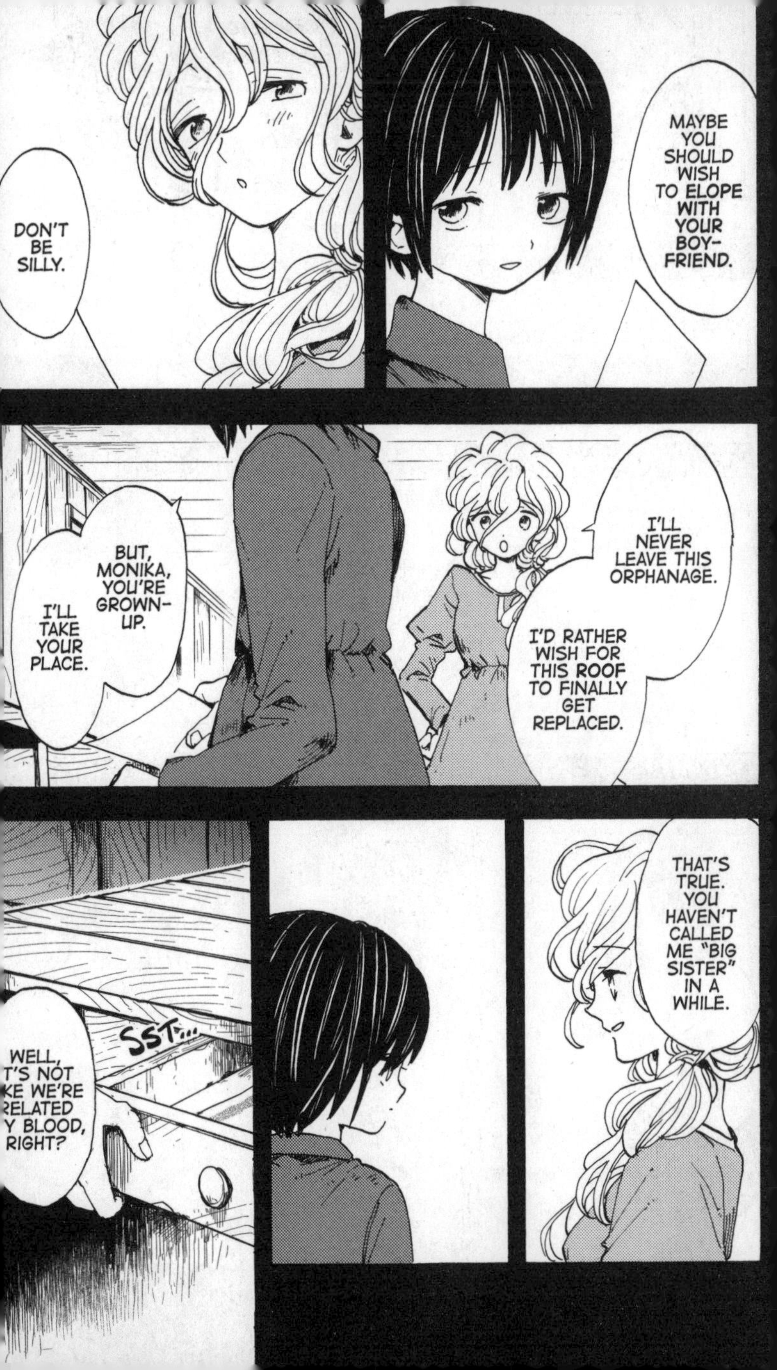
MAYBE YOU SHOULD WISH TO ELOPE WITH YOUR BOY-FRIEND.
DON'T BE SILLY.
I'LL NEVER LEAVE THIS ORPHANAGE.
I'D RATHER WISH FOR THIS ROOF TO FINALLY GET REPLACED.
BUT, MONIKA, YOU'RE GROWN-UP.
I'LL TAKE YOUR PLACE.
THAT'S TRUE. YOU HAVEN'T CALLED ME "BIG SISTER" IN A WHILE.
SST...
WELL, T'S NOT KE WE'RE RELATED Y BLOOD, RIGHT?

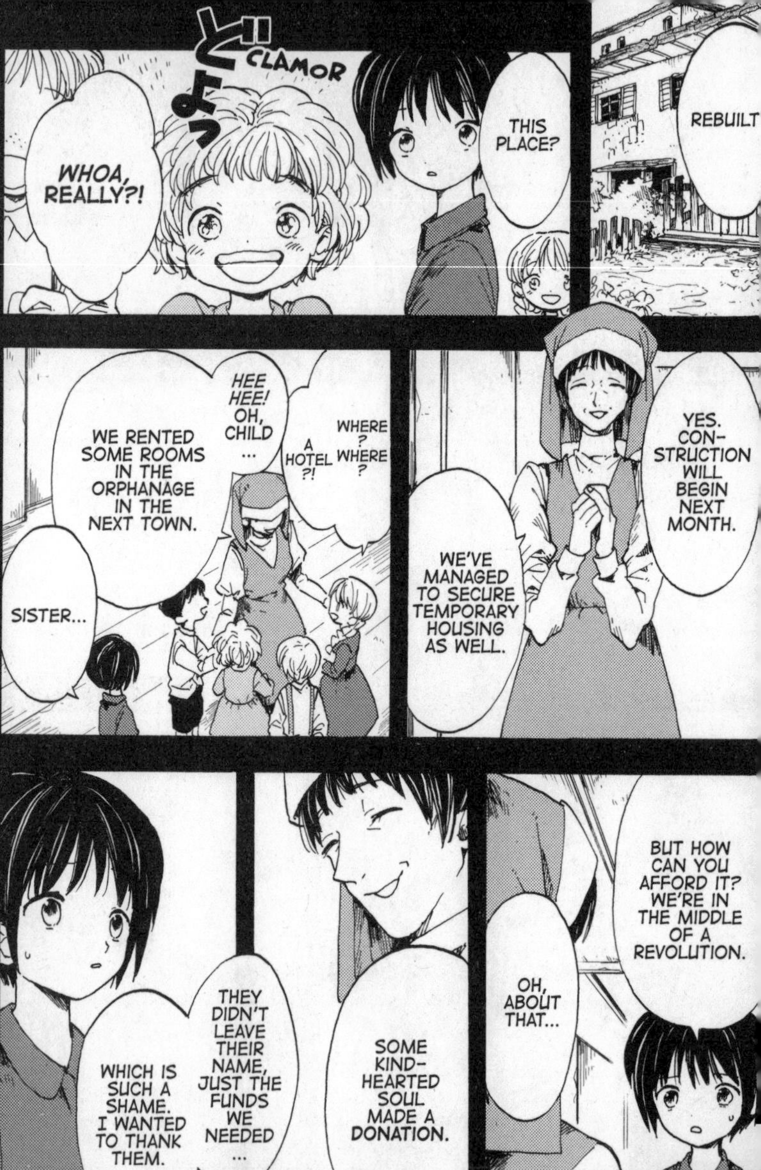
REBUILT
THIS PLACE?
どよっ CLAMOR
WHOA, REALLY?!
YES. CONSTRUCTION WILL BEGIN NEXT MONTH.
WE'VE MANAGED TO SECURE TEMPORARY HOUSING AS WELL.
WHERE? WHERE?
A HOTEL?!
HEE HEE! OH, CHILD...
WE RENTED SOME ROOMS IN THE ORPHANAGE IN THE NEXT TOWN.
SISTER...
BUT HOW CAN YOU AFFORD IT? WE'RE IN THE MIDDLE OF A REVOLUTION.
OH, ABOUT THAT...
SOME KIND-HEARTED SOUL MADE A DONATION.
THEY DIDN'T LEAVE THEIR NAME, JUST THE FUNDS WE NEEDED...
WHICH IS SUCH A SHAME. I WANTED TO THANK THEM.

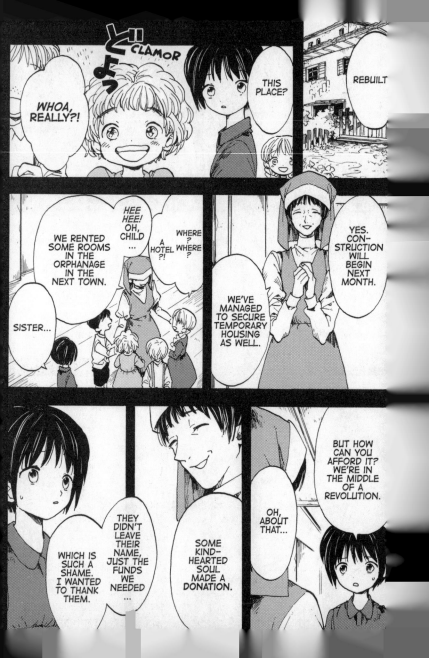

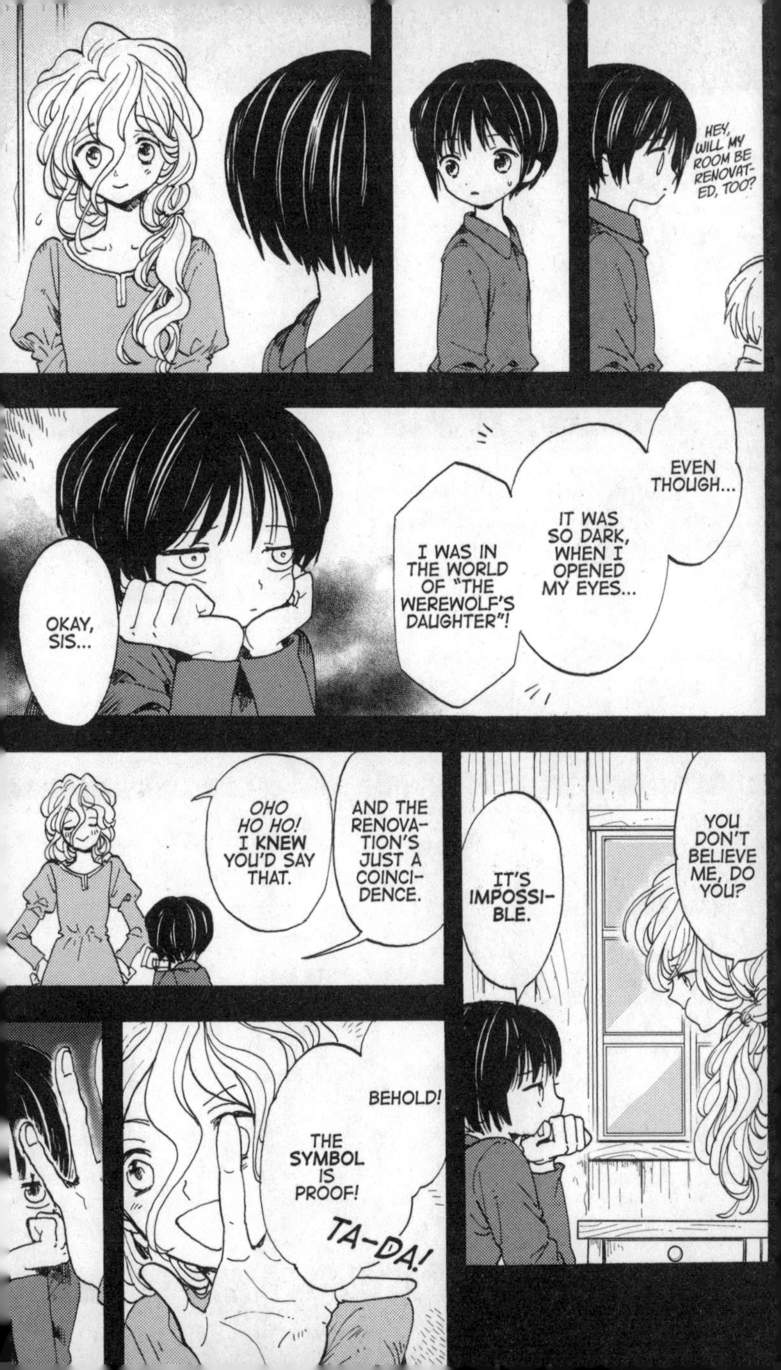
HEY, WILL MY ROOM BE RENOVATED, TOO?
EVEN THOUGH...
IT WAS SO DARK, WHEN I OPENED MY EYES...
I WAS IN THE WORLD OF "THE WEREWOLF'S DAUGHTER"!
OKAY, SIS...
YOU DON'T BELIEVE ME, DO YOU?
IT'S IMPOSSIBLE.
AND THE RENOVATION'S JUST A COINCIDENCE.
OHO HO HO! I KNEW YOU'D SAY THAT.
BEHOLD!
THE SYMBOL IS PROOF!
TA-DA!

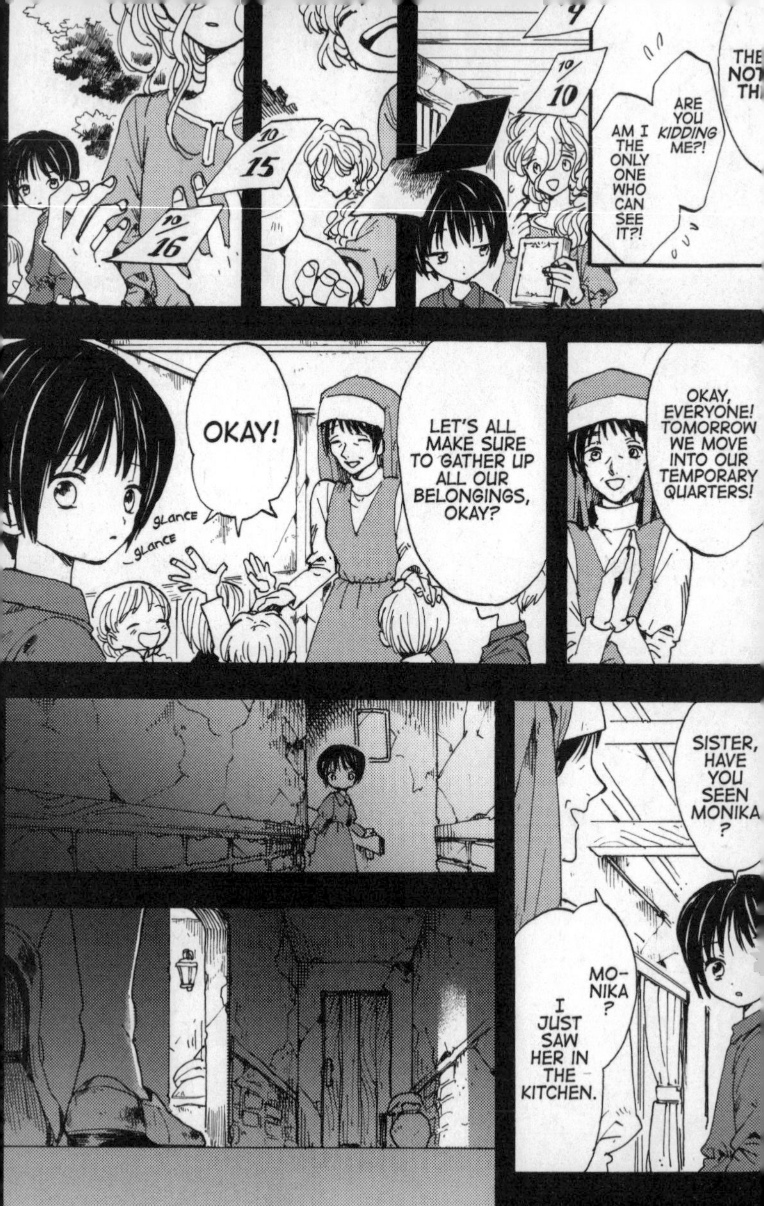
THE NOT TH
ARE YOU KIDDING ME?!
AM I THE ONLY ONE WHO CAN SEE IT?!
4
10/10
10/15
10/16
OKAY, EVERYONE! TOMORROW WE MOVE INTO OUR TEMPORARY QUARTERS!
LET'S ALL MAKE SURE TO GATHER UP ALL OUR BELONGINGS, OKAY?
OKAY!
GLANCE GLANCE
SISTER, HAVE YOU SEEN MONIKA?
MONIKA? I JUST SAW HER IN THE KITCHEN.

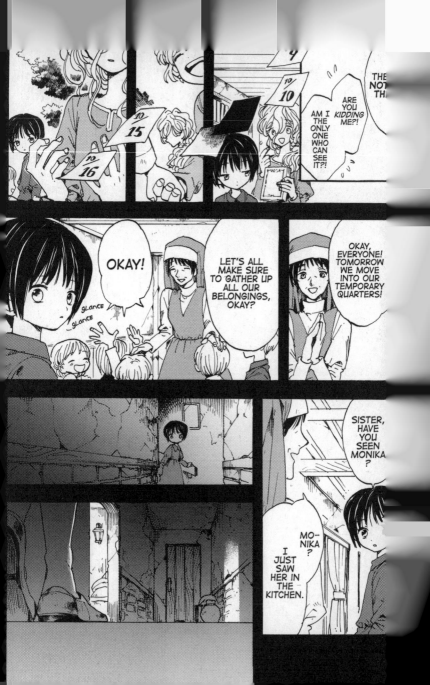

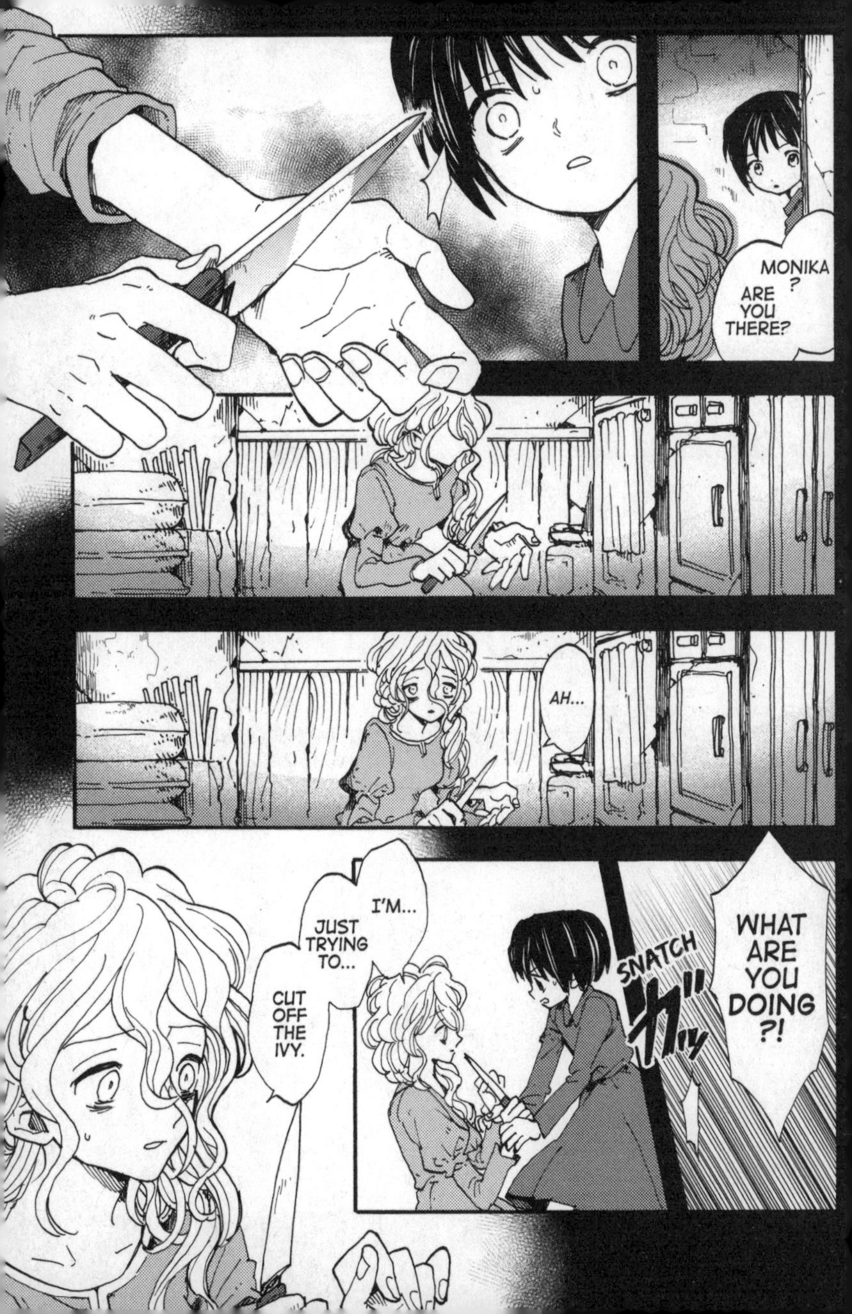
MONIKA? ARE YOU THERE?
AH...
WHAT ARE YOU DOING?!
SNATCH
I'M... JUST TRYING TO...
CUT OFF THE IVY.

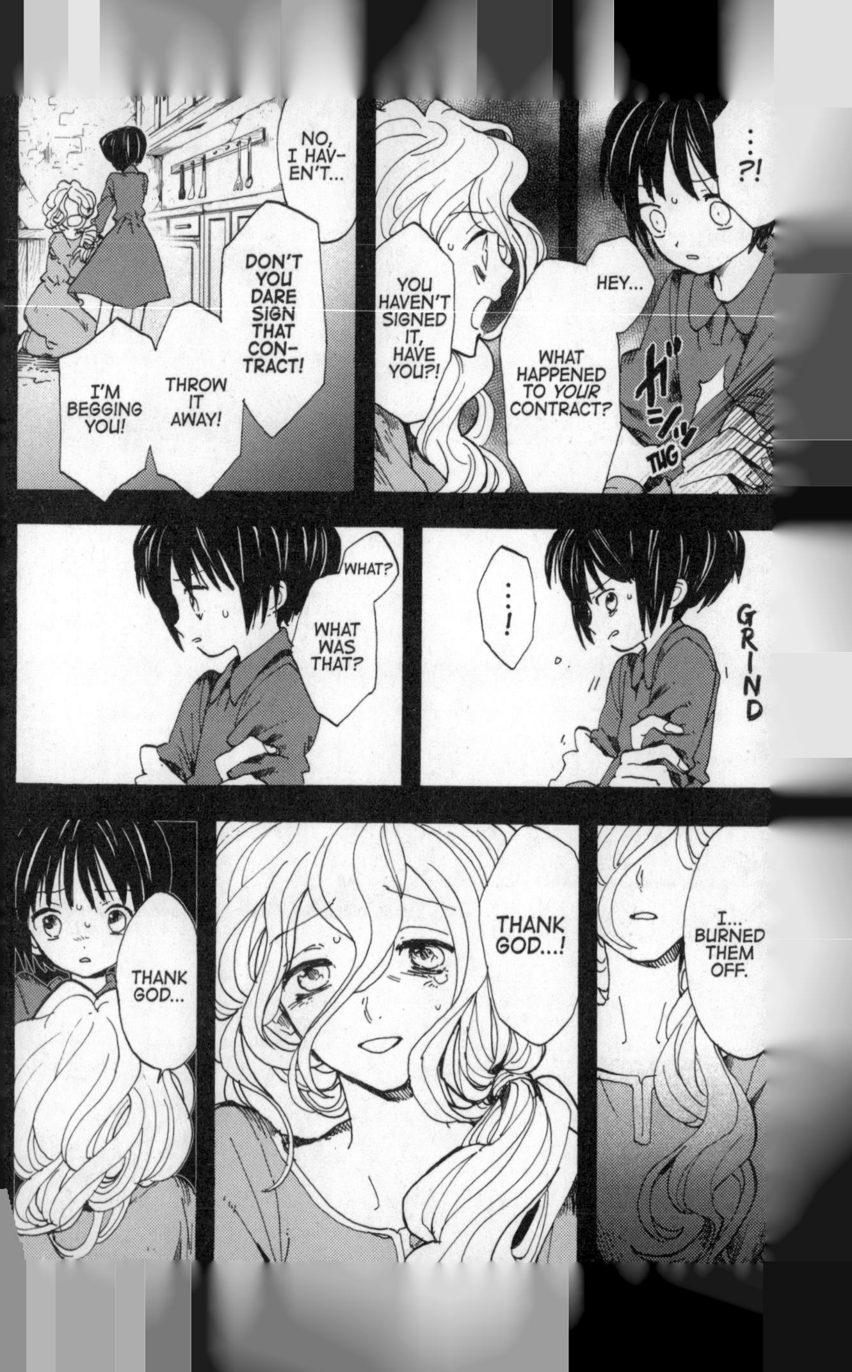
…?!
HEY…
WHAT HAPPENED TO YOUR CONTRACT?
TUG
YOU HAVEN'T SIGNED IT, HAVE YOU?!
NO, I HAV-EN'T…
DON'T YOU DARE SIGN THAT CONTRACT!
THROW IT AWAY!
I'M BEGGING YOU!
…!
GRIND
WHAT?
WHAT WAS THAT?
I… BURNED THEM OFF.
THANK GOD…!
THANK GOD…

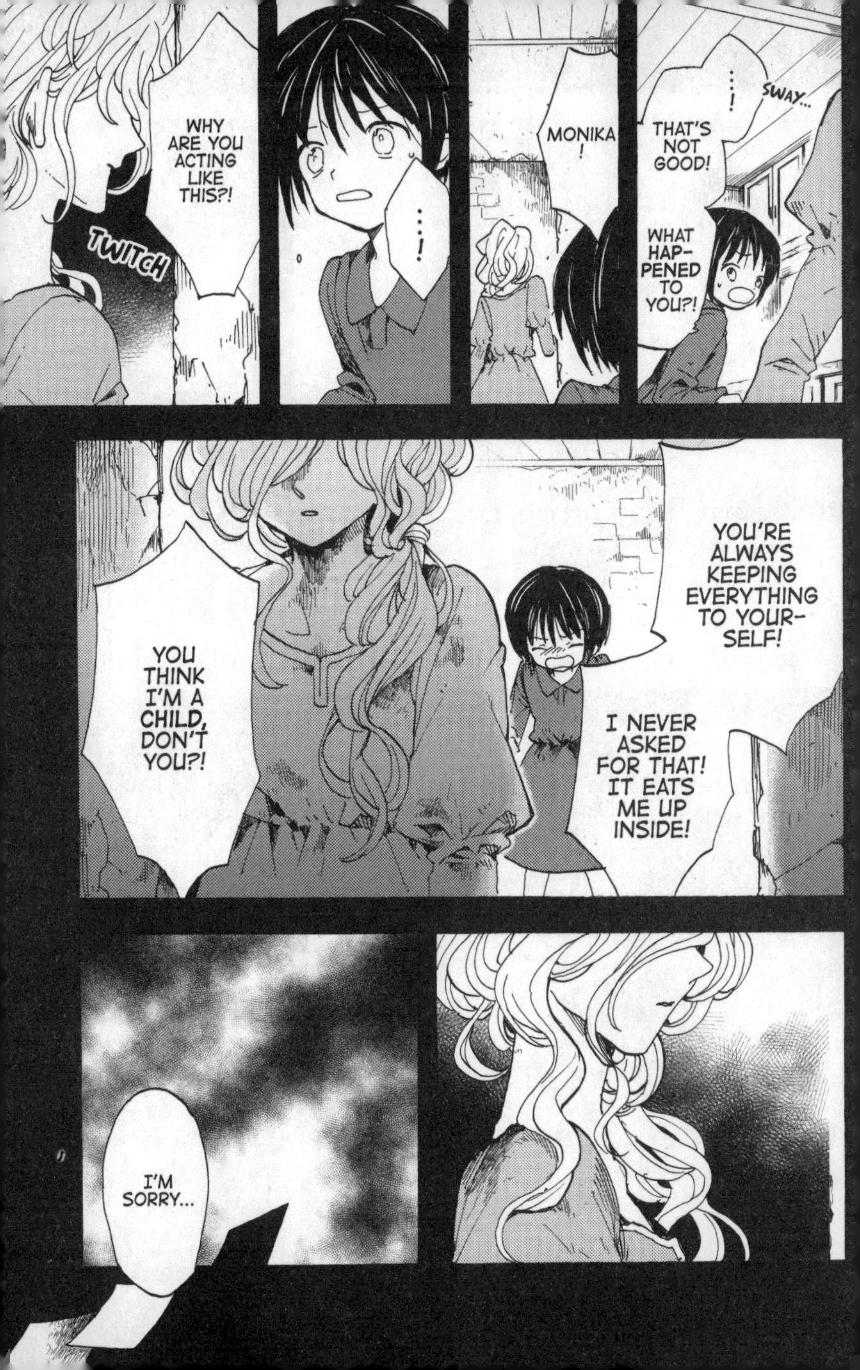
SWAY...
...!
THAT'S NOT GOOD!
WHAT HAPPENED TO YOU?!
MONIKA!
...!
WHY ARE YOU ACTING LIKE THIS?!
TWITCH
YOU'RE ALWAYS KEEPING EVERYTHING TO YOURSELF!
I NEVER ASKED FOR THAT! IT EATS ME UP INSIDE!
YOU THINK I'M A CHILD, DON'T YOU?!
I'M SORRY...

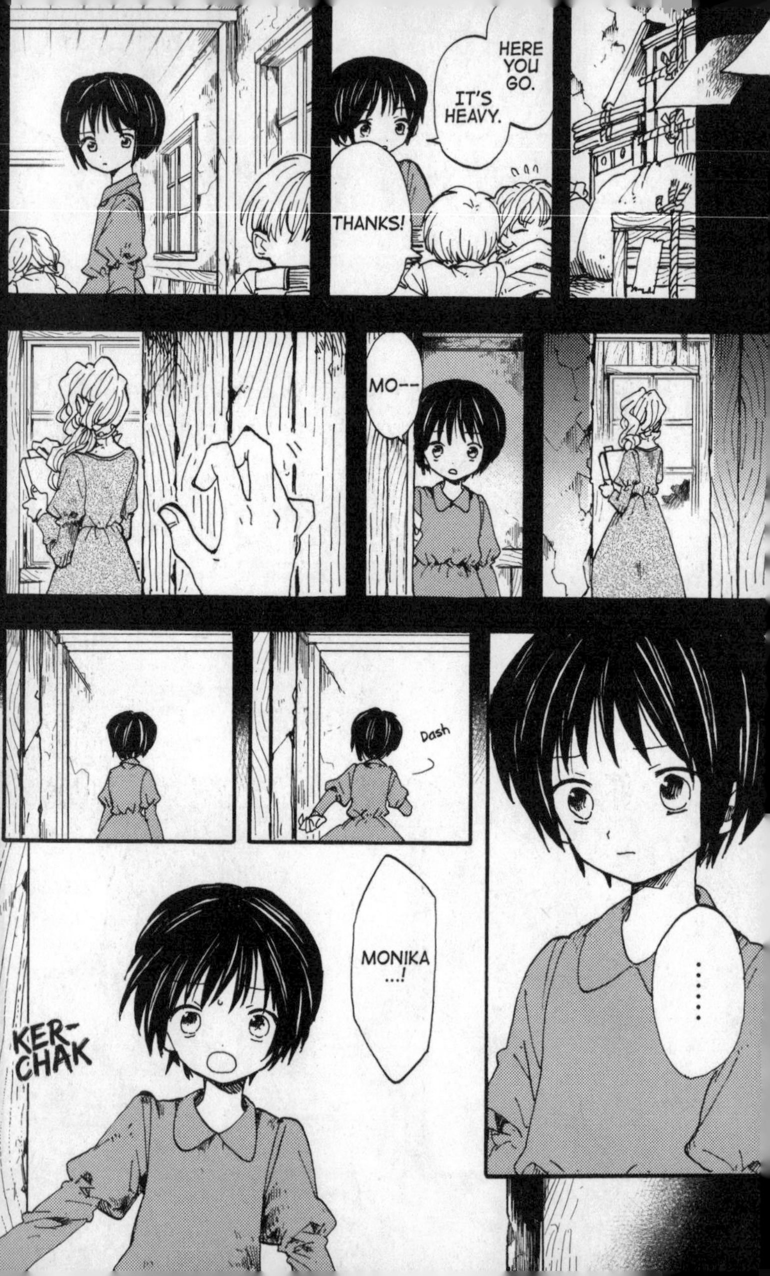
HERE YOU GO. IT'S HEAVY.
THANKS!
MO--
......
Dash
MONIKA ...!
KER-CHAK

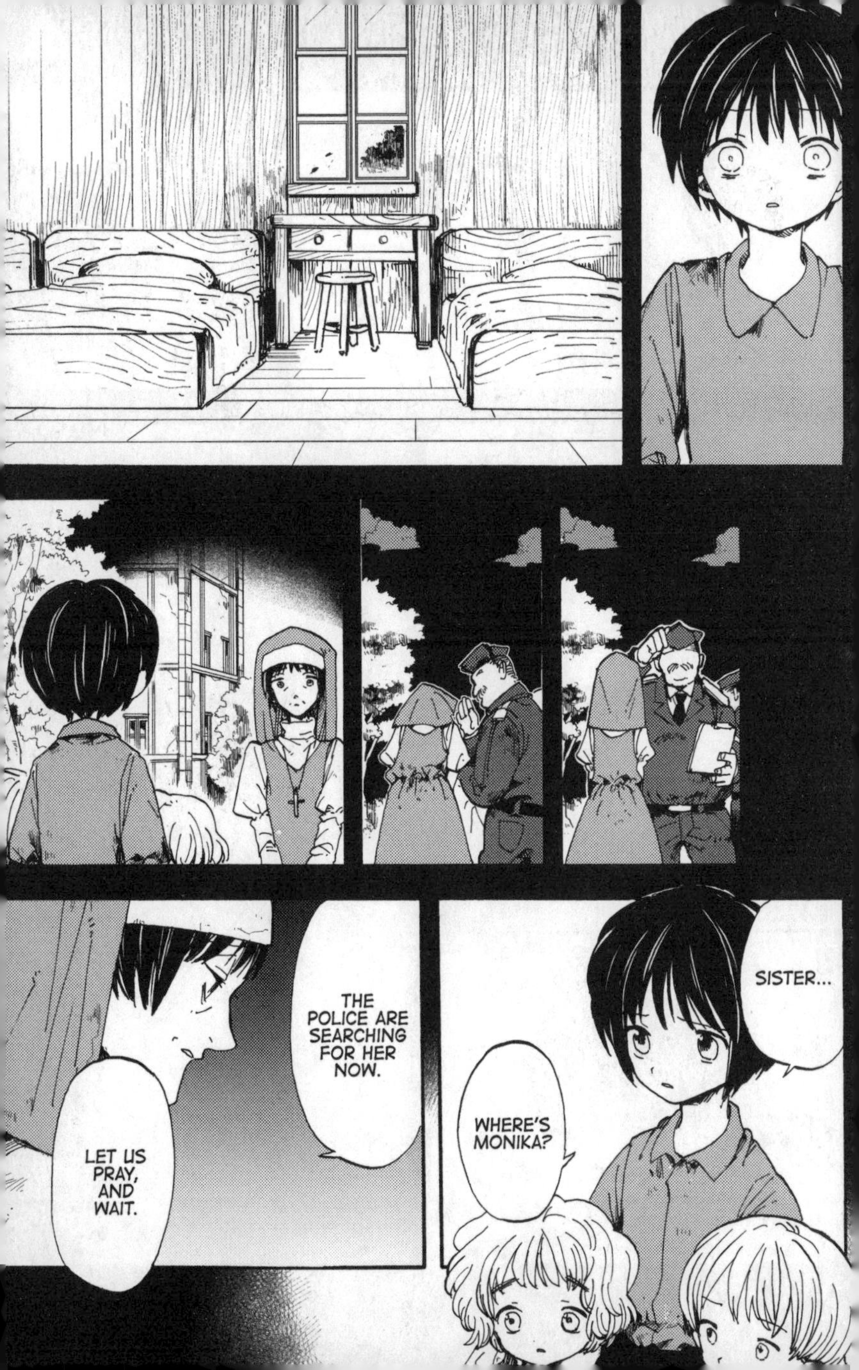
SISTER...
WHERE'S MONIKA?
THE POLICE ARE SEARCHING FOR HER NOW.
LET US PRAY, AND WAIT.

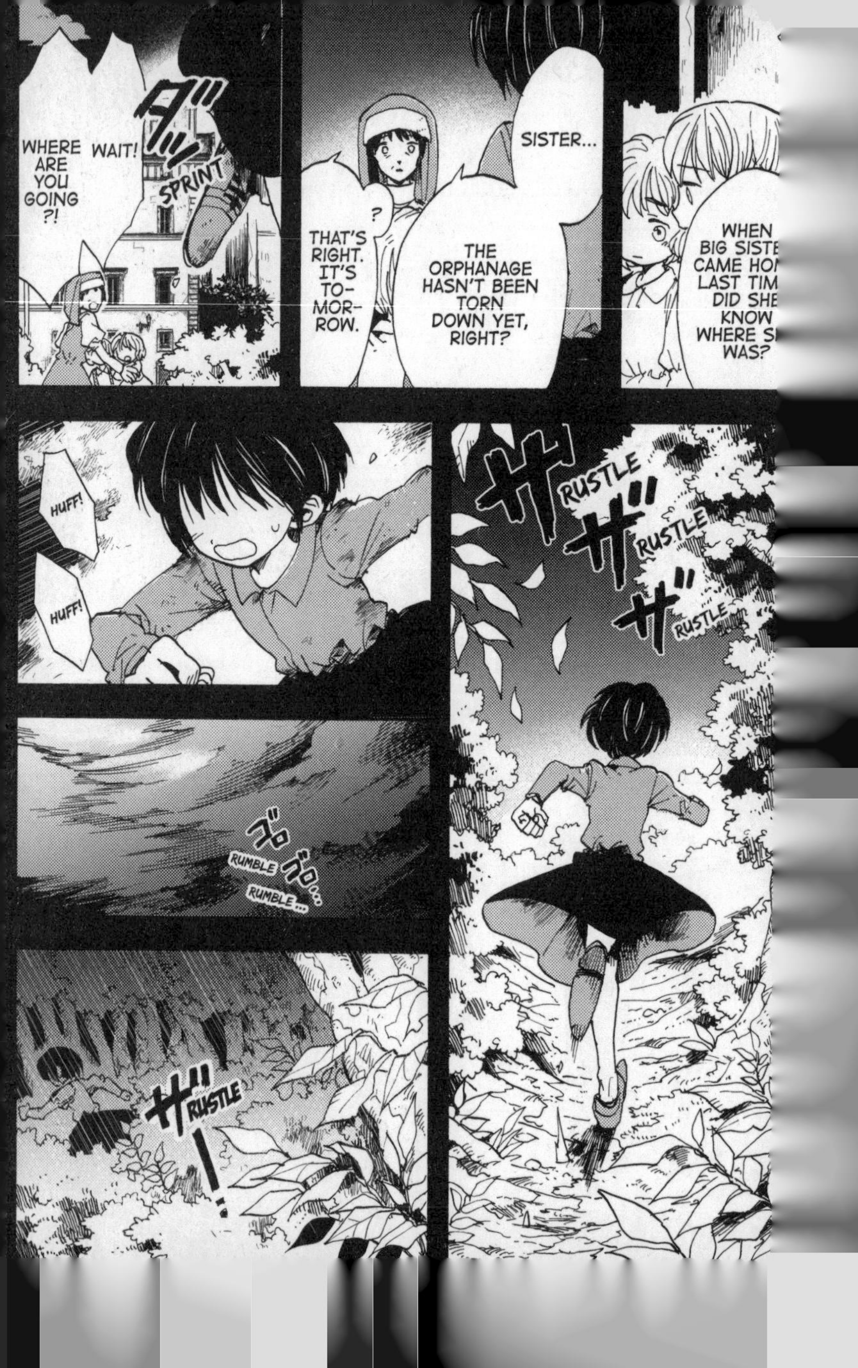
WHEN BIG SISTE CAME HOM LAST TIM DID SHE KNOW WHERE S WAS?
SISTER...
THE ORPHANAGE HASN'T BEEN TORN DOWN YET, RIGHT?
?
THAT'S RIGHT. IT'S TO-MOR-ROW.
ダッ
SPRINT
WAIT!
WHERE ARE YOU GOING ?!
ザッ
RUSTLE
ザッ
RUSTLE
ザッ
RUSTLE
HUFF!
HUFF!
ゴロ
RUMBLE
ゴロ...
RUMBLE...
ザッ
RUSTLE
!!

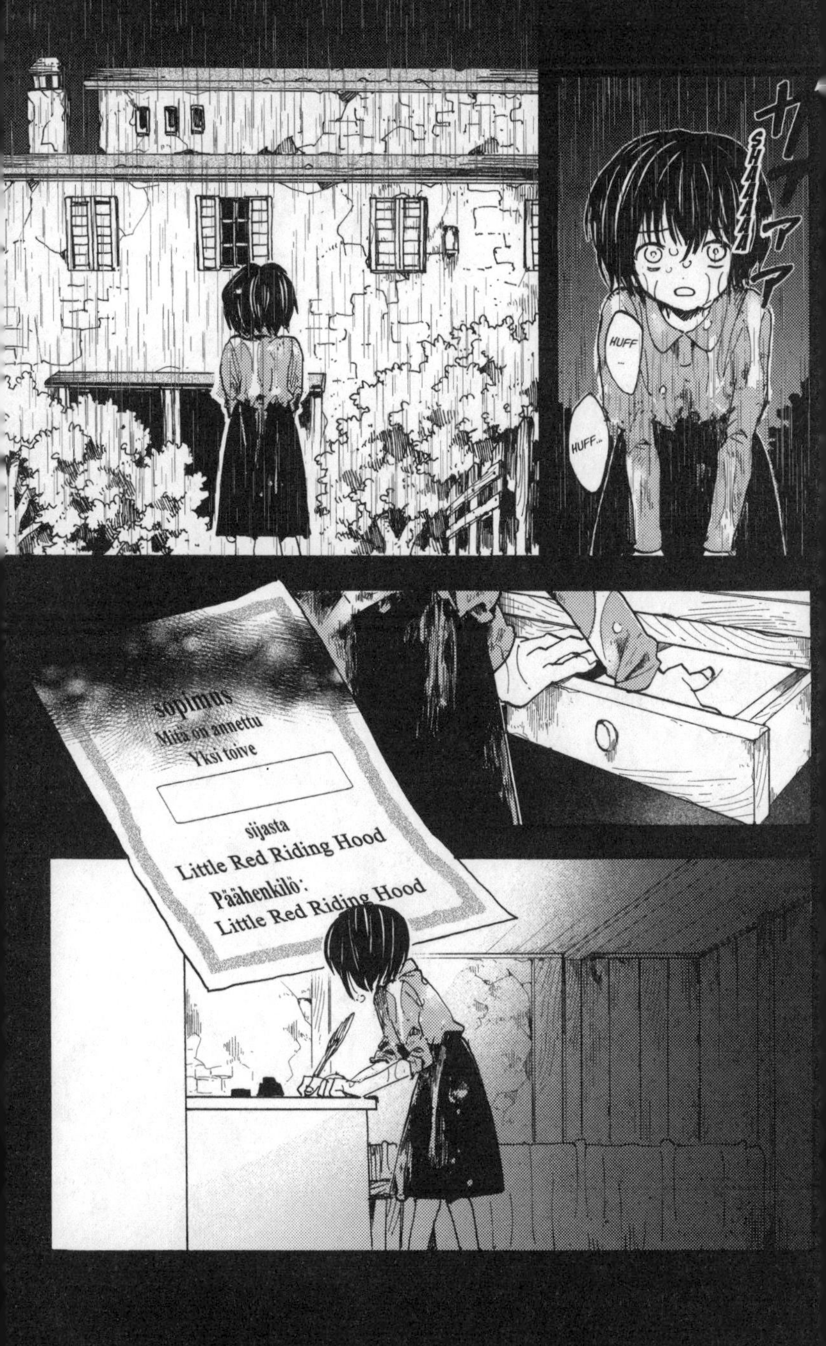
SHAAAAAA
HUFF...
HUFF...
sopimus
Mitä on annettu
Yksi toive
sijasta
Little Red Riding Hood
Päähenkilö:
Little Red Riding Hood

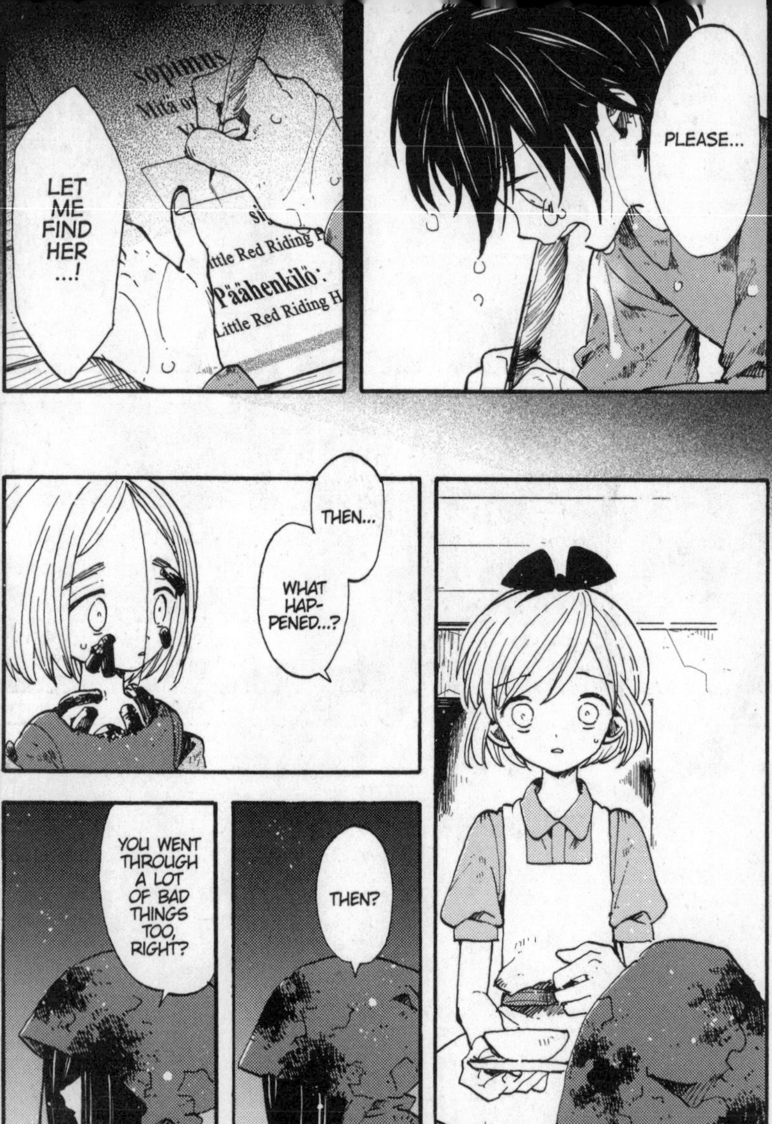
PLEASE...
Sopimus
Päähenkilö:
LET ME FIND HER ...!
THEN...
WHAT HAP-PENED...?
THEN?
YOU WENT THROUGH A LOT OF BAD THINGS TOO, RIGHT?

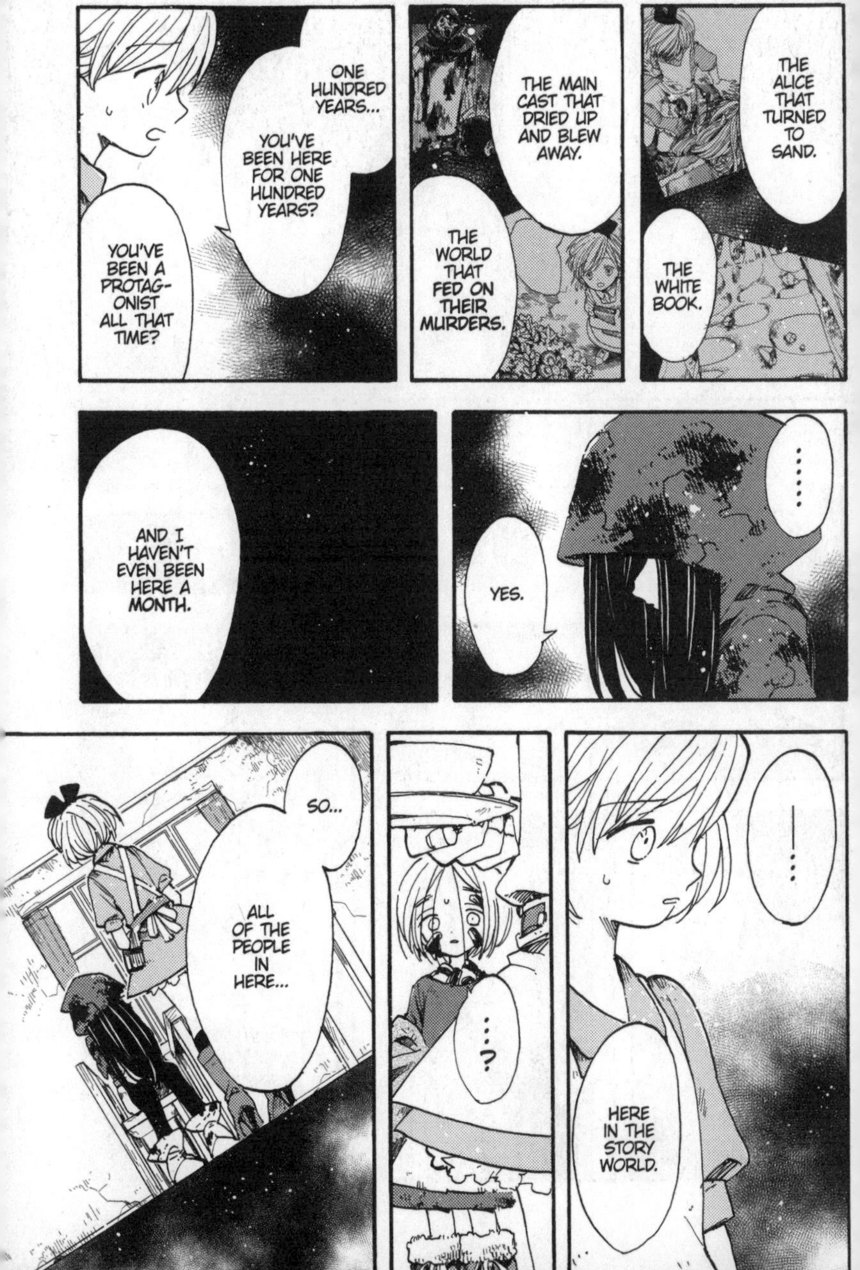
THE ALICE THAT TURNED TO SAND.
THE WHITE BOOK.
THE MAIN CAST THAT DRIED UP AND BLEW AWAY.
THE WORLD THAT FED ON THEIR MURDERS.
ONE HUNDRED YEARS...
YOU'VE BEEN HERE FOR ONE HUNDRED YEARS?
YOU'VE BEEN A PROTAG-ONIST ALL THAT TIME?
......
YES.
AND I HAVEN'T EVEN BEEN HERE A MONTH.
—......
HERE IN THE STORY WORLD.
...?
SO...
ALL OF THE PEOPLE IN HERE...

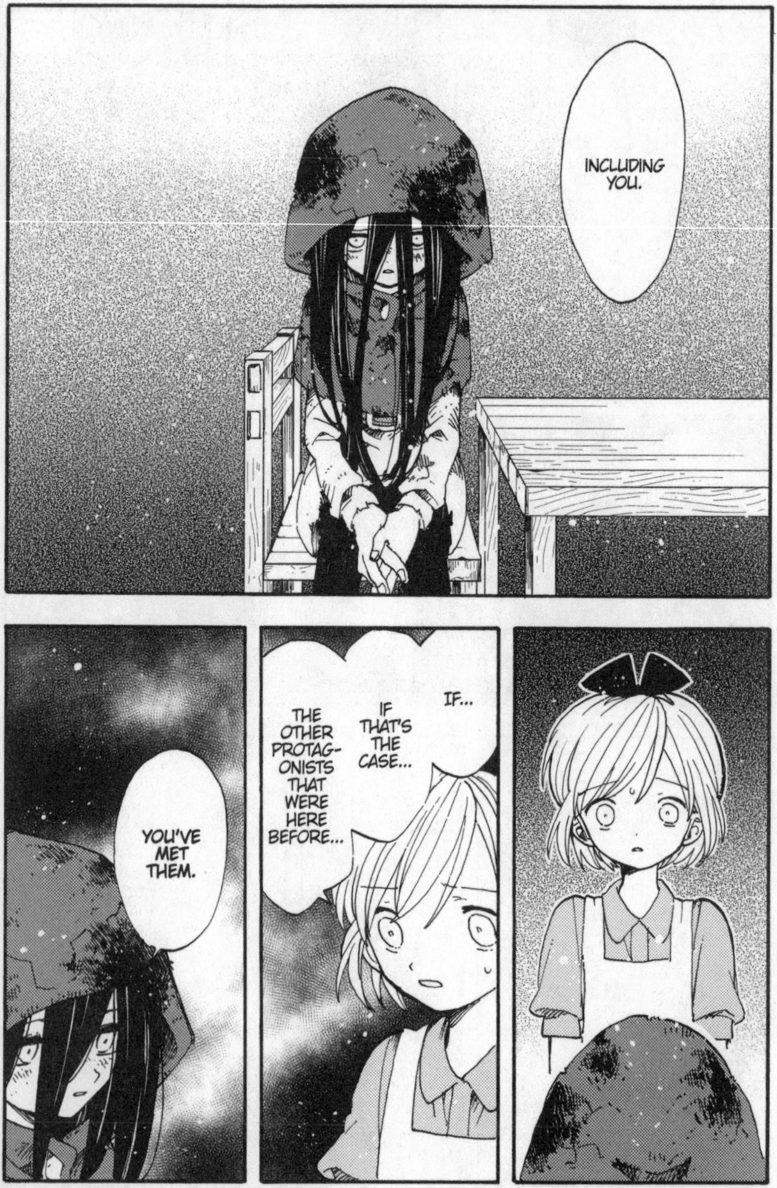
INCLUDING YOU.
IF...
IF THAT'S THE CASE...
THE OTHER PROTAGONISTS THAT WERE HERE BEFORE...
YOU'VE MET THEM.

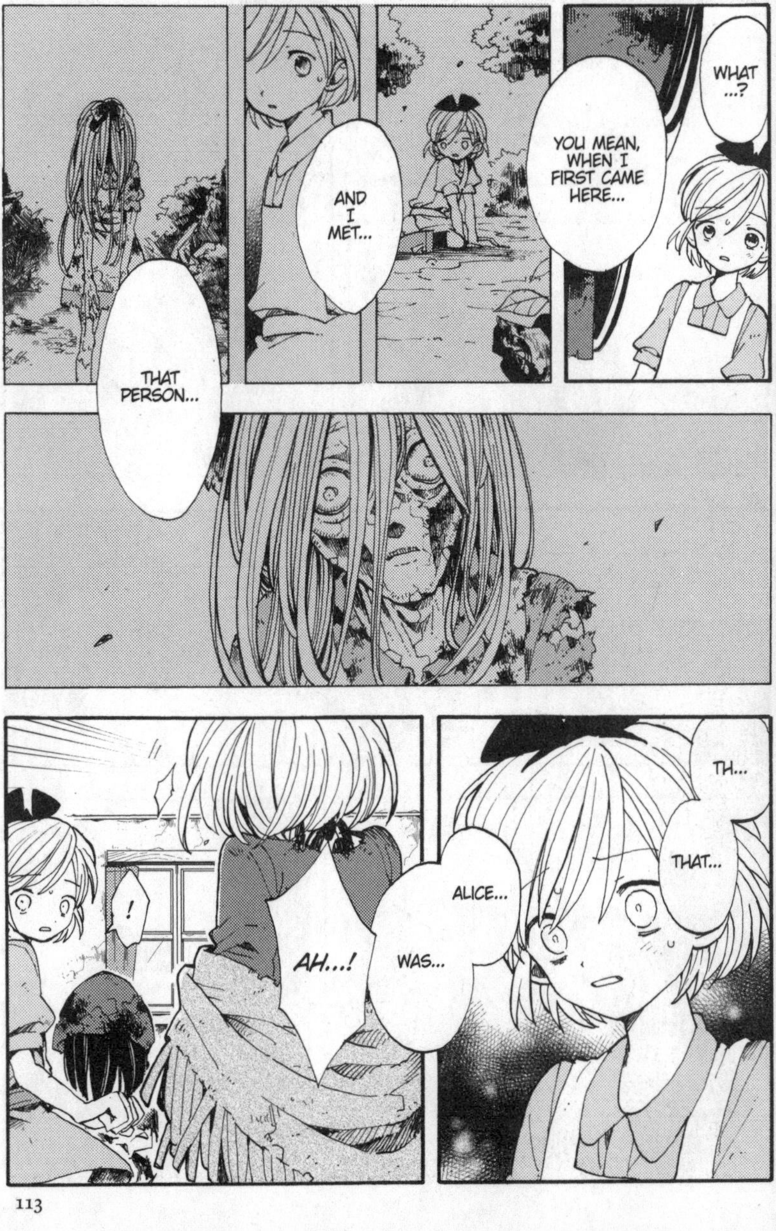
WHAT ...?
YOU MEAN, WHEN I FIRST CAME HERE...
AND I MET...
THAT PERSON...
TH...
THAT...
ALICE...
WAS...
AH...!
!

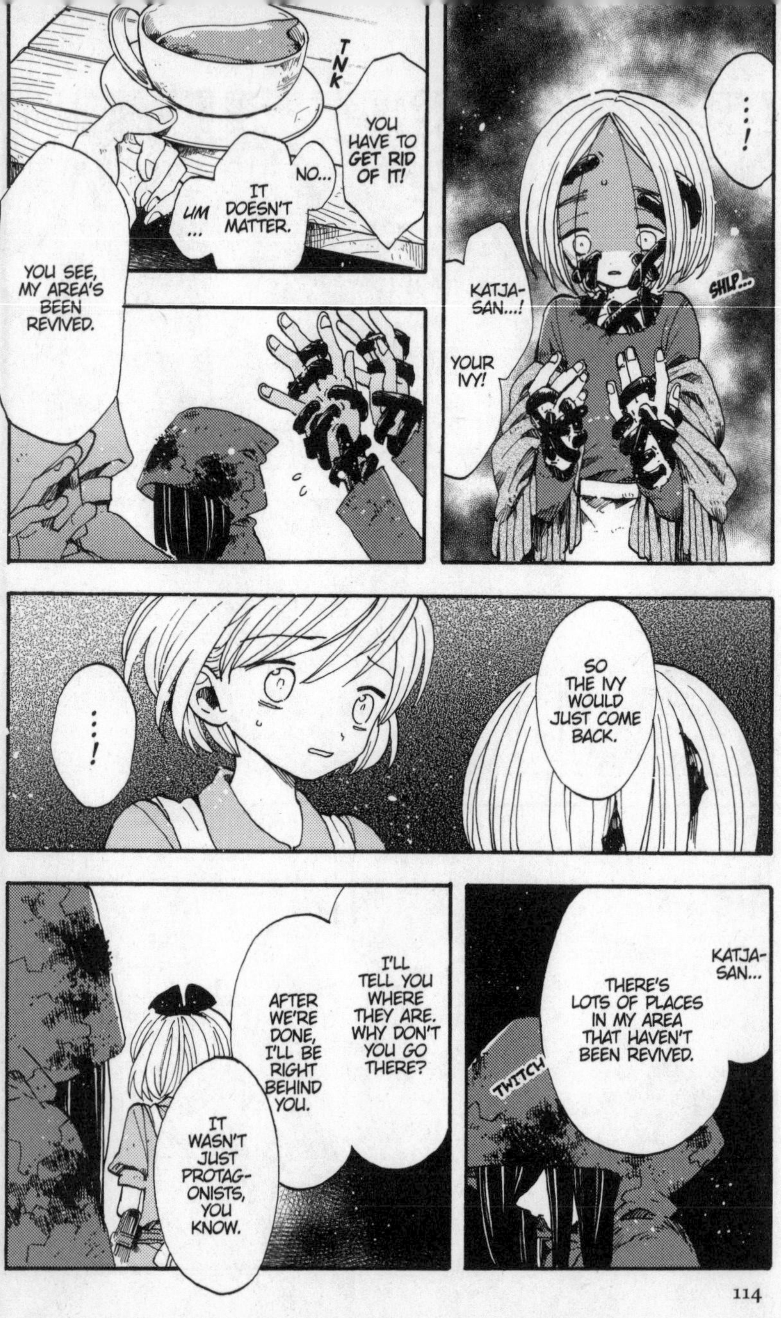
...!
KATJA-SAN...!
YOUR IVY!
SHLP...
TNK
YOU HAVE TO GET RID OF IT!
NO...
IT DOESN'T MATTER.
UM ...
YOU SEE, MY AREA'S BEEN REVIVED.
SO THE IVY WOULD JUST COME BACK.
...!
KATJA-SAN...
THERE'S LOTS OF PLACES IN MY AREA THAT HAVEN'T BEEN REVIVED.
TWITCH
I'LL TELL YOU WHERE THEY ARE. WHY DON'T YOU GO THERE?
AFTER WE'RE DONE, I'LL BE RIGHT BEHIND YOU.
IT WASN'T JUST PROTAG-ONISTS, YOU KNOW.

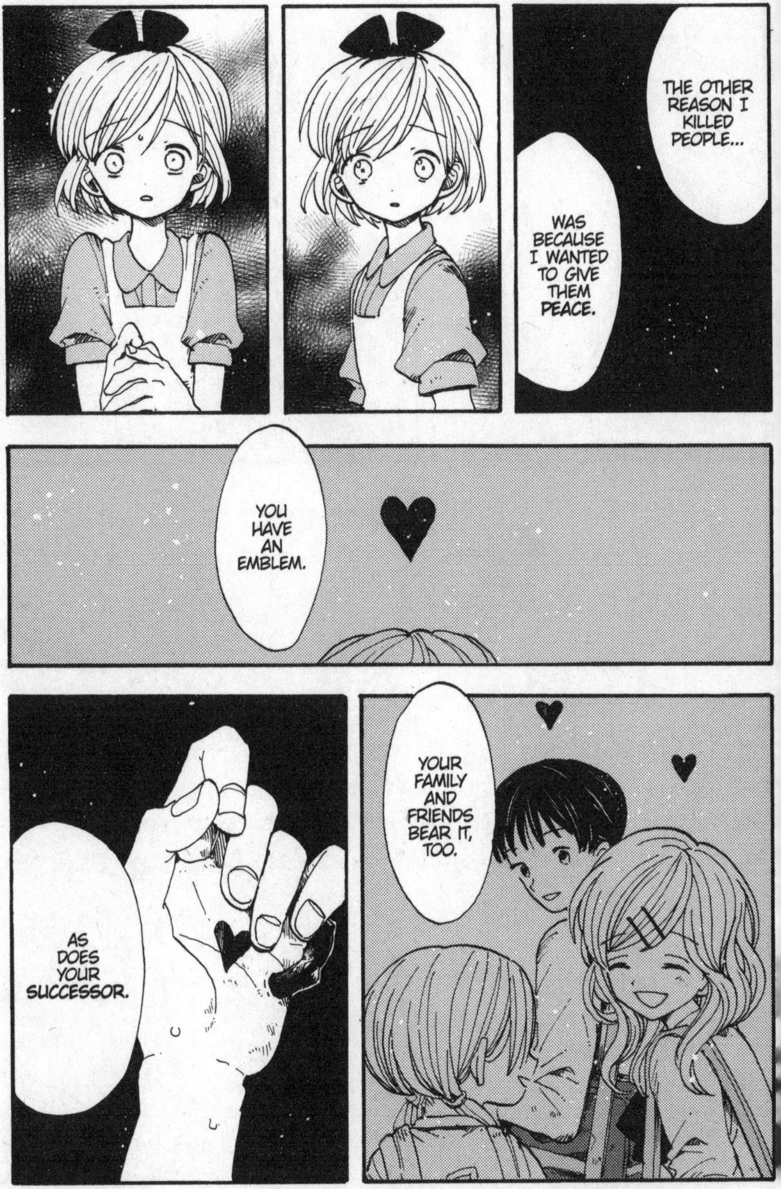
THE OTHER REASON I KILLED PEOPLE...
WAS BECAUSE I WANTED TO GIVE THEM PEACE.
YOU HAVE AN EMBLEM.
YOUR FAMILY AND FRIENDS BEAR IT, TOO.
AS DOES YOUR SUCCESSOR.

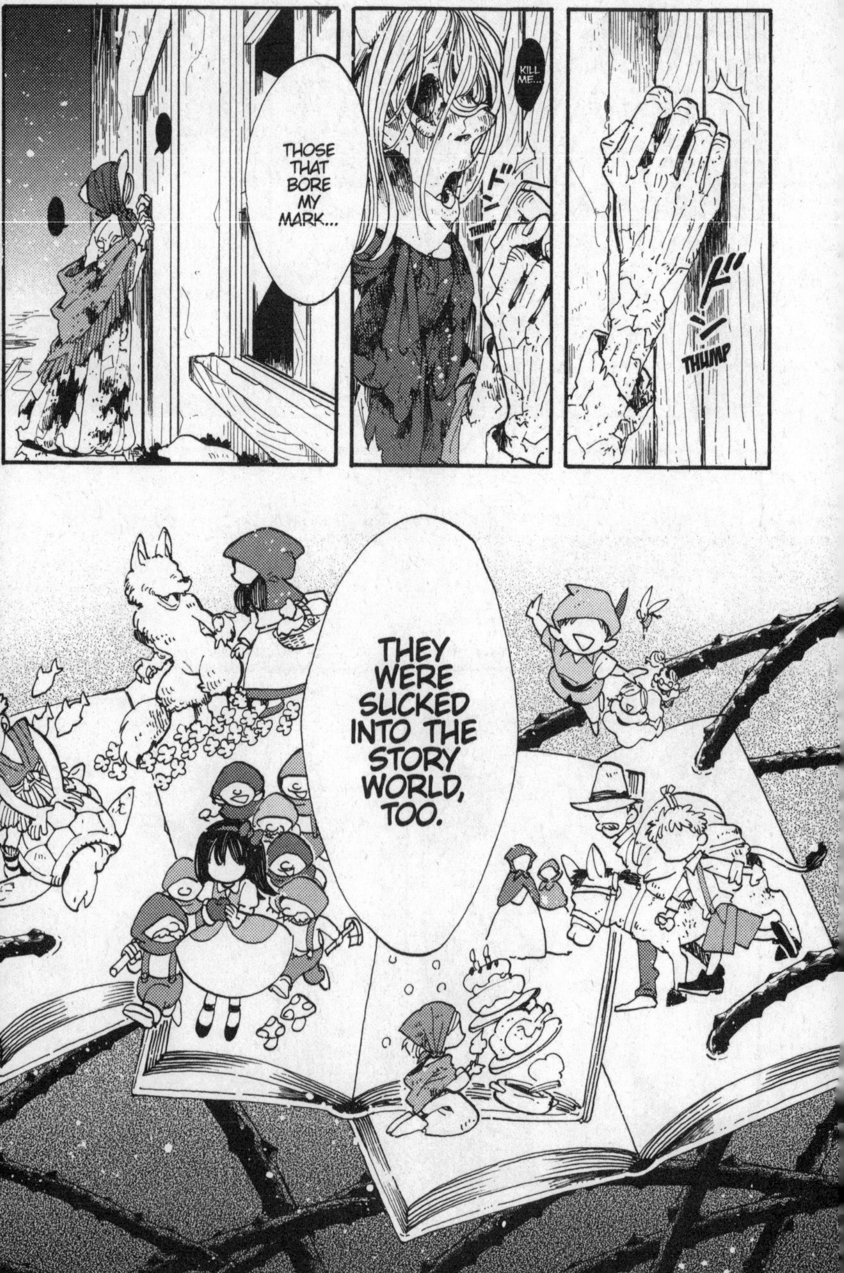
ドン
THUMP
KILL ME...
THOSE THAT BORE MY MARK...
ドン
THUMP
THEY WERE SUCKED INTO THE STORY WORLD, TOO.

FAIRY
TALE
BATTLE
ROYALE

FAIRY TALE BATTLE ROYALE

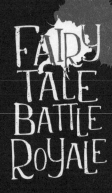

Chapter 16: Farewell

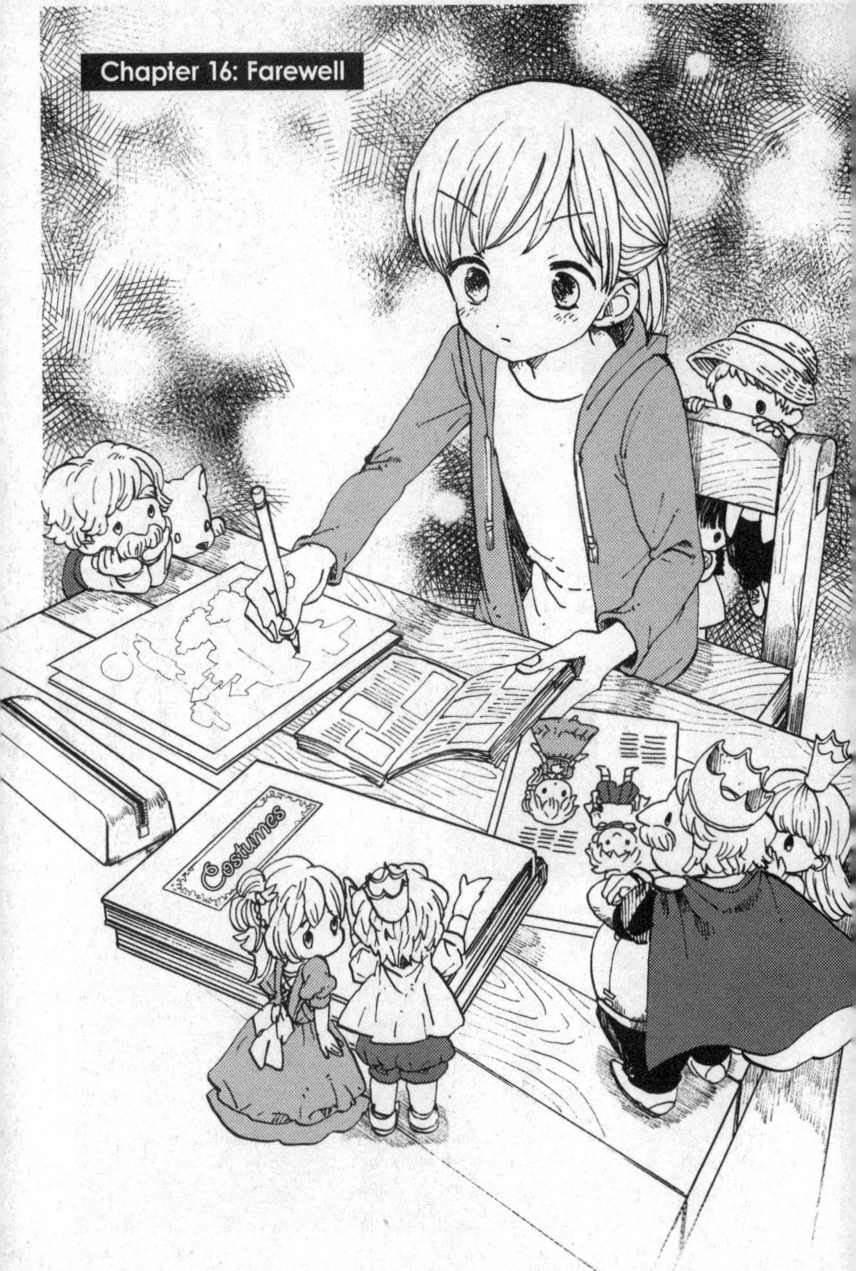
Costumes

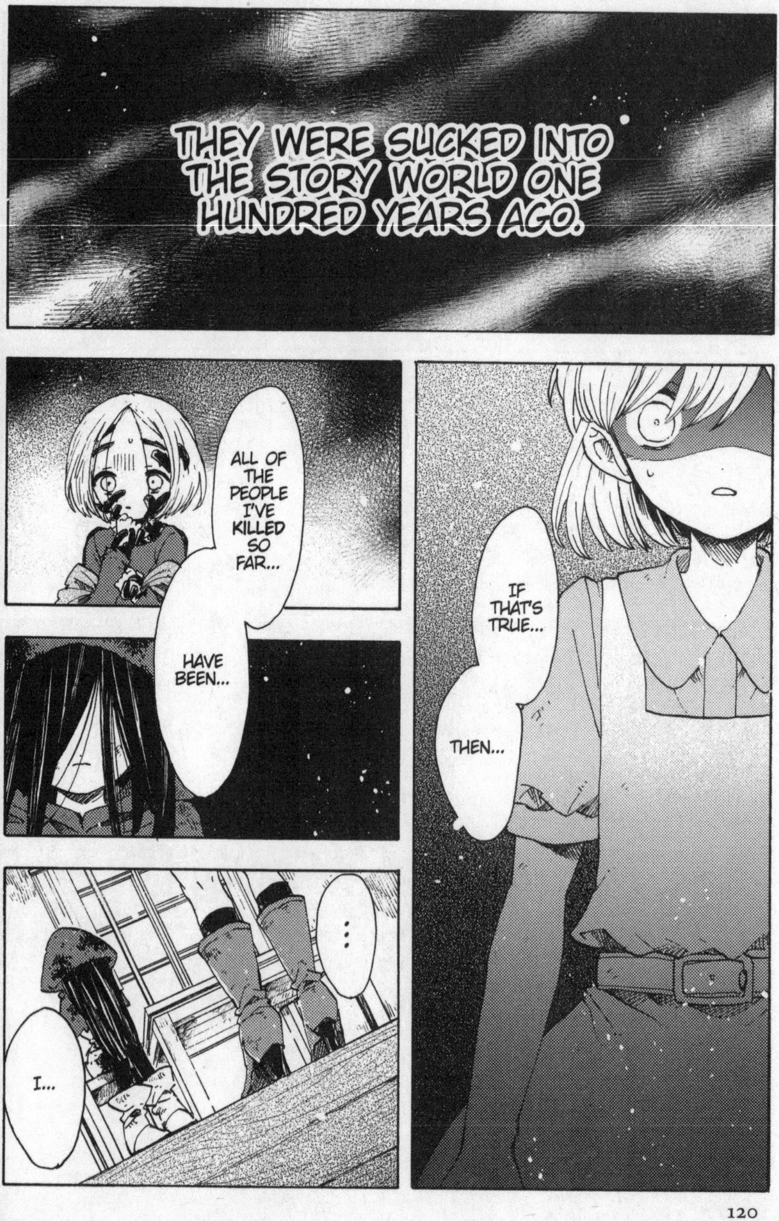
THEY WERE SUCKED INTO THE STORY WORLD ONE HUNDRED YEARS AGO.
IF THAT'S TRUE...
THEN...
ALL OF THE PEOPLE I'VE KILLED SO FAR...
HAVE BEEN...
...
I...

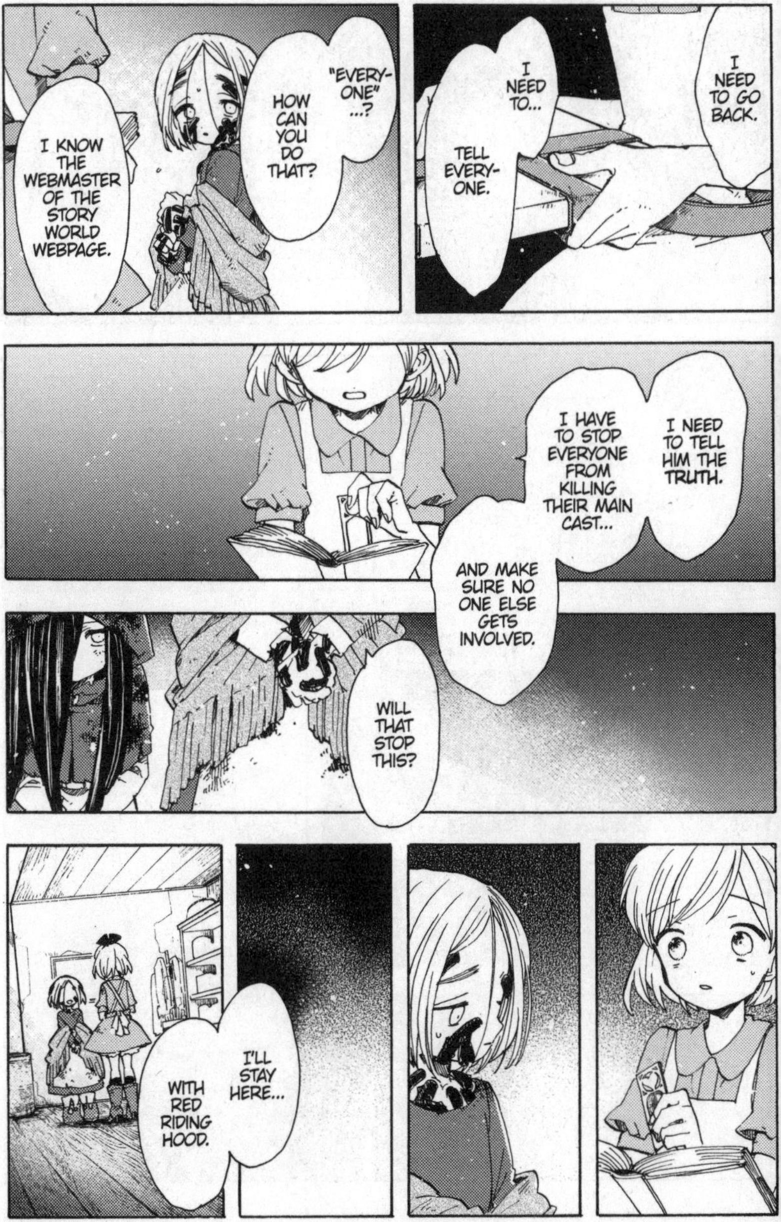
I NEED TO GO BACK.
I NEED TO...
TELL EVERY-ONE.
"EVERY-ONE"...?
HOW CAN YOU DO THAT?
I KNOW THE WEBMASTER OF THE STORY WORLD WEBPAGE.
I NEED TO TELL HIM THE TRUTH.
I HAVE TO STOP EVERYONE FROM KILLING THEIR MAIN CAST...
AND MAKE SURE NO ONE ELSE GETS INVOLVED.
WILL THAT STOP THIS?
I'LL STAY HERE...
WITH RED RIDING HOOD.

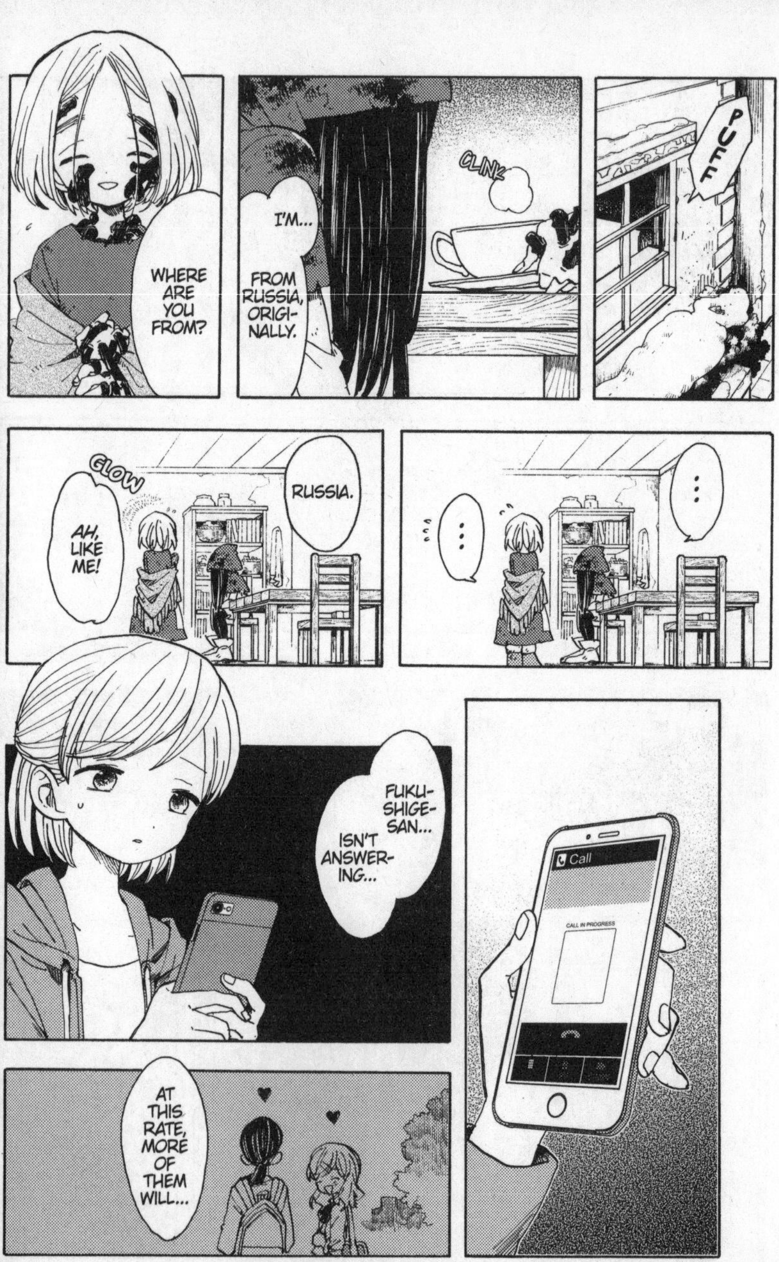
WHERE ARE YOU FROM?
I'M...
FROM RUSSIA, ORIGI-NALLY.
CLINK
PUFF
RUSSIA.
GLOW
AH, LIKE ME!
...
...
FUKU-SHIGE-SAN... ISN'T ANSWER-ING...
AT THIS RATE, MORE OF THEM WILL...
Call
CALL IN PROGRESS

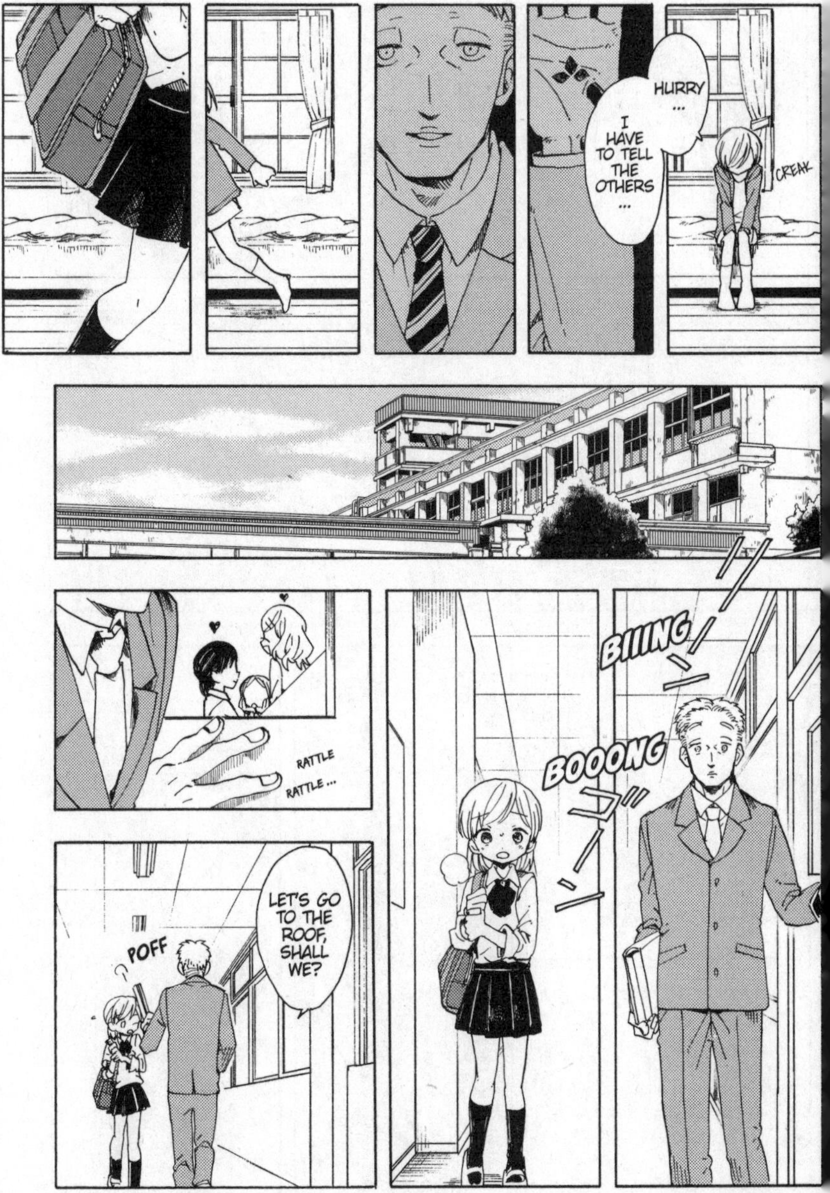
HURRY ... I HAVE TO TELL THE OTHERS ...
CREAK
BIIING
BOOONG
RATTLE
RATTLE ...
LET'S GO TO THE ROOF, SHALL WE?
POFF

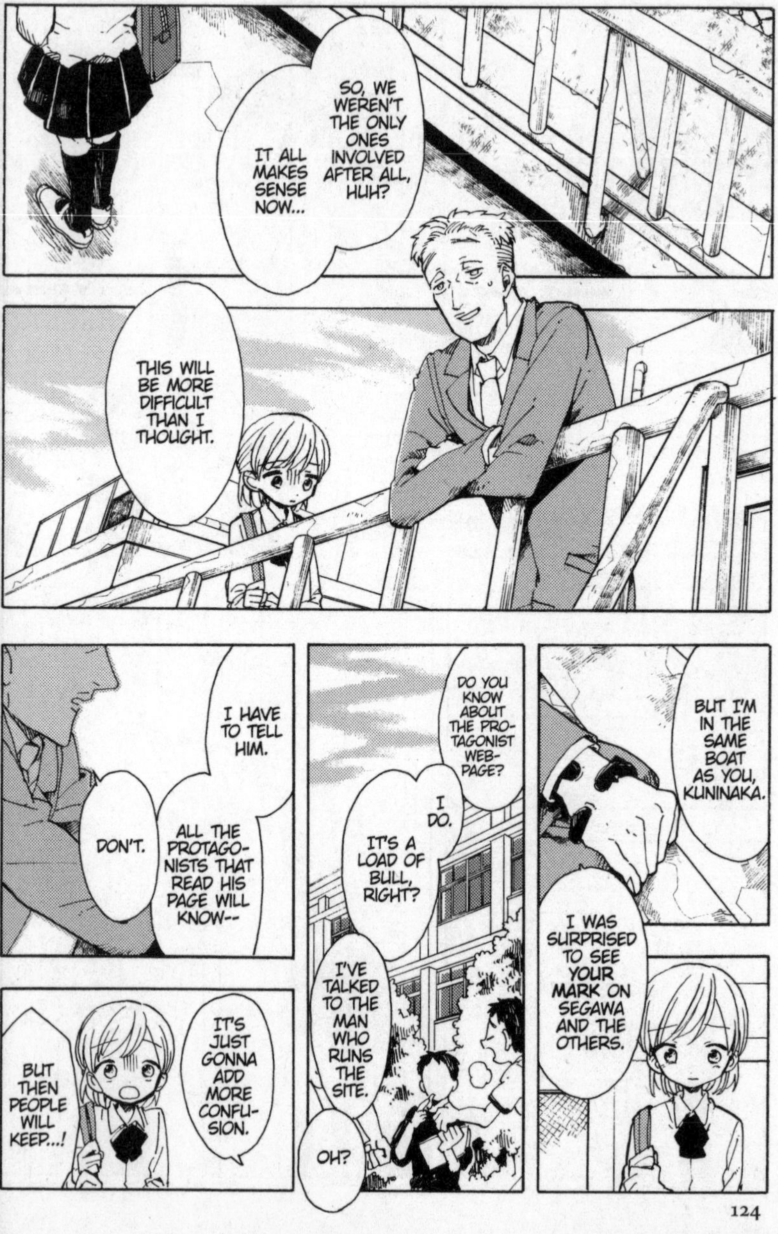
SO, WE WEREN'T THE ONLY ONES INVOLVED AFTER ALL, HUH?
IT ALL MAKES SENSE NOW...
THIS WILL BE MORE DIFFICULT THAN I THOUGHT.
BUT I'M IN THE SAME BOAT AS YOU, KUNINAKA.
I WAS SURPRISED TO SEE YOUR MARK ON SEGAWA AND THE OTHERS.
DO YOU KNOW ABOUT THE PROTAGONIST WEB-PAGE?
I DO.
IT'S A LOAD OF BULL, RIGHT?
I'VE TALKED TO THE MAN WHO RUNS THE SITE.
OH?
I HAVE TO TELL HIM.
ALL THE PROTAGO-NISTS THAT READ HIS PAGE WILL KNOW--
DON'T.
IT'S JUST GONNA ADD MORE CONFU-SION.
BUT THEN PEOPLE WILL KEEP...!

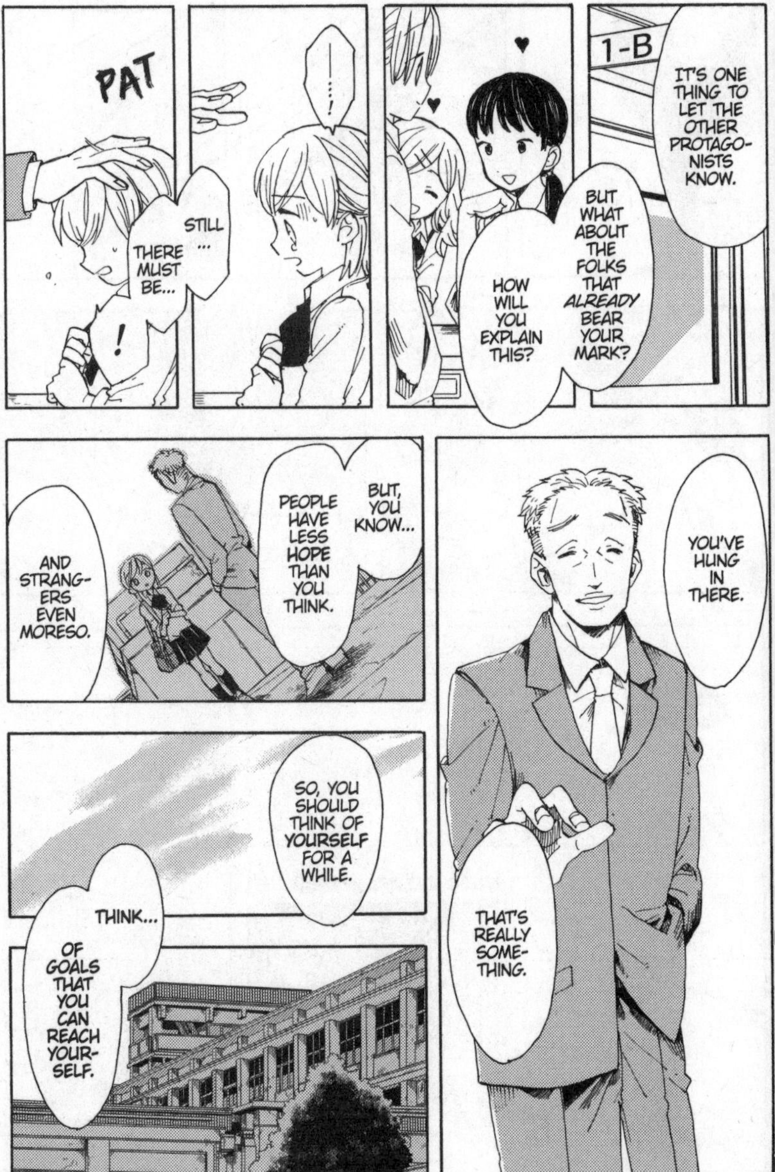
1-B
IT'S ONE THING TO LET THE OTHER PROTAGO- NISTS KNOW.
BUT WHAT ABOUT THE FOLKS THAT *ALREADY* BEAR YOUR MARK?
HOW WILL YOU EXPLAIN THIS?
—...!
PAT
STILL...
THERE MUST BE...
!
YOU'VE HUNG IN THERE.
THAT'S REALLY SOME- THING.
BUT, YOU KNOW...
PEOPLE HAVE LESS HOPE THAN YOU THINK.
AND STRANG- ERS EVEN MORESO.
SO, YOU SHOULD THINK OF YOURSELF FOR A WHILE.
THINK...
OF GOALS THAT YOU CAN REACH YOUR- SELF.

I'M SORRY I COULDN'T HELP.

GO HOME, KUNINAKA.

AND I WILL, TOO.

THUD

FWUMP

YOU DON'T HAVE MUCH TIME LEFT.

HOW DID THINGS...

GET LIKE THIS ...?

ALICE

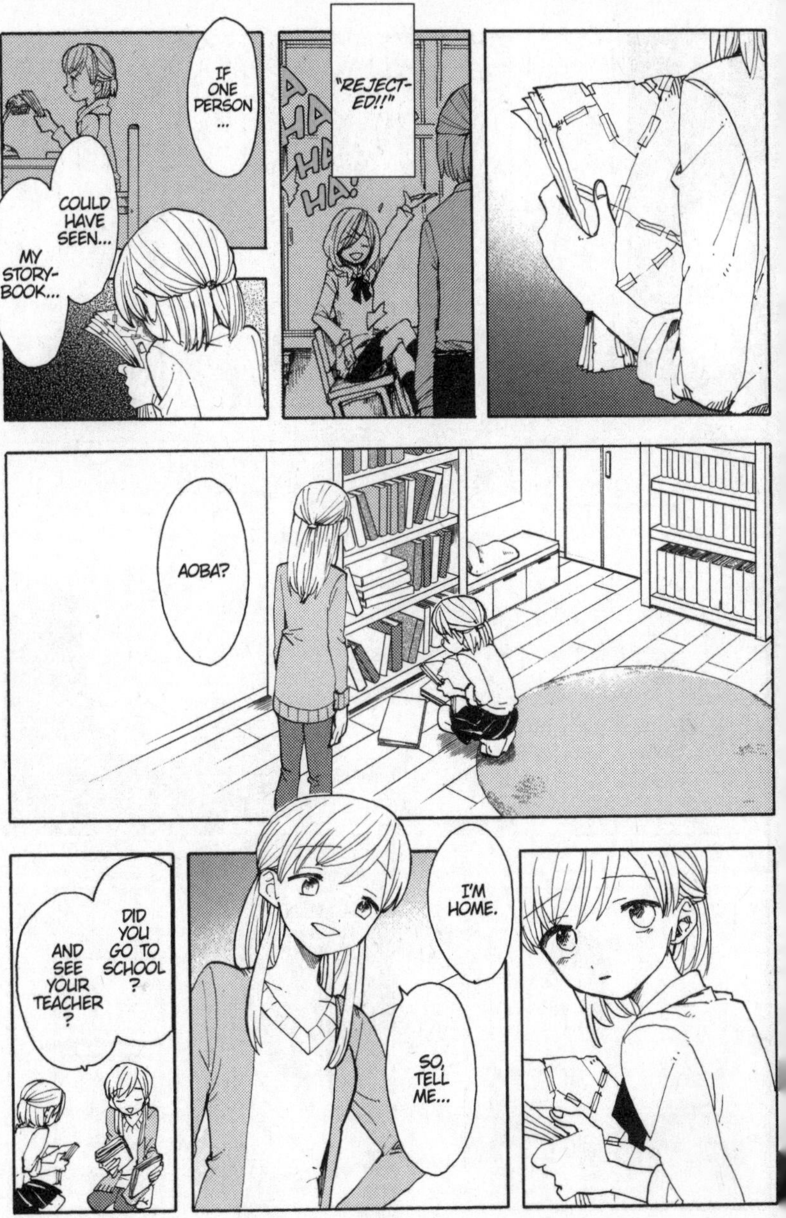
"REJECTED!!"
HA HA HA!
IF ONE PERSON...
COULD HAVE SEEN...
MY STORYBOOK...
AOBA?
I'M HOME.
SO, TELL ME...
DID YOU GO TO SCHOOL?
AND SEE YOUR TEACHER?

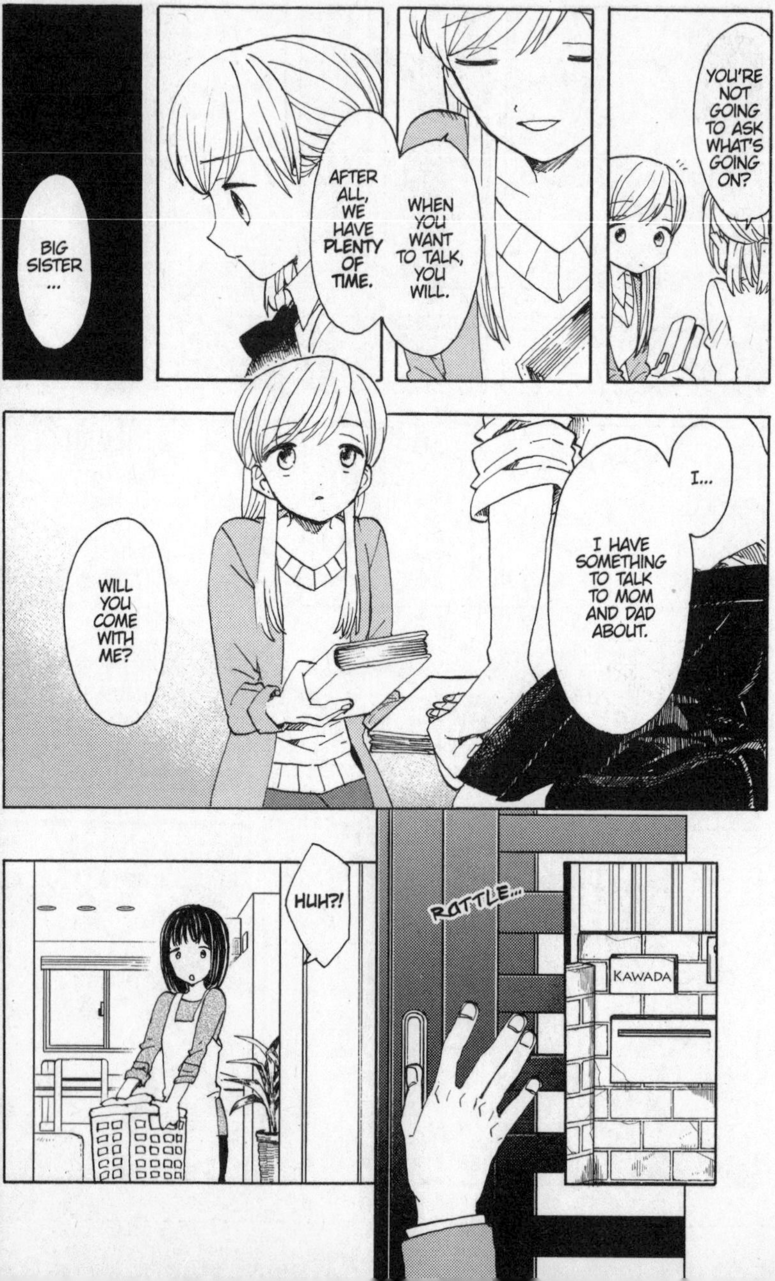

YOU'RE NOT GOING TO ASK WHAT'S GOING ON?
WHEN YOU WANT TO TALK, YOU WILL.
AFTER ALL, WE HAVE PLENTY OF TIME.
BIG SISTER...
I...
I HAVE SOMETHING TO TALK TO MOM AND DAD ABOUT.
WILL YOU COME WITH ME?
KAWADA
RATTLE...
HUH?!

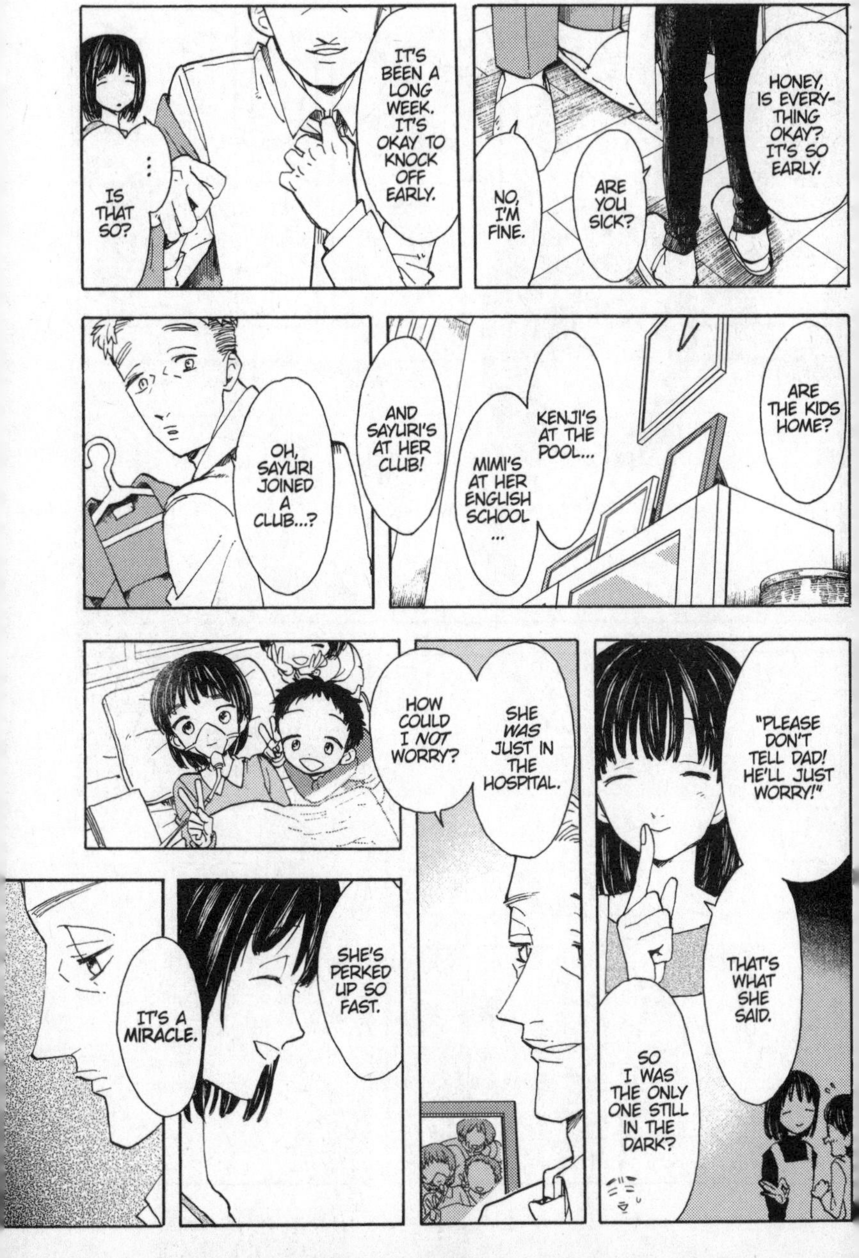
HONEY, IS EVERYTHING OKAY? IT'S SO EARLY.
ARE YOU SICK?
NO, I'M FINE.
IT'S BEEN A LONG WEEK. IT'S OKAY TO KNOCK OFF EARLY.
...
IS THAT SO?
ARE THE KIDS HOME?
KENJI'S AT THE POOL...
MIMI'S AT HER ENGLISH SCHOOL...
AND SAYURI'S AT HER CLUB!
OH, SAYURI JOINED A CLUB...?
"PLEASE DON'T TELL DAD! HE'LL JUST WORRY!"
THAT'S WHAT SHE SAID.
SO I WAS THE ONLY ONE STILL IN THE DARK?
SHE *WAS* JUST IN THE HOSPITAL.
HOW COULD I *NOT* WORRY?
SHE'S PERKED UP SO FAST.
IT'S A MIRACLE.

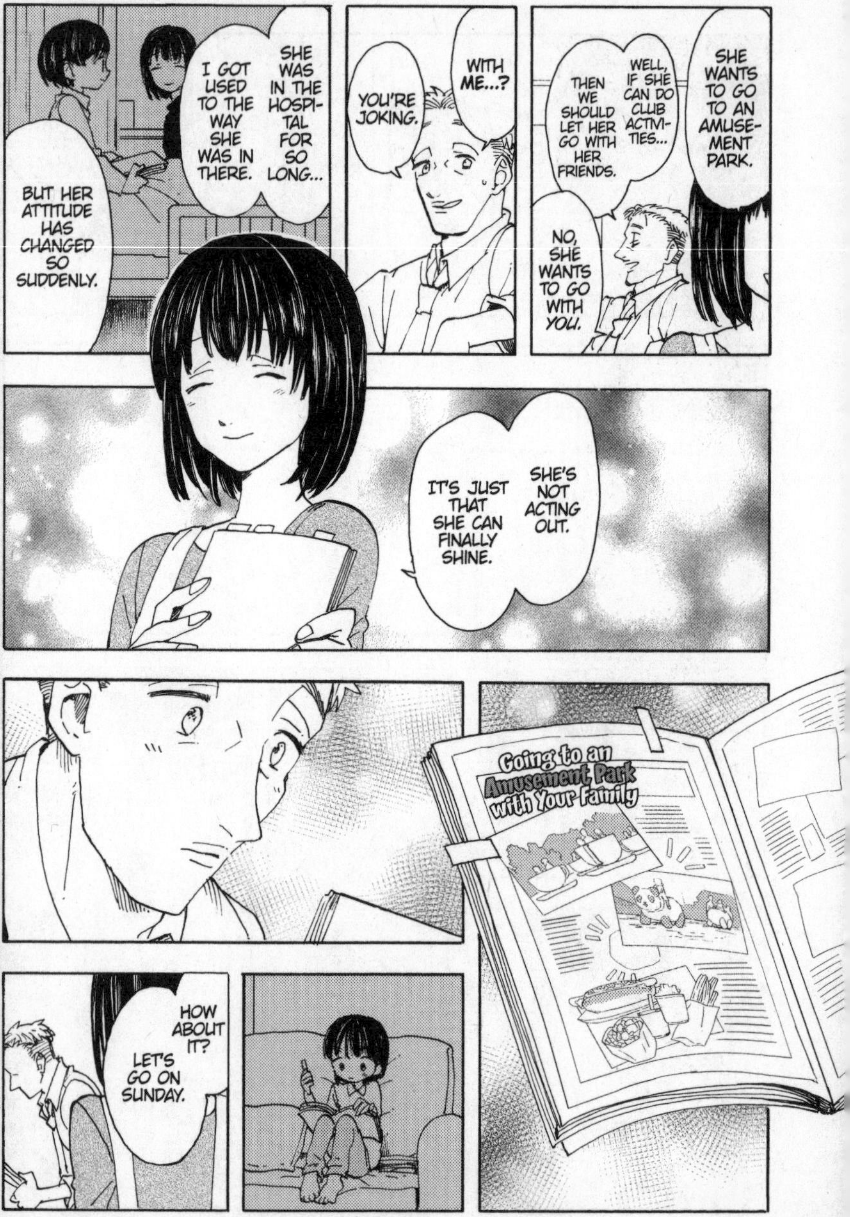
SHE WANTS TO GO TO AN AMUSEMENT PARK.
WELL, IF SHE CAN DO CLUB ACTIVITIES...
THEN WE SHOULD LET HER GO WITH HER FRIENDS.
NO, SHE WANTS TO GO WITH YOU.
WITH ME...?
YOU'RE JOKING.
SHE WAS IN THE HOSPITAL FOR SO LONG...
I GOT USED TO THE WAY SHE WAS IN THERE.
BUT HER ATTITUDE HAS CHANGED SO SUDDENLY.
SHE'S NOT ACTING OUT.
IT'S JUST THAT SHE CAN FINALLY SHINE.
Going to an Amusement Park with Your Family
HOW ABOUT IT?
LET'S GO ON SUNDAY.

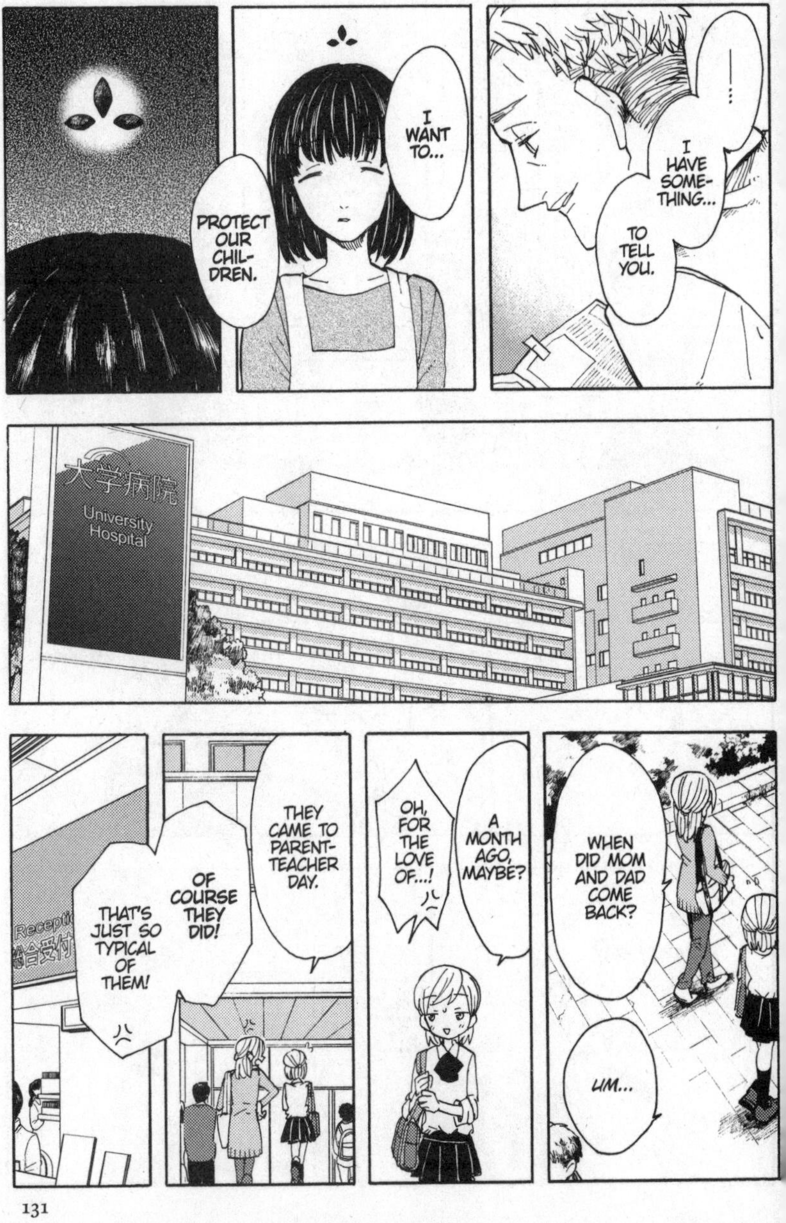
...!
I HAVE SOME-THING...
TO TELL YOU.
I WANT TO...
PROTECT OUR CHIL-DREN.
大学病院
University Hospital
WHEN DID MOM AND DAD COME BACK?
UM...
A MONTH AGO, MAYBE?
OH, FOR THE LOVE OF...!
THEY CAME TO PARENT-TEACHER DAY.
OF COURSE THEY DID!
THAT'S JUST SO TYPICAL OF THEM!

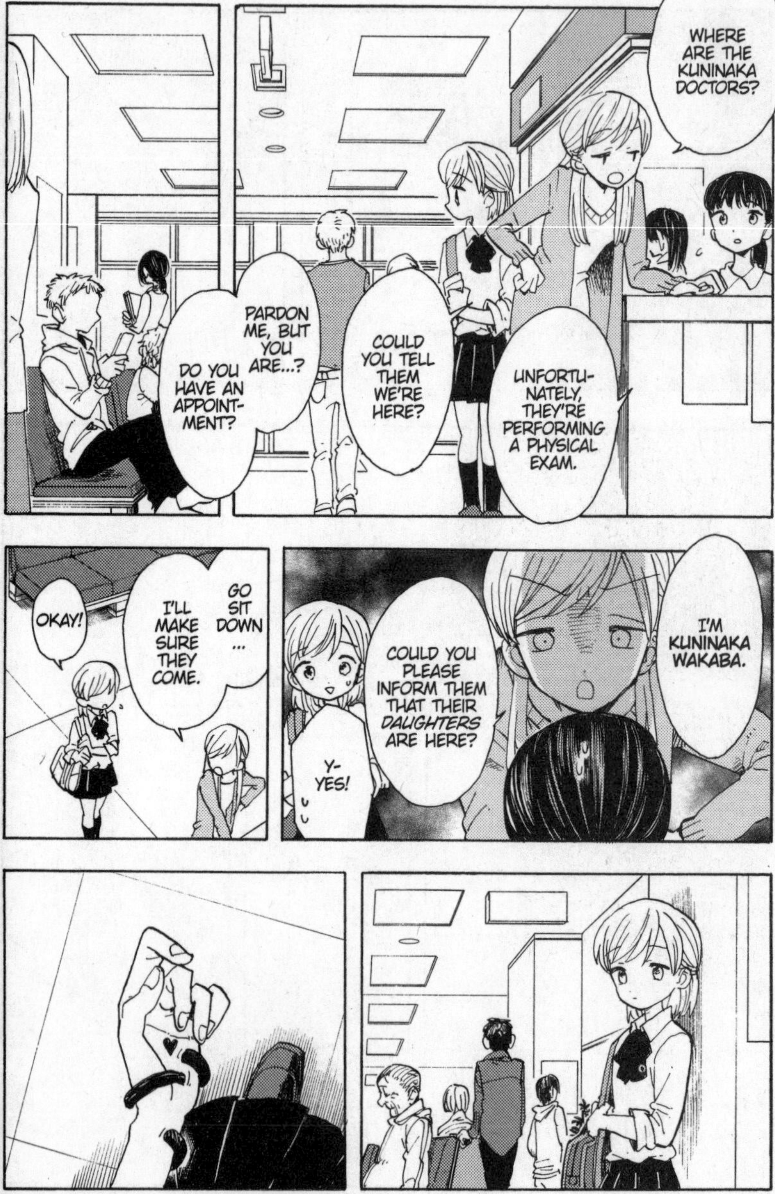
WHERE ARE THE KUNINAKA DOCTORS?
UNFORTUNATELY, THEY'RE PERFORMING A PHYSICAL EXAM.
COULD YOU TELL THEM WE'RE HERE?
PARDON ME, BUT YOU ARE...?
DO YOU HAVE AN APPOINTMENT?
I'M KUNINAKA WAKABA.
COULD YOU PLEASE INFORM THEM THAT THEIR *DAUGHTERS* ARE HERE?
Y-YES!
GO SIT DOWN...
I'LL MAKE SURE THEY COME.
OKAY!

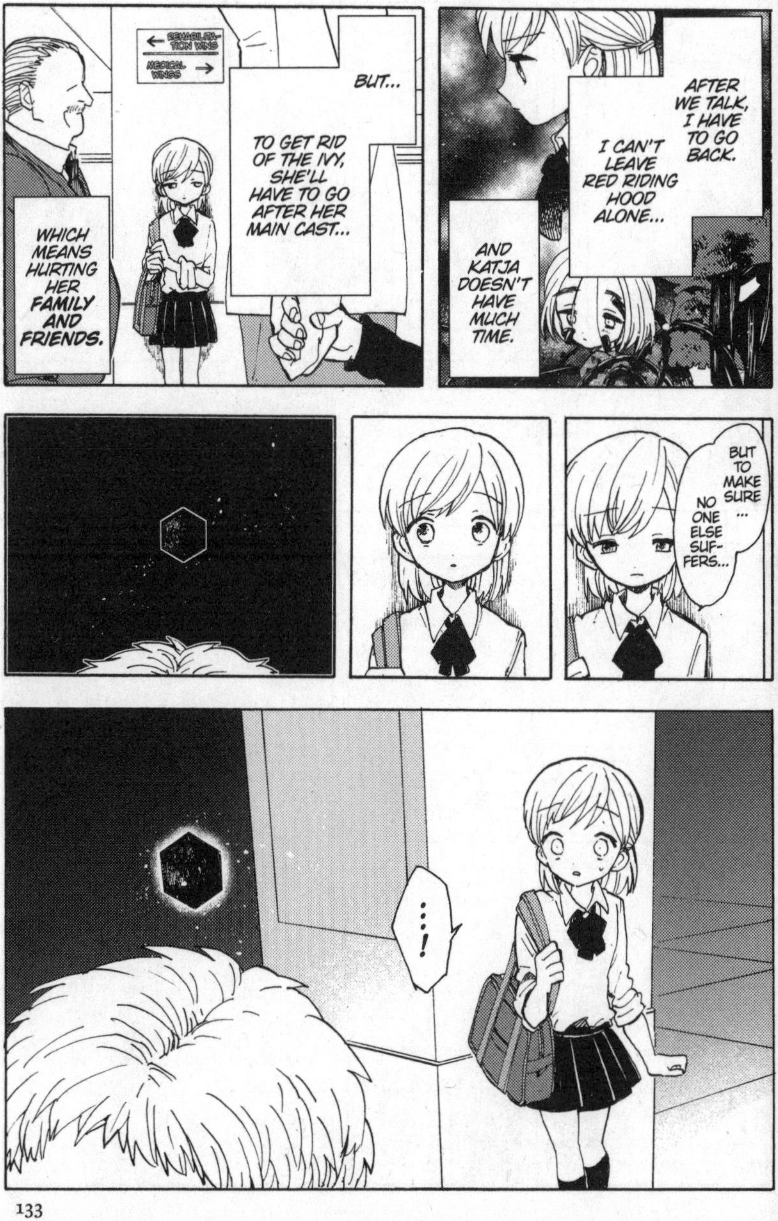
AFTER WE TALK, I HAVE TO GO BACK.
I CAN'T LEAVE RED RIDING HOOD ALONE...
AND KATJA DOESN'T HAVE MUCH TIME.
← REHABILITA-TION WING
MEDICAL WINGS →
BUT...
TO GET RID OF THE IVY, SHE'LL HAVE TO GO AFTER HER MAIN CAST...
WHICH MEANS HURTING HER FAMILY AND FRIENDS.
BUT TO MAKE SURE ...
NO ONE ELSE SUF-FERS...
...!

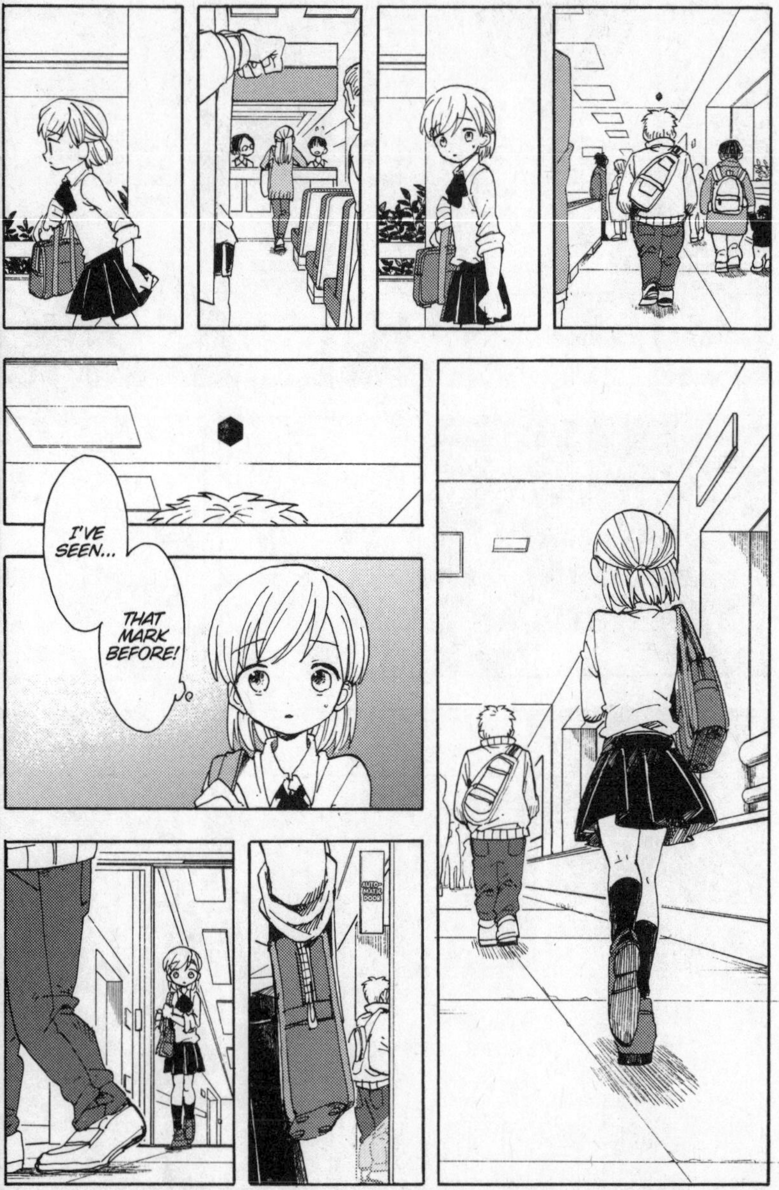
I'VE SEEN...
THAT MARK BEFORE!
AUTO-MATIC DOOR

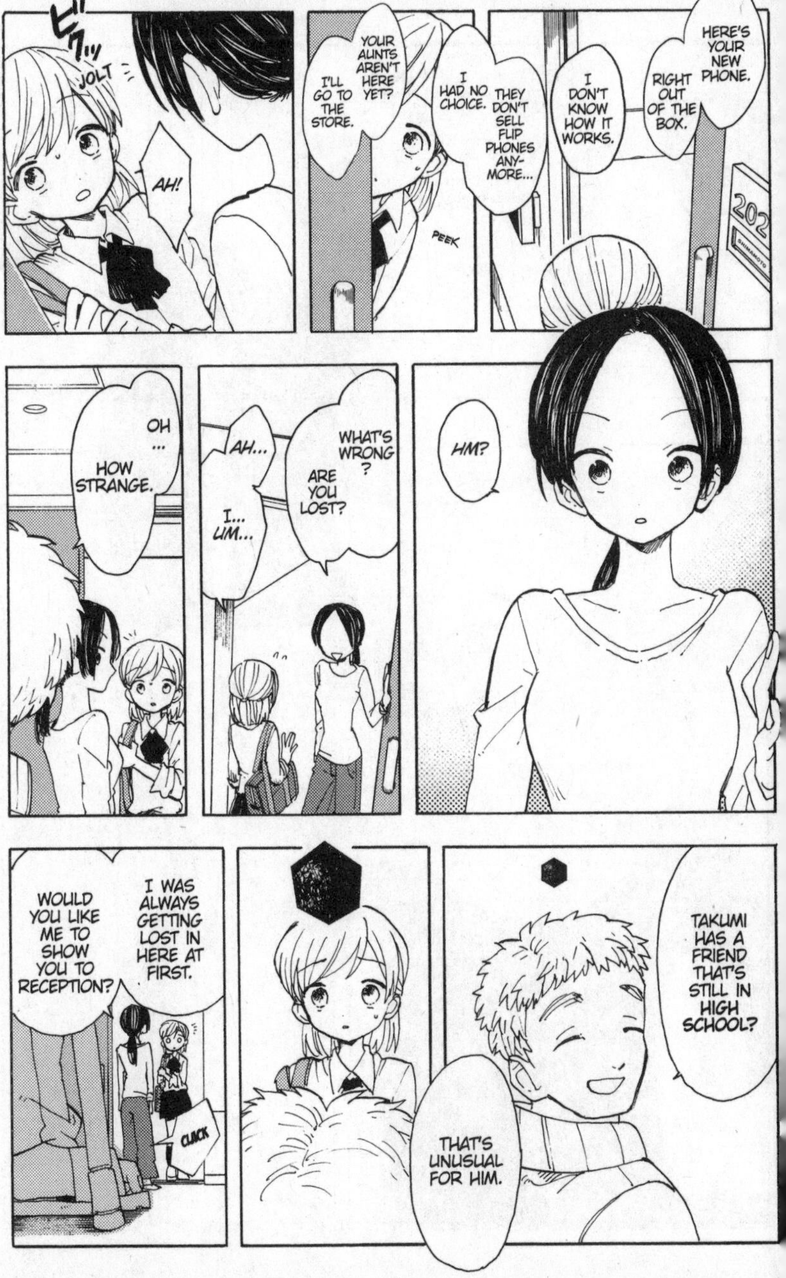
HERE'S YOUR NEW PHONE.
RIGHT OUT OF THE BOX.
I DON'T KNOW HOW IT WORKS.
202
SHIMAMOTO
I HAD NO CHOICE.
THEY DON'T SELL FLIP PHONES ANYMORE...
PEEK
YOUR AUNTS AREN'T HERE YET?
I'LL GO TO THE STORE.
ビクッ
JOLT
AH!
HM?
WHAT'S WRONG?
ARE YOU LOST?
AH...
I... UM...
OH... HOW STRANGE.
TAKUMI HAS A FRIEND THAT'S STILL IN HIGH SCHOOL?
THAT'S UNUSUAL FOR HIM.
I WAS ALWAYS GETTING LOST IN HERE AT FIRST.
WOULD YOU LIKE ME TO SHOW YOU TO RECEPTION?
CLICK

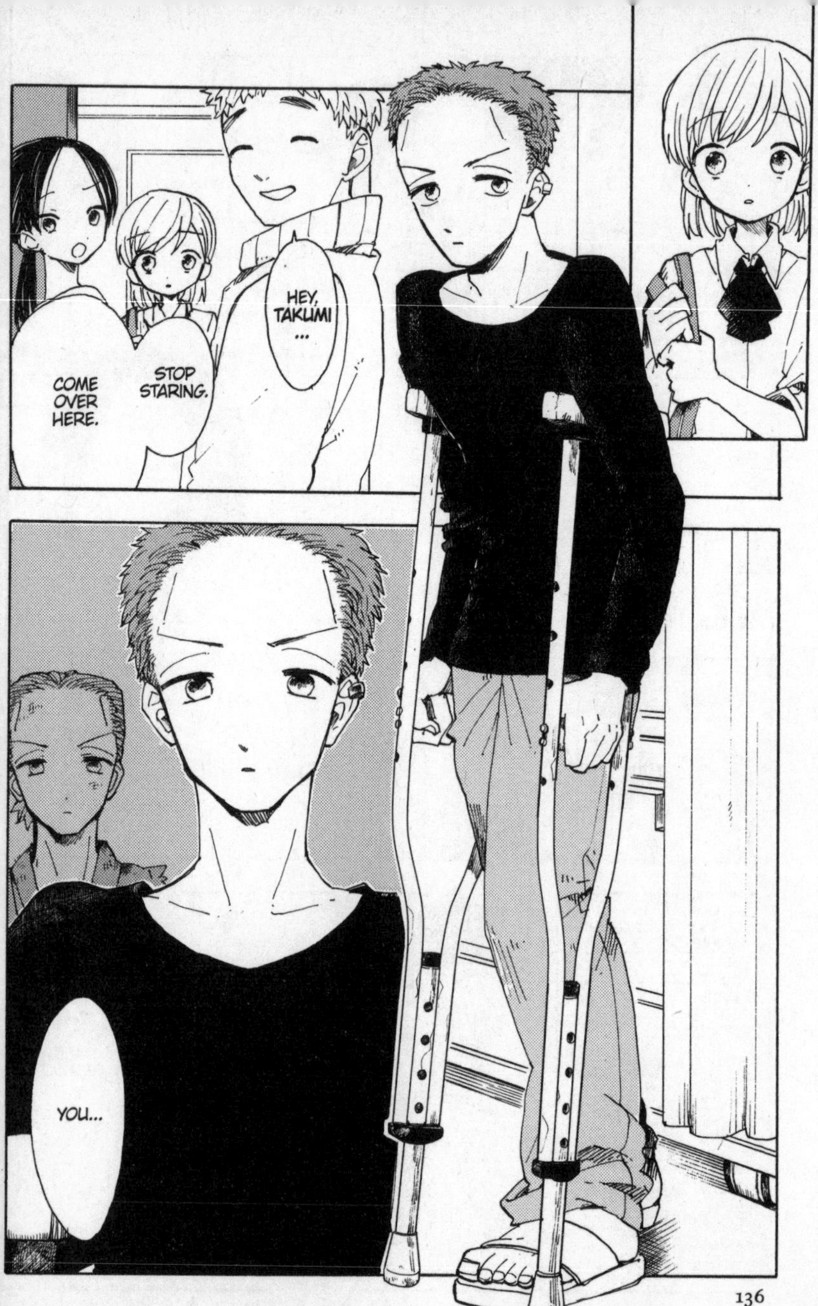
HEY, TAKUMI ...
STOP STARING.
COME OVER HERE.
YOU...

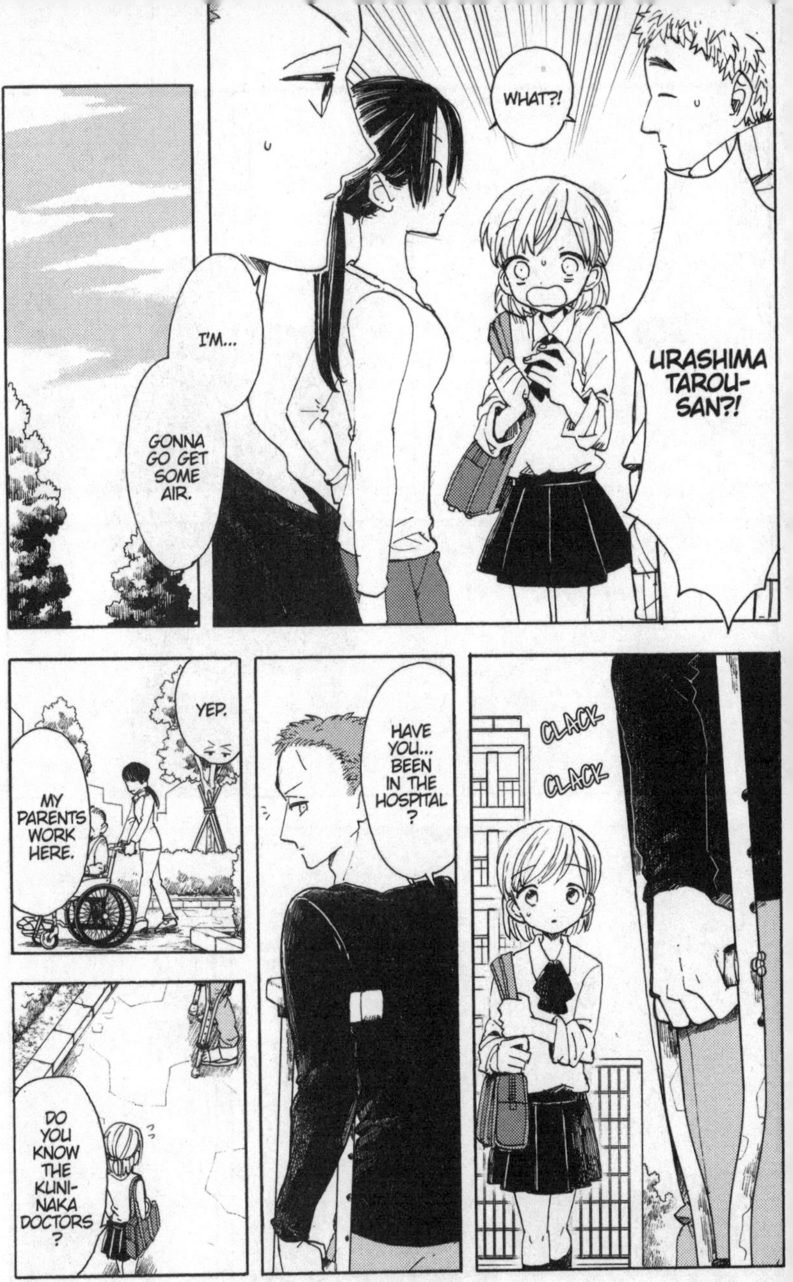
WHAT?!
URASHIMA TAROU-SAN?!
I'M...
GONNA GO GET SOME AIR.
CLACK
CLACK
HAVE YOU... BEEN IN THE HOSPITAL?
YEP.
MY PARENTS WORK HERE.
DO YOU KNOW THE KUNI-NAKA DOCTORS?

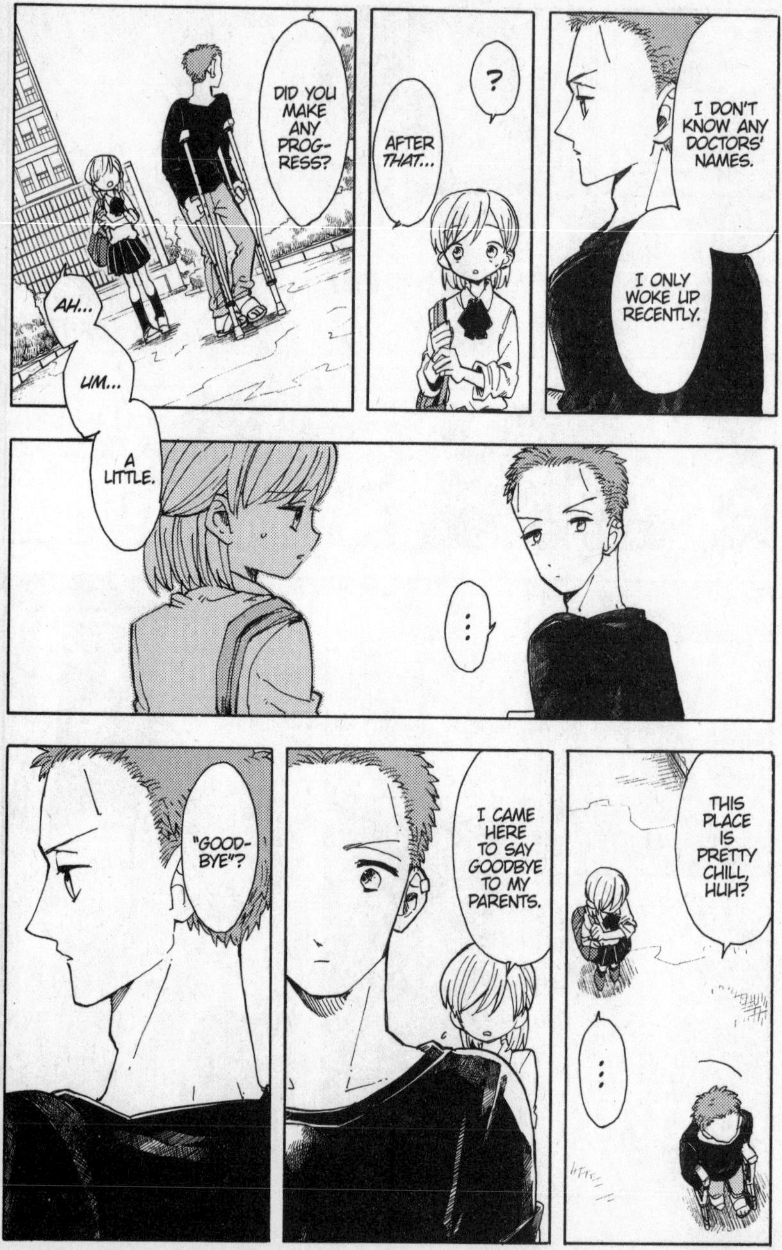
I DON'T KNOW ANY DOCTORS' NAMES.
I ONLY WOKE UP RECENTLY.
?
AFTER THAT...
DID YOU MAKE ANY PROG-RESS?
AH...
UM...
A LITTLE.
...
THIS PLACE IS PRETTY CHILL, HUH?
...
I CAME HERE TO SAY GOODBYE TO MY PARENTS.
"GOOD-BYE"?

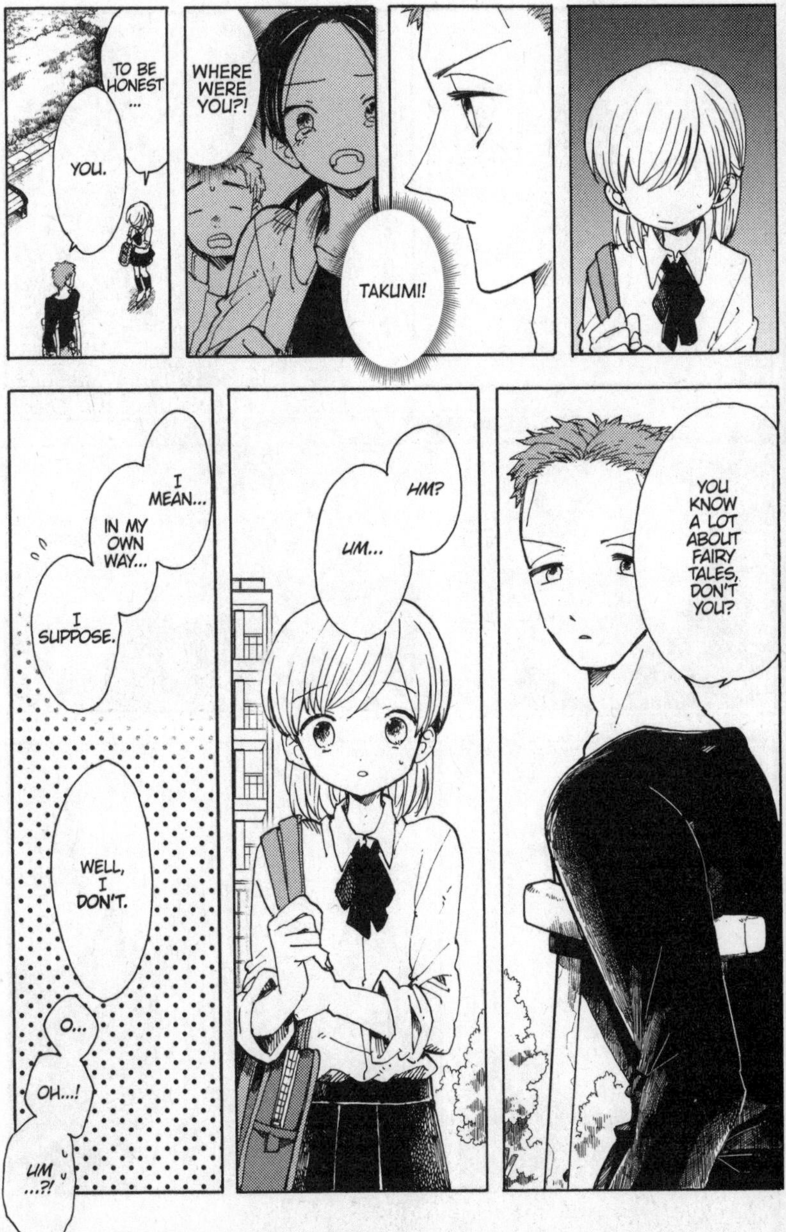
TAKUMI!
WHERE WERE YOU?!
TO BE HONEST...
YOU.
YOU KNOW A LOT ABOUT FAIRY TALES, DON'T YOU?
HM?
UM...
I MEAN...
IN MY OWN WAY...
I SUPPOSE.
WELL, I DON'T.
O...
OH...!
UM...?!

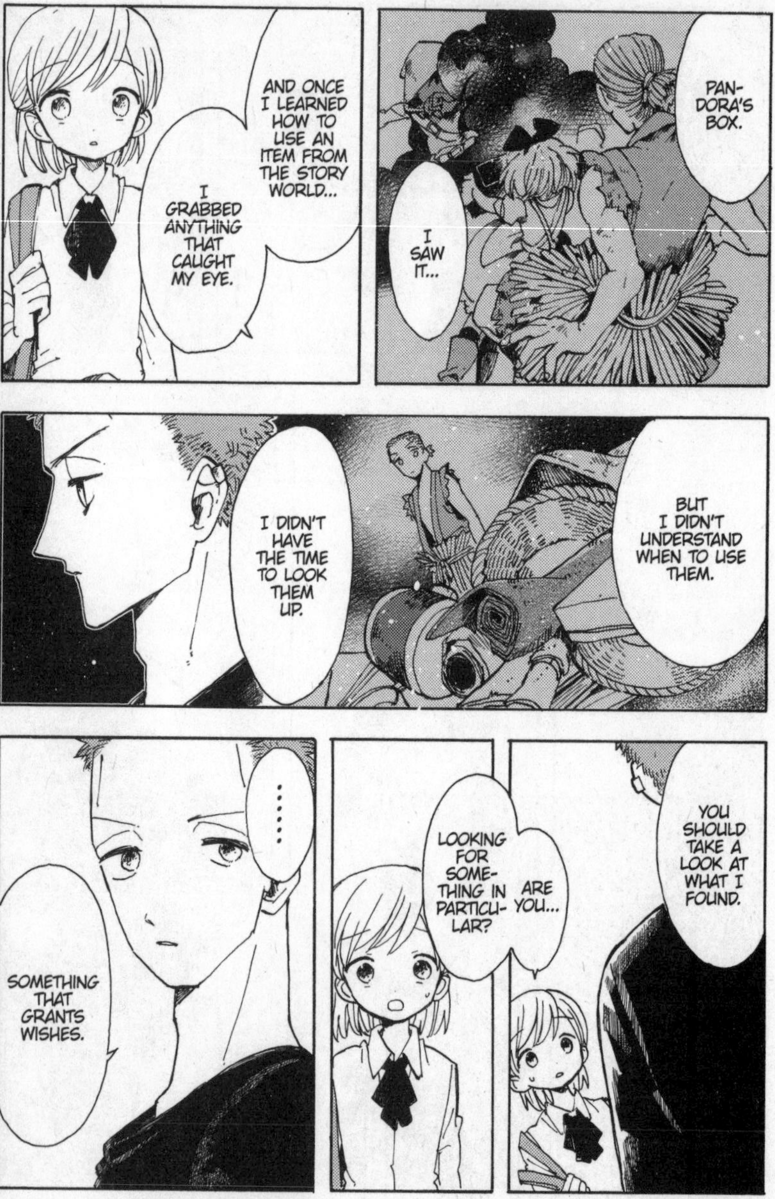
PAN-DORA'S BOX.
I SAW IT...
AND ONCE I LEARNED HOW TO USE AN ITEM FROM THE STORY WORLD...
I GRABBED ANYTHING THAT CAUGHT MY EYE.
BUT I DIDN'T UNDERSTAND WHEN TO USE THEM.
I DIDN'T HAVE THE TIME TO LOOK THEM UP.
YOU SHOULD TAKE A LOOK AT WHAT I FOUND.
LOOKING FOR SOME-THING IN PARTICU-LAR? ARE YOU...
......
SOMETHING THAT GRANTS WISHES.

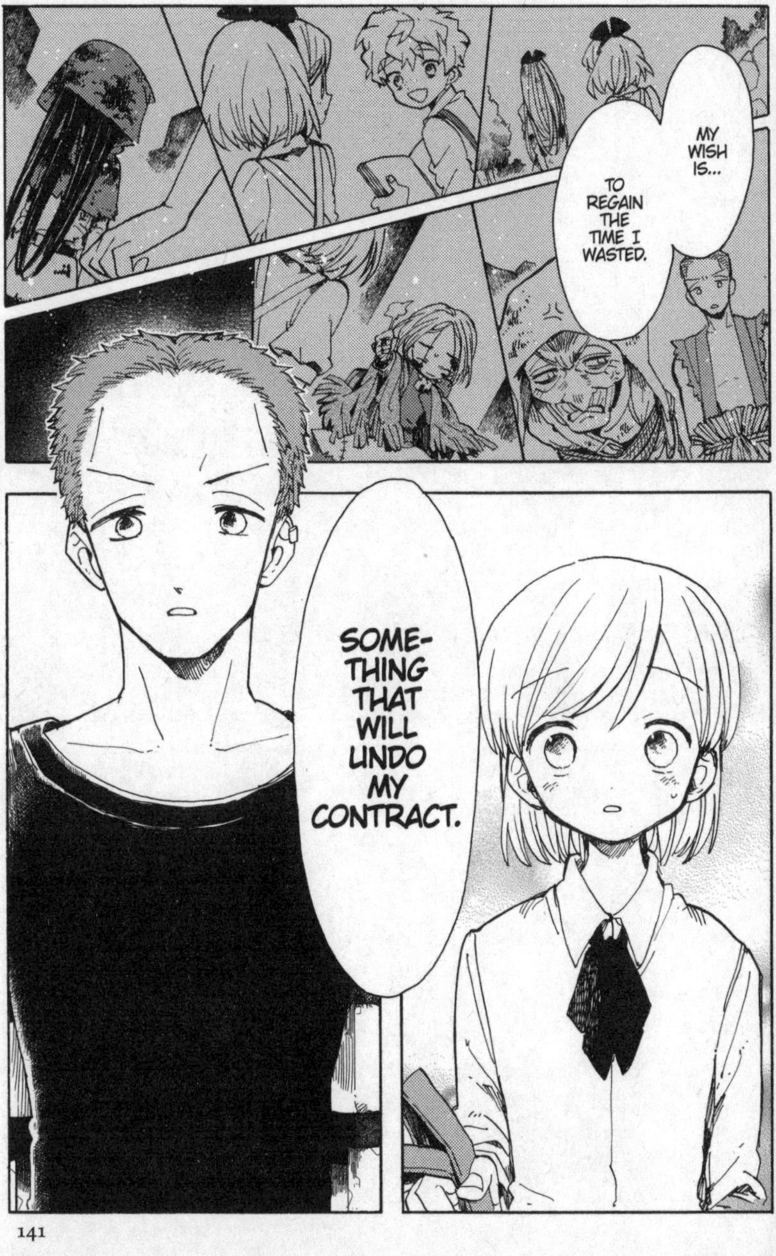
MY WISH IS...
TO REGAIN THE TIME I WASTED.
SOME-THING THAT WILL UNDO MY CONTRACT.

FAIRY
TALE
BATTLE
ROYALE

Chapter 17: Contact

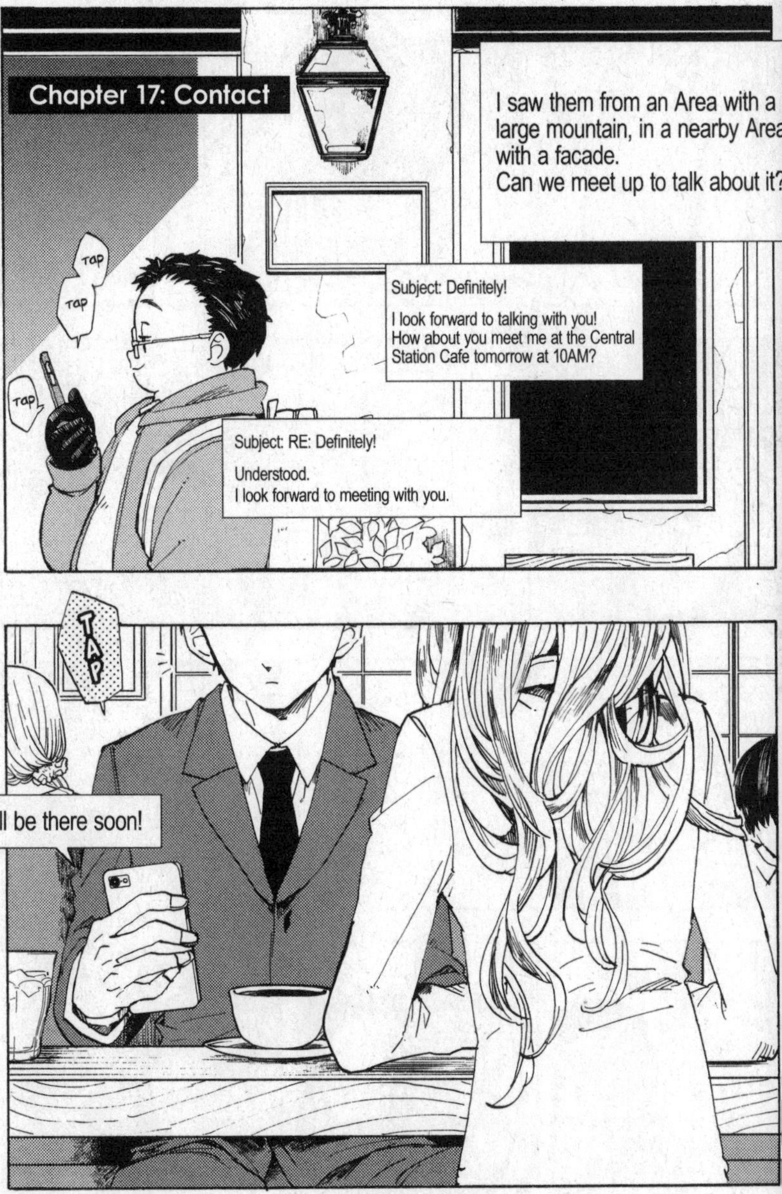
I saw them from an Area with a large mountain, in a nearby Area with a facade.
Can we meet up to talk about it?
Subject: Definitely!
I look forward to talking with you! How about you meet me at the Central Station Cafe tomorrow at 10AM?
Tap
Tap
Tap
Subject: RE: Definitely!
Understood. I look forward to meeting with you.
TAP
I'll be there soon!

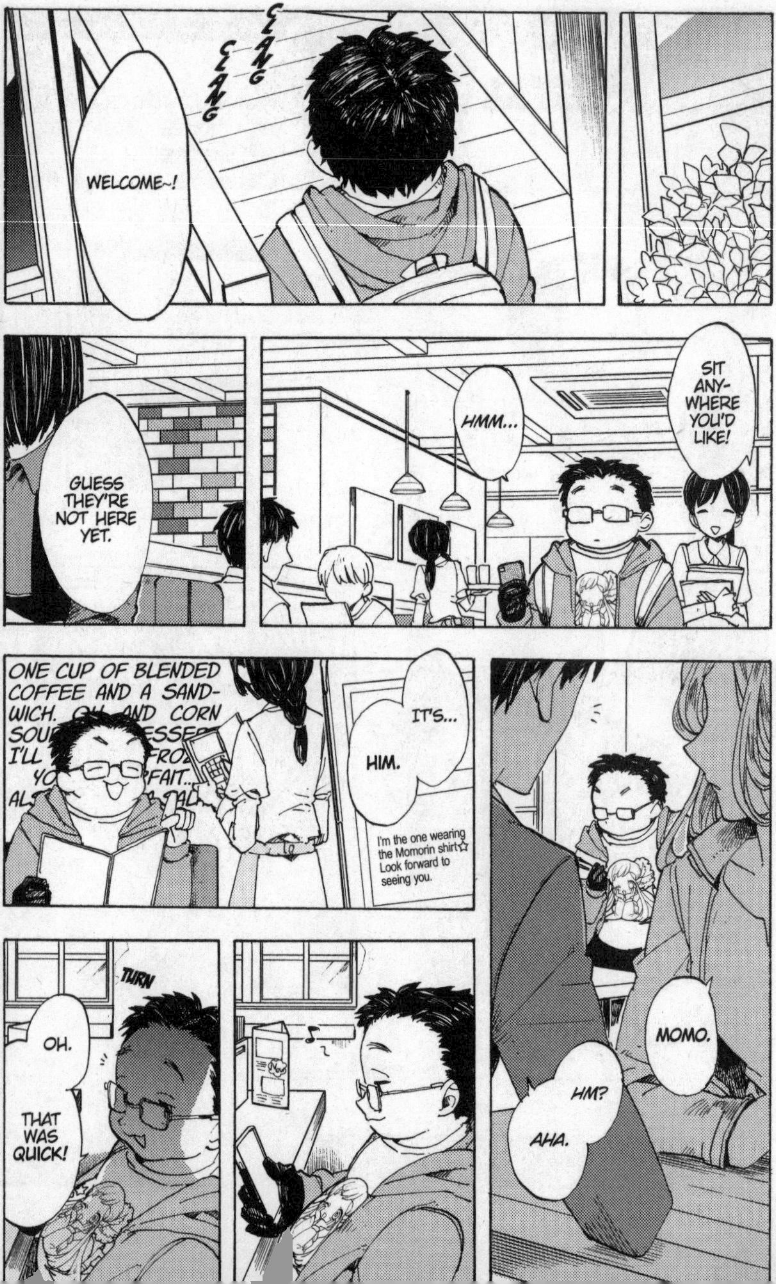
CLANG
CLANG
WELCOME~!
SIT ANY-WHERE YOU'D LIKE!
HMM...
GUESS THEY'RE NOT HERE YET.
MOMO.
HM?
AHA.
IT'S...
HIM.
ONE CUP OF BLENDED COFFEE AND A SAND-WICH.
I'm the one wearing the Momorin shirt☆ Look forward to seeing you.
TURN
OH.
THAT WAS QUICK!

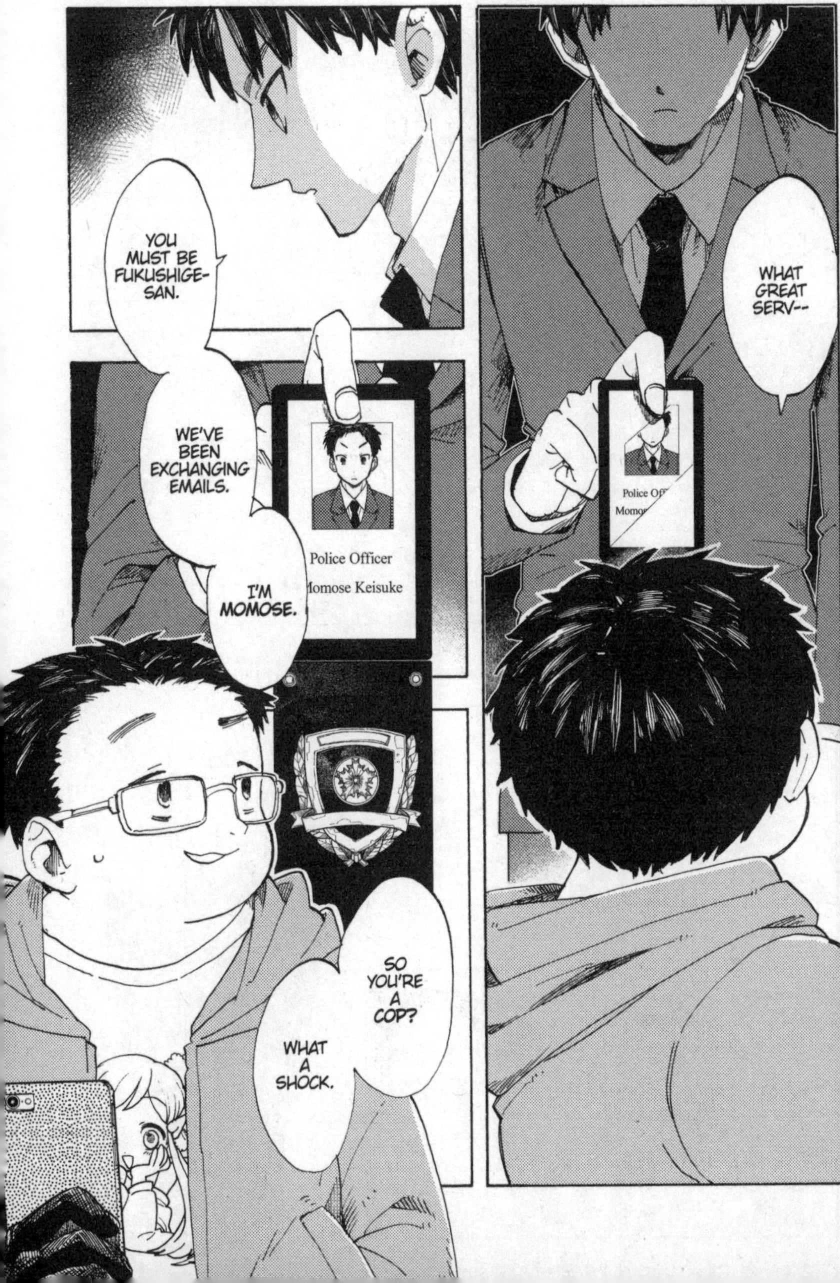
WHAT GREAT SERV--
Police Off
Momos
YOU MUST BE FUKUSHIGE-SAN.
WE'VE BEEN EXCHANGING EMAILS.
Police Officer
Momose Keisuke
I'M MOMOSE.
SO YOU'RE A COP?
WHAT A SHOCK.

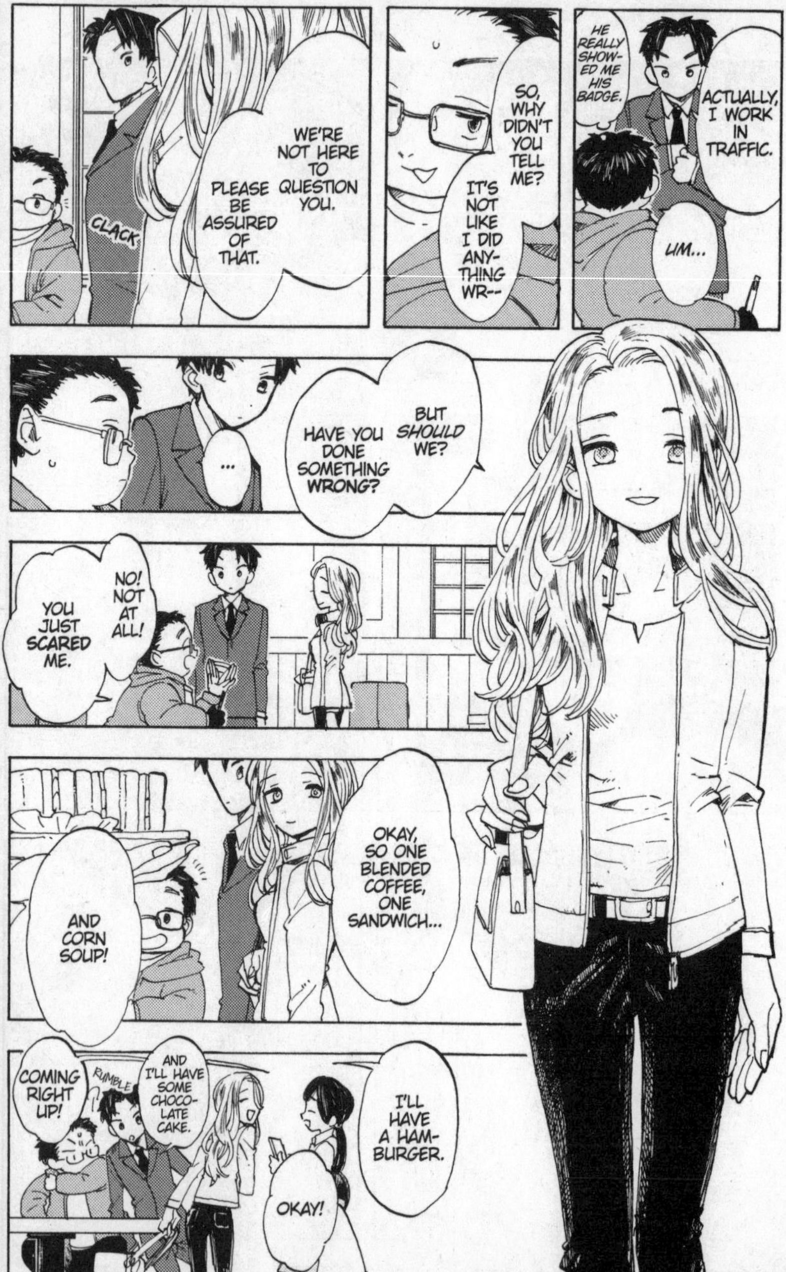
ACTUALLY, I WORK IN TRAFFIC.
HE REALLY SHOWED ME HIS BADGE.
UM...
SO, WHY DIDN'T YOU TELL ME?
IT'S NOT LIKE I DID ANYTHING WR--
WE'RE NOT HERE TO QUESTION YOU.
PLEASE BE ASSURED OF THAT.
CLACK
BUT *SHOULD* WE?
HAVE YOU DONE SOMETHING WRONG?
...
NO! NOT AT ALL!
YOU JUST SCARED ME.
OKAY, SO ONE BLENDED COFFEE, ONE SANDWICH...
AND CORN SOUP!
I'LL HAVE A HAMBURGER.
OKAY!
AND I'LL HAVE SOME CHOCOLATE CAKE.
RUMBLE
COMING RIGHT UP!

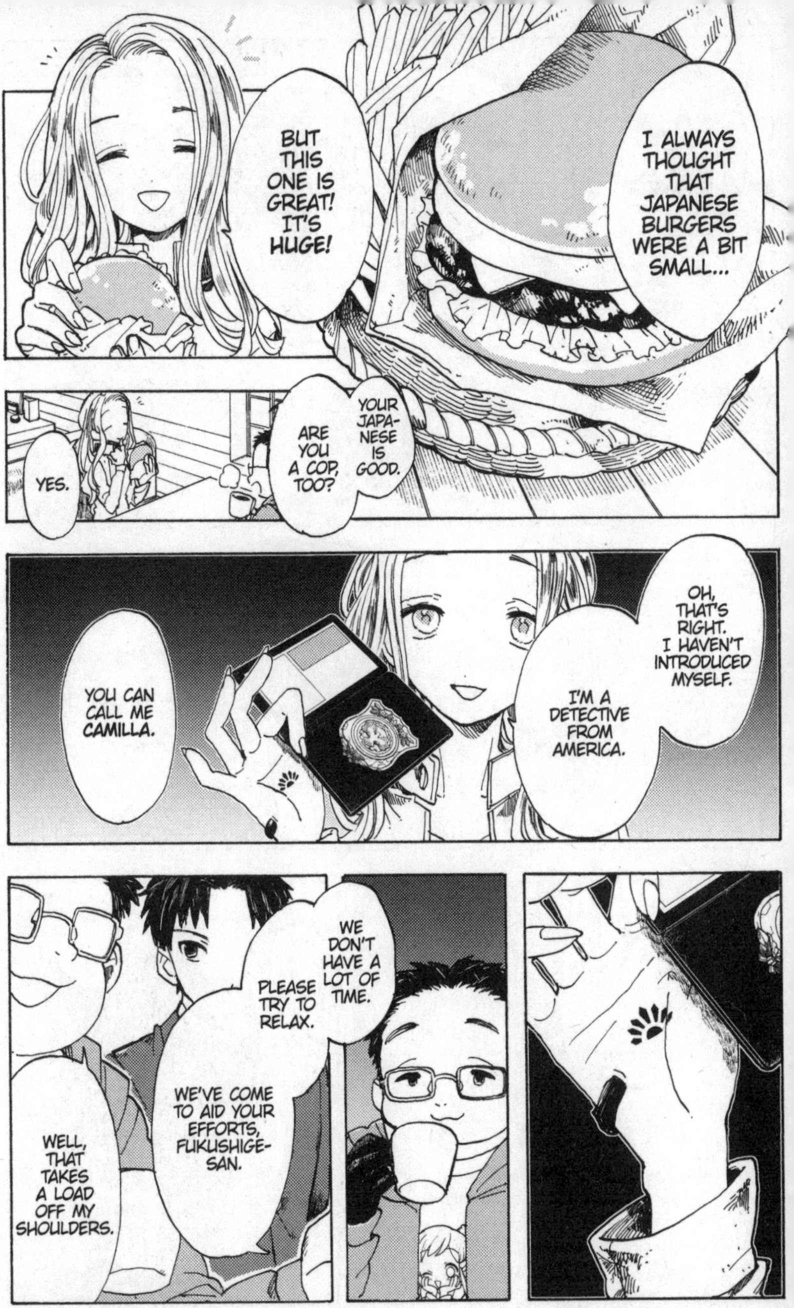
I ALWAYS THOUGHT THAT JAPANESE BURGERS WERE A BIT SMALL...
BUT THIS ONE IS GREAT! IT'S HUGE!
YOUR JAPANESE IS GOOD.
ARE YOU A COP, TOO?
YES.
OH, THAT'S RIGHT. I HAVEN'T INTRODUCED MYSELF.
I'M A DETECTIVE FROM AMERICA.
YOU CAN CALL ME CAMILLA.
WE DON'T HAVE A LOT OF TIME.
PLEASE TRY TO RELAX.
WE'VE COME TO AID YOUR EFFORTS, FUKUSHIGE-SAN.
WELL, THAT TAKES A LOAD OFF MY SHOULDERS.

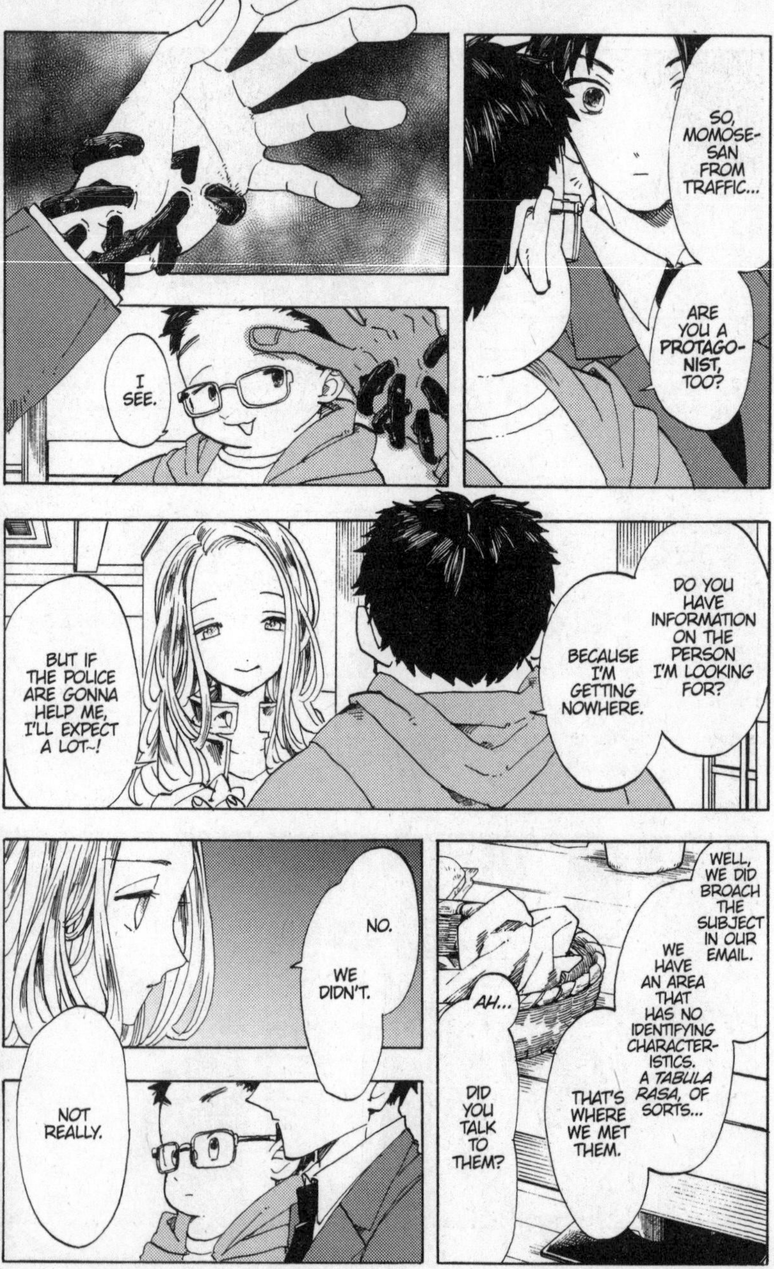
SO, MOMOSE-SAN FROM TRAFFIC...
ARE YOU A PROTAGONIST, TOO?
I SEE.
DO YOU HAVE INFORMATION ON THE PERSON I'M LOOKING FOR?
BECAUSE I'M GETTING NOWHERE.
BUT IF THE POLICE ARE GONNA HELP ME, I'LL EXPECT A LOT~!
WELL, WE DID BROACH THE SUBJECT IN OUR EMAIL.
WE HAVE AN AREA THAT HAS NO IDENTIFYING CHARACTERISTICS. A *TABULA RASA*, OF SORTS...
THAT'S WHERE WE MET THEM.
AH...
DID YOU TALK TO THEM?
NO.
WE DIDN'T.
NOT REALLY.

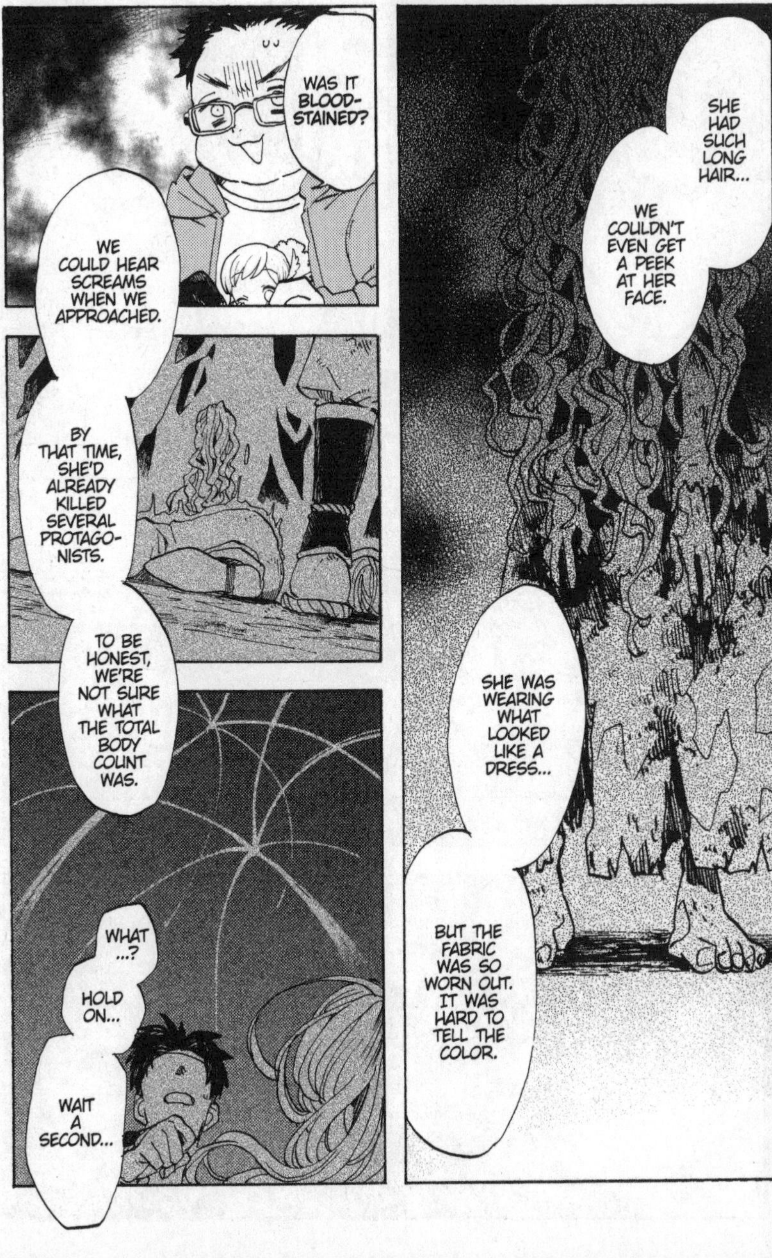
SHE HAD SUCH LONG HAIR...
WE COULDN'T EVEN GET A PEEK AT HER FACE.
SHE WAS WEARING WHAT LOOKED LIKE A DRESS...
BUT THE FABRIC WAS SO WORN OUT. IT WAS HARD TO TELL THE COLOR.
WAS IT BLOOD-STAINED?
WE COULD HEAR SCREAMS WHEN WE APPROACHED.
BY THAT TIME, SHE'D ALREADY KILLED SEVERAL PROTAGO-NISTS.
TO BE HONEST, WE'RE NOT SURE WHAT THE TOTAL BODY COUNT WAS.
WHAT ...?
HOLD ON...
WAIT A SECOND...

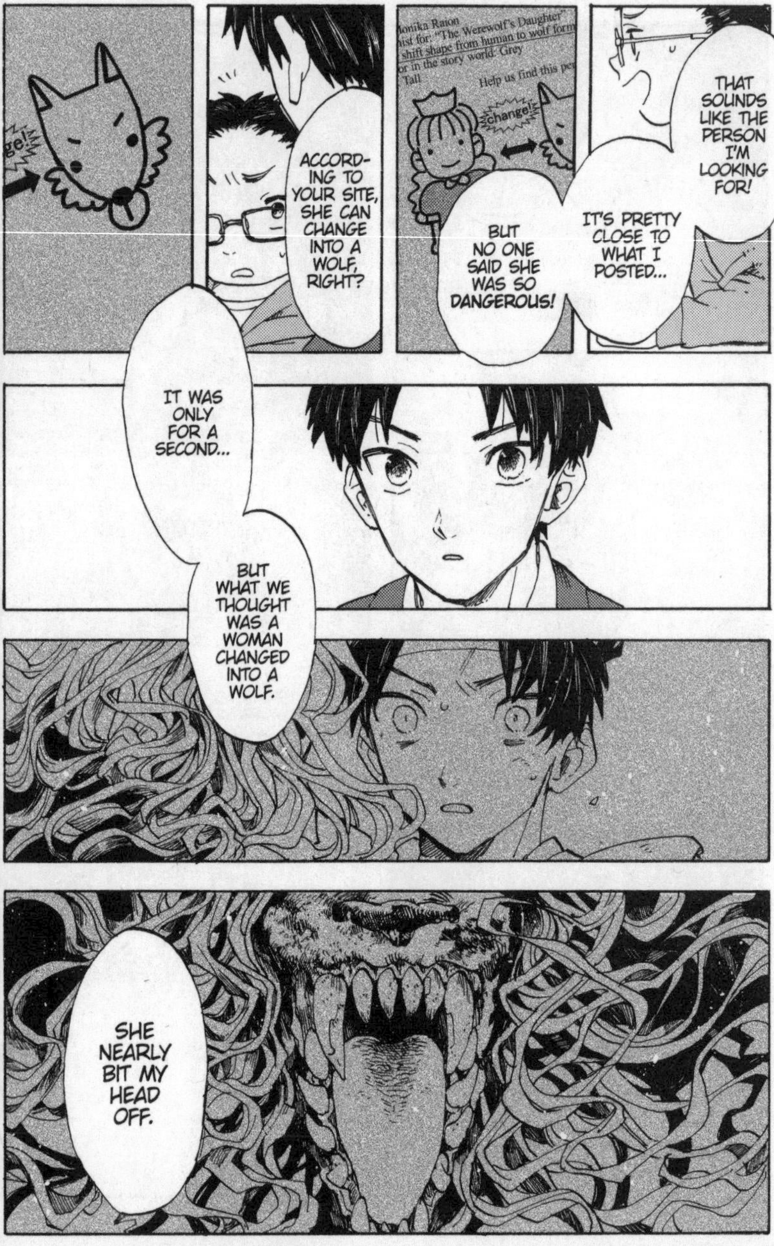
THAT SOUNDS LIKE THE PERSON I'M LOOKING FOR!
IT'S PRETTY CLOSE TO WHAT I POSTED...
BUT NO ONE SAID SHE WAS SO DANGEROUS!
change!
ACCORDING TO YOUR SITE, SHE CAN CHANGE INTO A WOLF, RIGHT?
IT WAS ONLY FOR A SECOND...
BUT WHAT WE THOUGHT WAS A WOMAN CHANGED INTO A WOLF.
SHE NEARLY BIT MY HEAD OFF.

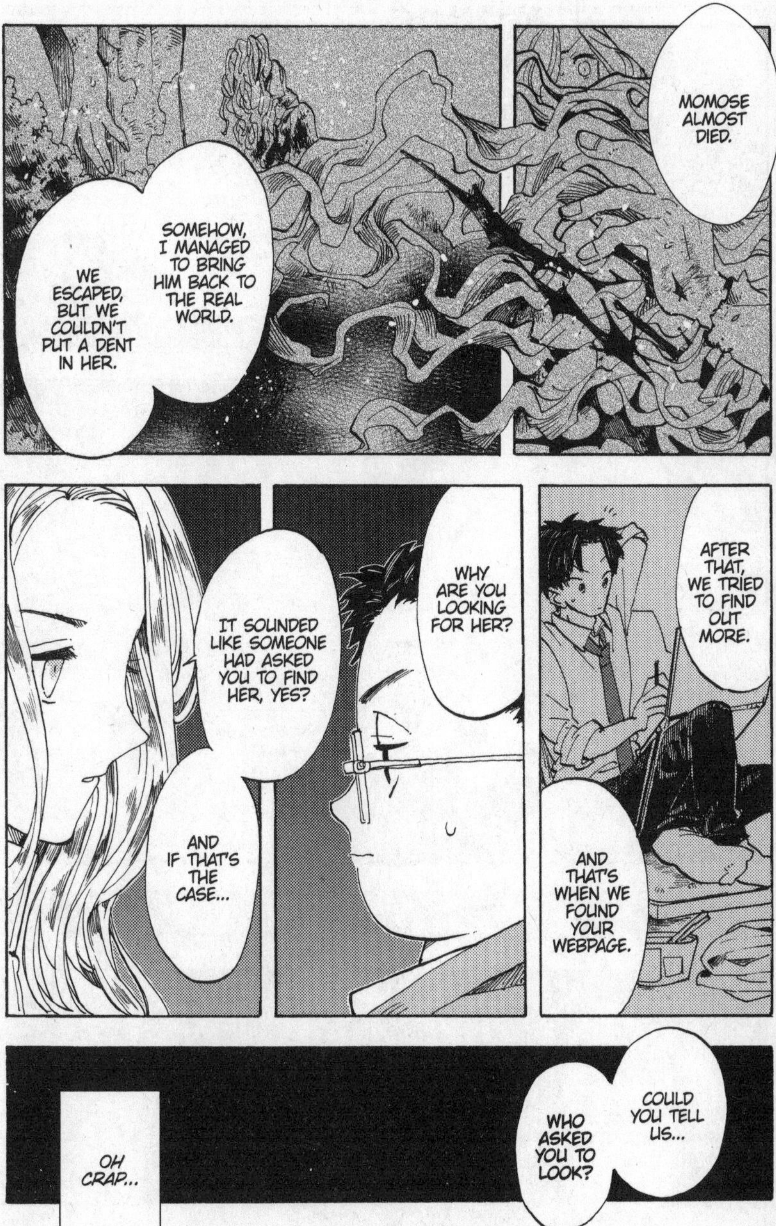
MOMOSE ALMOST DIED.
SOMEHOW, I MANAGED TO BRING HIM BACK TO THE REAL WORLD.
WE ESCAPED, BUT WE COULDN'T PUT A DENT IN HER.
AFTER THAT, WE TRIED TO FIND OUT MORE.
AND THAT'S WHEN WE FOUND YOUR WEBPAGE.
WHY ARE YOU LOOKING FOR HER?
IT SOUNDED LIKE SOMEONE HAD ASKED YOU TO FIND HER, YES?
AND IF THAT'S THE CASE...
COULD YOU TELL US...
WHO ASKED YOU TO LOOK?
OH CRAP...

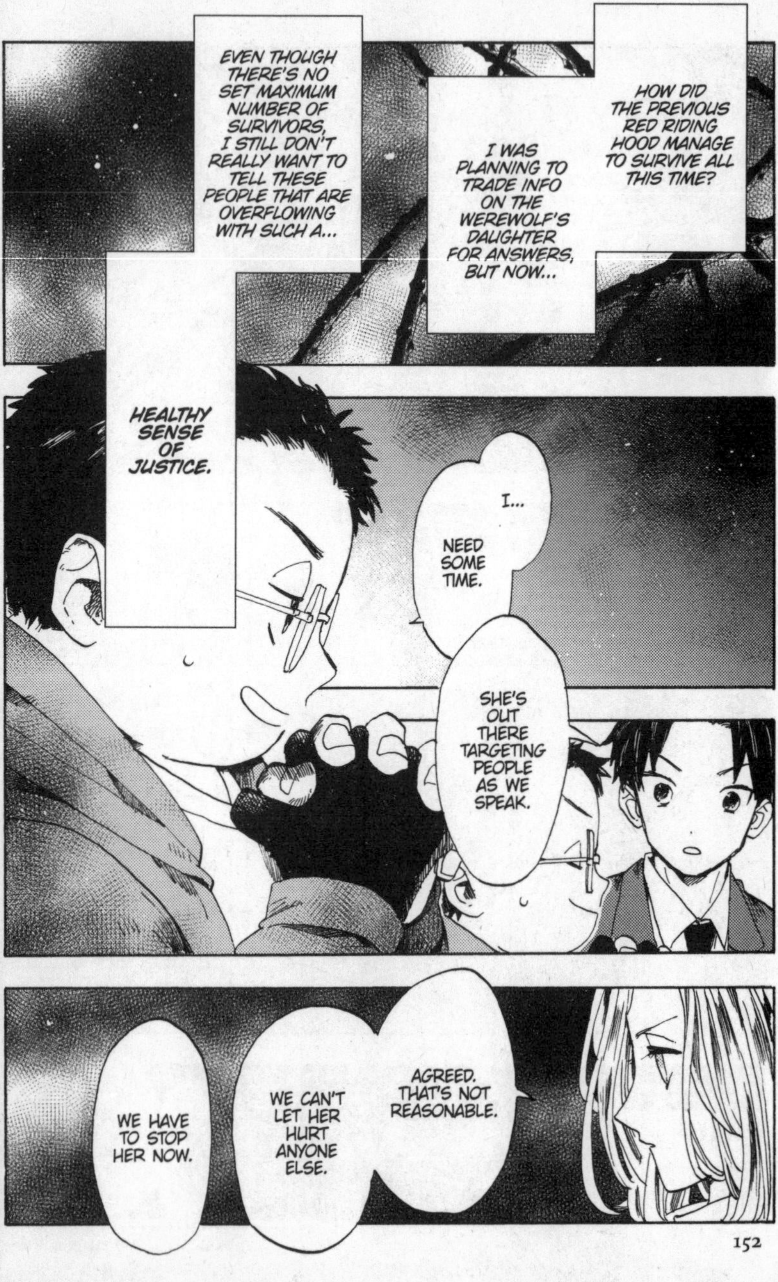
HOW DID THE PREVIOUS RED RIDING HOOD MANAGE TO SURVIVE ALL THIS TIME?
I WAS PLANNING TO TRADE INFO ON THE WEREWOLF'S DAUGHTER FOR ANSWERS, BUT NOW...
EVEN THOUGH THERE'S NO SET MAXIMUM NUMBER OF SURVIVORS, I STILL DON'T REALLY WANT TO TELL THESE PEOPLE THAT ARE OVERFLOWING WITH SUCH A...
HEALTHY SENSE OF JUSTICE.
I...
NEED SOME TIME.
SHE'S OUT THERE TARGETING PEOPLE AS WE SPEAK.
AGREED. THAT'S NOT REASONABLE.
WE CAN'T LET HER HURT ANYONE ELSE.
WE HAVE TO STOP HER NOW.

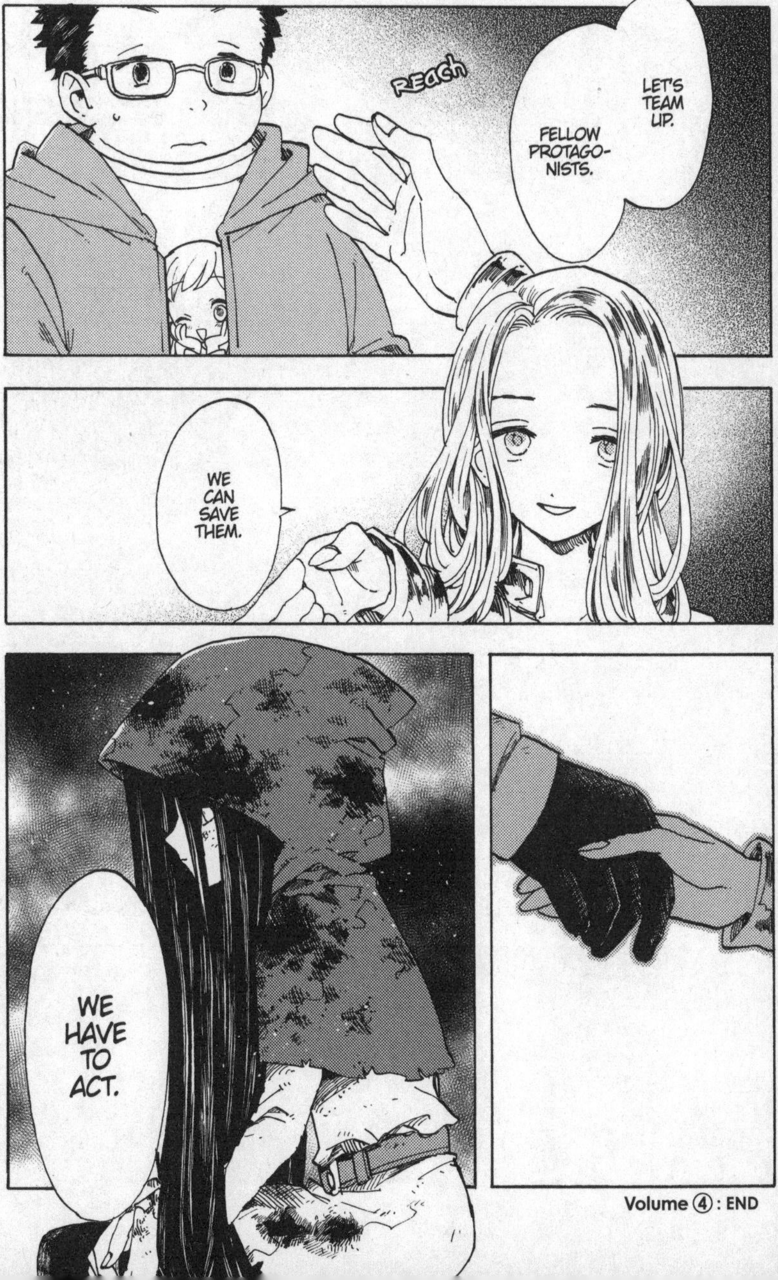
LET'S TEAM UP.
FELLOW PROTAGONISTS.
REACH
WE CAN SAVE THEM.
WE HAVE TO ACT.

Volume ④ : END

FAIRY
TALE
BATTLE
ROYALE

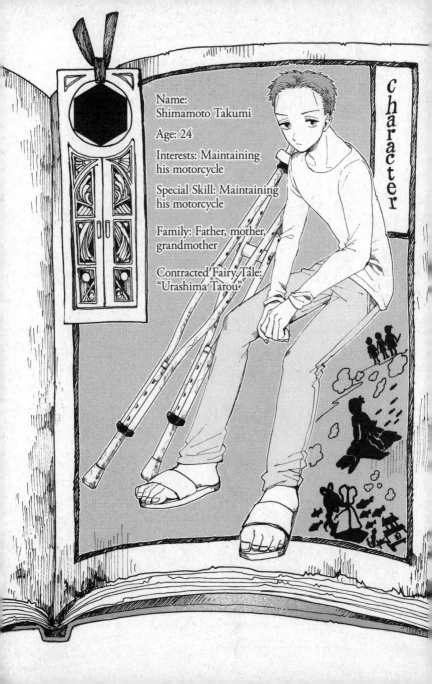

Name:
Shimamoto Takumi

Age: 24

Interests: Maintaining
his motorcycle

Special Skill: Maintaining
his motorcycle

Family: Father, mother,
grandmother

Contracted Fairy Tale:
"Urashima Tarou"

character

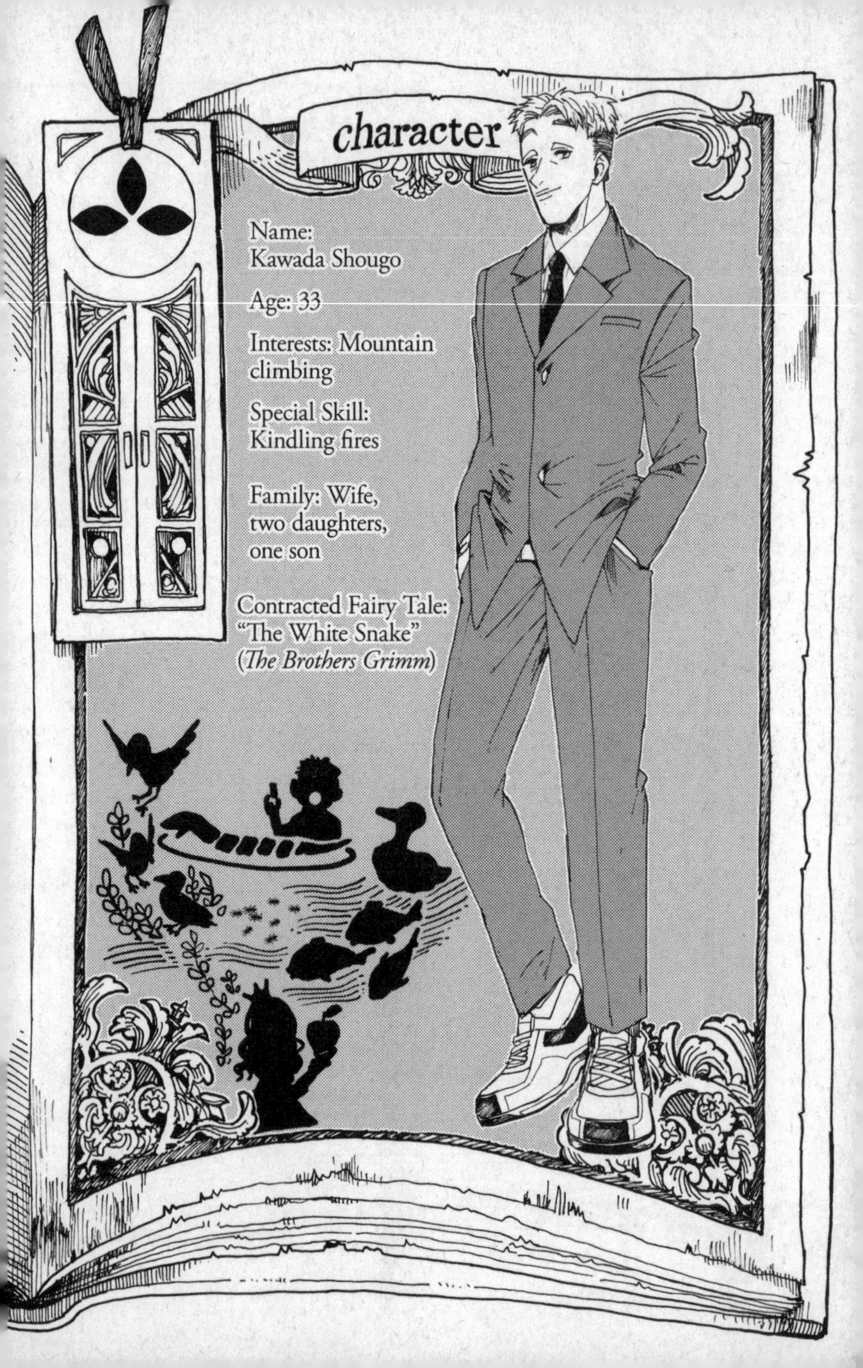
character
Name:
Kawada Shougo
Age: 33
Interests: Mountain climbing
Special Skill:
Kindling fires
Family: Wife, two daughters, one son
Contracted Fairy Tale:
"The White Snake"
(*The Brothers Grimm*)

FAIRY
TALE
BATTLE
ROYALE

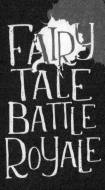

After Aoba returned to the real world.
THE TEA...
IT'S PROBABLY COLD BY NOW.
I'VE CAUSED SO MUCH TROUBLE...
I SHOULD MAKE IT UP TO HER.
I'M GONNA GO MAKE MORE TEA, OKAY?
I THINK THIS IS WHERE AOBA FOUND THE TEA LEAVES...
THUNK
GLUG
GLUG
RUMBLE
RUMBLE
RUMBLE
RATTLE
Thud
rumble
rumble
rumble...
CLANG...
CREAK
CREAK
CREAK
ALL RIGHT.
I MADE TEA!
wobble...
...
SHE WAS SO CLUMSY THAT THE NOISE...
ATTRACTED A GAGGLE OF MUMMIES.

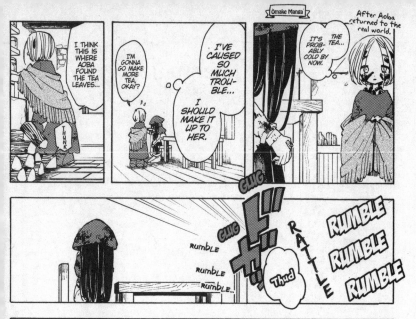

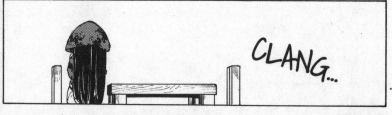

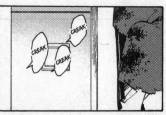

Afterword

Thank you for reading *Fairy Tale Battle Royale* Volume 4.

It's been nearly two years since Volume 3 went on sale. I feel this story is still worth telling and worth the effort that it took to draw.

I'm so sorry you had to wait so long to read it.

I'm not sure what shape this story will take in the future, but I absolutely want to finish it. If you could continue to read, that would make me very happy.

February 2000
Soraho Ina

FAIRY TALE BATTLE ROYALE

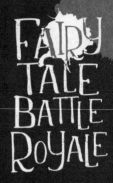

SEVEN SEAS ENTERTAINMENT PRESENTS

FAIRY TALE BATTLE ROYALE

Volume 4

story and art by **SORAHO INA**

TRANSLATION
Molly Rabbitt

ADAPTATION
Cae Hawksmoor

LETTERING AND RETOUCH
Alexandra Gunawan

INTERIOR LAYOUT
Christa Miesner

COVER DESIGN
Kris Aubin

PROOFREADER
Kurestin Armada

EDITOR
Shanti Whitesides

PREPRESS TECHNICIAN
Rhiannon Rasmussen-Silverstein

PRODUCTION MANAGER
Lissa Pattillo

MANAGING EDITOR
Julie Davis

ASSOCIATE PUBLISHER
Adam Arnold

PUBLISHER
Jason DeAngelis

OTOGIBANASHI BATTLE ROYALE Volume 4

First published in Japan in 2020 by KADOKAWA CORPORATION, Tokyo.
English translation rights arranged with KADOKAWA CORPORATION, Tokyo.

Seven Seas press and purchase enquiries can be sent to Marketing Manager Lianne Sentar at press@gomanga.com. Information regarding the distribution and purchase of digital editions is available from Digital Manager CK Russell at digital@gomanga.com.

ISBN: 978-1-64275-743-9

Printed in Canada

First Printing: October 2020

10 9 8 7 6 5 4 3 2 1

FOLLOW US ONLINE: ***www.sevenseasentertainment.com***

READING DIRECTIONS

This book reads from ***right to left***, Japanese style. If this is your first time reading manga, you start reading from the top right panel on each page and take it from there. If you get lost, just follow the numbered diagram here. It may seem backwards at first, but you'll get the hang of it! Have fun!!

1
2
3
4
5
6
7
8
9

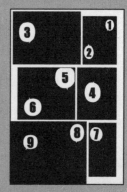